D1614371

CHILDHOOD IDENTITIES

CHILDHOOD IDENTITIES

*Self and Social Relationships in
the Experience of the Child*

ALLISON JAMES

EDINBURGH UNIVERSITY PRESS

For my parents

© Allison James, 1993

Edinburgh University Press Ltd
22 George Square, Edinburgh

Typeset in Linotronic Baskerville
by Speedspools, Edinburgh, and
printed and bound in Great Britain by
the University Press, Cambridge

A CIP record for this book is
available from the British Library

ISBN 0 7486 0456 1

Contents

Preface

This is a book about childhood. More specifically it is about children's experience of childhood and focuses on the difficulties which some children encounter in being children. It is also, then, a book which explores the wider issues of Selfhood, identity and belonging as they are faced by children. It raises questions about the experience of difference and disability, about the contexts and outcomes of bullying and other anti-social forms of behaviour, and explores processes of friendship making and friendship-breaking. In this sense this book addresses a number of substantive issues in children's lives. At the same time, however, it considers the problems and possibilities of addressing these issues theoretically. From within the debates of contemporary social anthropology, it examines processes of account-giving and interpretation in the light of the cultural and social construction of childhood.

For those seeking immediate and simple solutions to children's dilemmas this book offers little comfort, for it depicts the complexity of children's social lives which in the popular imagination is masked by an assumption of childishness. Through what Geertz (1975) terms the art of 'thick description', children's social relationships are explored in their unfolding and social actions contextualised in their specificity. This allows us to identify, not the causes, but the contexts of events and permits us to interpret, rather than explain, social action. Thus, although not detailing a policy-oriented piece of research, this book is written with the hope that the insights it provides into children's social lives will have some application.

In this claim, I am acknowledging the considerable debt I owe to the parents, children and teachers who so generously spared time to talk with me about some of the problems and difficulties which children face and to those others who provided me with information and personal accounts which formed the starting point for this research. I hope that the understandings of childhood which I present in this book remain faithful to the spirit of the project in which I engaged their interest. To the children and staff of 'Hilltop' school I am especially grateful for my long and happy sojourn. Most of the children and some of the staff have, by now, moved on to other schools and cities. They will, no doubt, have forgotten the anthropologist who came to stay. However, as is the nature of anthropological work, the ethnographic present remains for me and I will not forget their enthusiasm and good will towards me. Thanks are also due to professionals in the health service and the staff and children from other schools with whom I had more fleeting but nevertheless important contact. While all these individuals and institutions must inevitably remain anonymous in the text, their individuality hidden by pseudonyms, their thoughts and ideas have shaped the direction which this book has taken. For this I am indebted. I alone am responsible for its final form.

To the British Academy I owe many thanks for financial backing through the award of a Post-doctoral Fellowship, held between 1988–91 at Southbank University. My colleagues in the Community Health and Nursing Department were always welcoming and supportive and, in particular, Val Chapman and Alan Prout encouraged me during the early stages of research. Since that time I have had many opportunities to present different aspects of my research in departmental seminars, medical sociology and anthropology conferences. Through critical debate and discussion I have been led to develop and then refine my ideas. This means that many other voices have an implicit, but important, presence in the text. For this contribution I am grateful.

Finally, some special thanks are in order. These go first to Nigel Rapport, who expended much effort on my behalf, commenting on working papers and draft chapters, and with whom I talked long and hard about my research. His perceptive critiques sharpened both my analysis and writing. Jenny Hockey, Malcolm Young and David Brooks, as ever, cushioned the research process, advising and consoling. Thanks too to Jenny Kitzinger and Kate Hunt for the contribution of additional material which confirmed my interpretation of children's attitudes to the body and to Tony Cohen for encouraging me to publish. Lastly, as befits the subject-matter of this book, I must thank Jeremy, Daniel and Peter James for putting up with me in my own multiple and changing identities: as wife, mother, researcher and writer.

ONE

In Search of the Self and Other

Memories and Imagination

A memory. In the hot summer of 1984 my second son was born. His small body was beautiful, his face fringed with thick dark hair, eyes wide open and sparkling. But the lower part of his face was unrecognisably distorted. He had a cleft lip and palate and, in that moment, it seemed impossible that anything could be done to repair his damaged face. But, four years and two operations later, only photographs recalled for us the shock of that summer evening as, in the autumn of 1988, he set off, mischievous and grinning, to spend his first day at school. The miracle of modern surgical techniques meant that his face was by now visibly transformed. Only a slight scar, a raised lump on his lip and a downward twist to his nose hinted at past problems. Of more concern was his speech which, although understood by family and friends and much improved by therapy, could still at times be unclear to strangers.

What, I wondered, would other children make of him? Would he easily find friends at school or would his slight disability prove to be a social handicap? Would his school experiences be happy or not? Such parental thoughts surely accompany many children as they leave the domestic world to make their own way in the playground. For me, this time, they had more urgency. I felt I had more grounds for concern.

A second memory. Earlier, on that morning of his first school day, my son had stood in front of a full-length mirror looking at himself as a 'school-boy'. Dressed, like his brother, in navy-blue jumper, light-blue shirt, striped tie and grey shorts and socks, his finger moved slowly to touch his scar. 'Why have I got this?' he asked. Having often been told in the past about his cleft lip and palate, why at that moment did he choose to ask a question to which he already had the answer? Did he think, I wondered, that by donning a uniform his face could, like his social body, be magically transformed?

It was in pondering thoughts such as these, that some research ideas began slowly to coalesce in the manner which C. Wright-Mills described, many years ago now, as being integral to the sociological imagination. In his view it is the task of social scientists 'to translate personal troubles into public issues and public issues into the terms of their human meaning for a variety of individuals' (1959: 187). The promise of social science, he suggested, lies in the fact that what may feel to be simply 'personal troubles are very often also problems shared by others, and more importantly, not capable of solution by any one individual but only by modifications of the structure of the groups in which he lives' (1959: 187).

This book is a testimony to this vision in its account of cultural ideas of Otherness and identity in childhood which grew out of a most personal encounter with impairment.[1] It is a theme which is doubly encoded. First, it is expressed through a practical concern with childhood identities. Drawing on conversations with children, parents, teachers and health professionals living and working in a large English town, I chart in subsequent chapters the progress of a dialogue of research questions about the ways in which children conceive and mark out their own and other social identities. These range from the practical and particular to the more general and philosophic. How significant are personal attributes such as physical appearance or ability in shaping children's friendships? Do social and cultural differences – gender, ethnicity and class, for example – impact decisively or minimally on their choice of friends? Are the differences which children attribute to one another simply reflections of the stigmas and prejudices of the adult world, thus testifying to a process of passive cultural continuity, or is significance differently attributed by children to diversity among their peers? If so, do age and gender have a part to play in shaping this cognition? How are the subtleties of prejudice learnt and their social import recognised, and what significance might the acknowledgement of difference have for a child's developing sense of Self and for his or her social identity? Such questions begged others and, initially centring on processes of social classification and cognition, the search broadened into an exploration of how children's sense of Self, identity and personhood develop in and through the patterning of their social encounters. In this way, I was able to confirm that, as Goffman suspected, an understanding of stigma really requires 'a language of relationships, not attributes'

(1968: 13). Recognition of the significance of differences by children arises through the particularities of their relationships with one another.

Thus it was through asking specific and pragmatic questions about the ways in which young children come to conceptualise and generate ideas of difference in their everyday social relations that, later, I was able to address theoretically the ways in which the more generalised process of socialisation takes place, and to consider the forms through which it might be possible to chart its process and progress. It was the experience of doing long-term participant observation fieldwork in a Midlands' primary school, alongside more formal interviews with adults and children, which gave me the clues. Gradually, I learnt – as the children did – which differences make a difference (Bateson, 1973). Listening to the tenor of children's rhymes and teases, watching their games of chase and chance, hearing with sympathy of their troubles, squabbles and fallings-out, I was made conscious of the diverse and powerful socialising processes through which the children qualified each other's childhoods. Working with children of different ages highlighted the inherent temporality of childhood, alerting me to the gradual unfolding of children's sense of Self in relation to Others over time (James and Prout, 1990b). I became conscious of the subtlety of social maturation as I was led slowly to see how children come literally to embody the limits and possibilities of culture. And I was taught, gently but sometimes more rudely and distressingly, to appreciate the very different consequences which that cognitive embodiment can have for individual children. My path of reflective questioning thus enabled me to see quite clearly that, as Ardener has argued, 'the social is, in virtue of its categorizing and classifying structures, a space that "identifies"' (1987: 39). The social space I explored was that of childhood which 'identifies' children and within which children 'identify' one another and themselves.

The 'thick descriptions' of childhood relationships, which are inscribed in this volume, stem from the kind of field research described by Geertz (1975) as being integral to the practice of social anthropology. Through observation of and occasional participation in the minutiae of their everyday encounters, I learnt about the distinctions and discriminations which the children used to negotiate their relationships. Through close attention to their patterned use of language and social space, gradually, I was able to envisage, and later to explain, not only how children become social, but also how they socialise one another.

From this it is clear that the interpretive approach to social life which shapes my understanding of childhood and childhood identities is not in the business of discovering facts. Indeed, in this account they are few in number. The claim is, instead, more humble: it is to be good at 'guessing at meanings, assessing the guesses and drawing explanatory conclusions from the better guesses' (Geertz, 1975: 20). But, as Geertz observes, nevertheless, it:

> is with the kind of material produced by long-term, mainly (though not exclusively) qualitative, highly participative, and almost obsessively fine-comb field study in confined contexts that the mega-concepts with which contemporary social science is afflicted – legitimacy, modernization, integration, conflict, charisma, structure . . . meaning – can be given the sort of sensible actuality that makes it possible to think not only realistically and concretely about them, but, what is more important, creatively and imaginatively with them. (1975: 23)

If the style of my day-to-day encounters with children and adults during the research project necessarily contextualised the theoretical understanding which I gradually developed, it follows that my account of children's experience of the social world and of their part in its continuance is, likewise, shaped by the research process. As will become clear it informs, for example, the emphasis laid upon the culture of childhood as a socialising context, above those other contexts of home and school (Musgrave, 1987). This is evidenced by the seriousness with which, in later chapters, children's own accounts of their social relationships are taken as adequate testimony of the cultural experience which adults term childhood. Like any other account of childhood, then, mine must properly be seen as both peculiar and partisan (see Chapter 3).

This highlights the second encoding of the themes of Otherness and identity running through this volume: the process of 'accounting for' children. This refers to the multitude of ways in which children are identified as children and as children of particular kinds. Whether through visual or verbal images, through protective laws or welfare practices, accounts of what children are or should be map out for children themselves a cultural space within which they are identified as children. It is a process of categorising no less pertinent to the act of research. Thus, integral to my ethnographic account of the processes of cognition and socialisation during childhood – the main substance of this book – is the ontological status of the understanding of childhood which I present. It is this which I turn to first as, in the following three chapters, I ask how knowledge about children is generated, and what kinds of knowledge it is which makes the 'child' a cultural symbol of Otherness in contemporary British society. I begin this task here by setting out the intimate relationship which exists between personal anthropology, fieldwork practice and the construction of anthropological accounts.

Reflexivity and Anthropology: the Self and Others

The reflexive potential of research in the social sciences, which Wright Mills drew attention to some thirty years ago, is now commonly acknowledged in the discourse of anthropologists (Clifford and Marcus, 1986; Caplan, 1988). No longer is the 'Self' – the I – of the anthropologist to be buried quietly within the written text or allowed fleetingly to appear as a sign of authenticity or authority (Geertz, 1988). Nor is it now necessary for the very personal experience of encountering the Other to be relegated, in seeming embarrassment, to footnotes and appendices or semi-fictional accounts (Okely, 1992). It has been acknowledged that, wherever anthropologists stray, their reliance on long-term participatory fieldwork as a main methodology inevitably involves 'constructing texts ostensibly scientific out of experiences broadly biographical' on their return home (Geertz, 1988: 10).

However, as Okely (1992) observes, the implications of autobiography for research, which the movement towards a more reflexive approach to the study of social life acknowledges, has not been universally welcomed. Some are dismissive, seeing little heuristic value to be gained from what they regard as a form of navel-gazing, while others recoil from what they darkly suspect this consciousness of the Self to be really about: at best, a sort of do-it-yourself psychoanalysis; at worst, simple self-indulgence. Such reactions are informative. They point to a failure to see or, more intriguingly, an unwillingness to acknowledge that the strength and distinctiveness of anthropological approaches to understanding social life lies, fundamentally, in the Self's relationship with other Selves. Those who would hope to staunch the rising tide of reflexivity in anthropology register a particular anxiety in their alarm: that the open admittance of the inter-subjectivity of anthropological practice risks a number of important epistemological issues which, in turn, may lead to a questioning of the very enterprise itself.

For example, Okely's (1992) observation that, through its reliance on participant observation as a research method, social anthropology is always about social relationships, although perhaps self-evident, appears radical in the light of the history of the discipline. By and large, the classic texts of anthropology, whilst relying heavily on social relationships in the field, have taken scant regard of them in the final polished texts. Thus, although Malinowski (1922) highlights social relationships in his pioneering monograph through the notion of the privileged informant, and more explicitly discusses these relationships in his diary (Geertz, 1983), he did not explore the significance of it being his own, rather than another's, encounter with the argonauts of the Western Pacific. The actual daily doing of anthropology (when such relationships might have been fruitfully examined) later became all but edited out of anthropological accounts (Clifford, 1988). Thus, whilst the joys and sorrow of fieldwork relations were privately shared with friends and colleagues at home, quickly coalescing into anthropology's own mythology (Barley, 1986), details of the anthropologist as a person amongst other people abroad were rarely made public. If they were, it was to mark the ethnographic account with tracks of being-there-ness (Geertz, 1988). As Clifford notes (1988), this obfuscation was partly a function of the ready acceptance which ethnographic fieldwork quickly achieved. The 'validity' of participant observation as a method for getting to know about 'other' cultures had become established and proven by the early 1940s. Providing details of what it actually involved, on a day-to-day and one-to-one basis, seemed perhaps unnecessary for those anthropologists who followed after.

However, the erasing of the person of the anthropologist can also be accounted for by the disciplinary status which anthropology aspired to during the first half of the twentieth century. As has by now been well-documented (Okely, 1975) the prevailing model was that of the natural sciences. The 'peculiar amalgam of intense personal experience and scientific analysis' which participant observation became meant that the people anthropologists made relationships with in the field had necessarily to become objectified as Other and distanced from the Self (Clifford, 1988: 34). And one way to do that was to disguise the nature of the relationships out of which anthropological understanding arose. Thus, as Fabian's (1983) critique has illustrated, in many of the early anthropological writings about 'primitive' cultures, the relationship between Self and Other was rephrased as a dichotomy between 'us' and 'them', between 'white' culture and 'savage' culture. And in this rephrasing there passed unnoticed a myriad of implicit assumptions about the nature of power, supremacy and Nature itself which later formed the basis for the colonial framing of anthropology (Okely, 1975).

The consequences of this stylistic blending and disguising of the social relations of anthropology remain problematic for contemporary anthropologists as is evidenced by the language which anthropologists use in their writings about Other cultures (Campbell, 1989: 6–12). Although in idle conversation they may speak with affection of their friends abroad, in their academic writings many anthropologists, uncritically, switch voices. They adopt an 'ethnographic' language or, more properly, the traditional language of 'ethnography'. Implicitly, this reconciles an unspoken or even unacknowledged quest for objectivity – for some kind of scientific recognition or 'truth' – with the overwhelmingly subjective experience of living amongst strangers. As Campbell points out terms such as 'informant', 'the field' and 'data' mask the subjectivity of friendships made in faraway places and makes 'their' ideas, casual remarks and preferred opinions more solid stuff which can be 'gathered' and 'collated' for 'our' understanding of 'them'. The very technicality of these terms helps to specify social roles, denote cultural processes and to define social groups. Anecdotes become reified as 'data' and the part which the Self of the anthropologist has had in the production of anthropological knowledge about Others is simultaneously disguised (Fabian, 1983; Clifford, 1988). Furthermore, these terms work to perpetuate and create a post-hoc formalism in ethnographic research which contrasts with the messy, often serendipidous and unstructured reality which daily unravels in the 'field' (Young, 1990). Thus, the carving out of a specialist and technical lexicon both distances research participants and places, redescribes the process of ethnographic work and privileges

the interpreter's account above that of the interpreted. As
Geertz has observed, at times this makes anthropology seem
like 'a variety of long-distance mind reading or cannibal-isle
fantasising' from which the anthropologist emerges as interpretive hero, seeming to know more about other people than
those Others know about themselves (1975: 14; Hayes and
Hayes, 1970).

By contrast, the contemporary emphasis upon reflexive
approaches works towards a rejection of the separations and
distinctions which such a terminology embodies and engenders.
First mooted in 1973 by Pocock, the idea of a personal anthropology has developed into a more fully fledged commitment to
make clear, rather than obviate, the inherent subjectivity of
anthropology. It is acknowledged that anthropological research
begins, as well as ends, with the anthropologist. Most importantly this shift has entailed the recognition that the Self of the
anthropologist critically informs the interpretations s/he makes
of other people's culture. Despite best efforts to suspend judgement and disbelief, who one is, what one believes and does,
implicitly and ineluctably shapes the process and products of
research: 'our past is present in us as a project' and impacts
upon our future (Fabian, 1983: 93). Accordingly, it must also
be accounted for.

Reformulated in this way, the process of 'doing fieldwork'
and depicting the Other need no longer be disguised as an
'objective' and 'scientific' method of gathering 'data' from 'informants' in the 'field'. Rather, it can be revealed as what it is:
a process of endeavouring to understand the form and process
of social relationships fostered in largely unfamiliar contexts.
Put this way, it becomes quite obvious that whilst doing fieldwork, the Self of the anthropologist is inevitably drawn into
intimate companionship with other Selves. This need not,
however, be some kind of mutual intimacy. As Geertz (1983)
reminds us, the sociality between Self and Other in the 'field'
can be variously framed, conceived and experienced. It can
range from quite formal relationships between guest and host,
sponsor and sponsored, through to a close companionship,
verging on friendship. To claim to see things from 'the native's
point of view' it is not necessary for anthropologists also to 'claim
some unique form of psychological closeness, a sort of trans-
cultural identification with [their] subjects' (Geertz, 1983: 56).
What matters is that the precise nature of that relationship is

acknowledged and explored as it unfolds through 'concrete experience and communicative interaction' (Fabian, 1983). It is this process which is integral to the generation of anthropological knowledge.

But the relationship between Self and Other does not cease when fieldwork ends. As I have already hinted it becomes inscribed in and through the written record. Acknowledging this involvement is not, however, just a matter of choosing words more carefully. More correctly, it entails recognising what a particular choice of words reveals (Campbell, 1989: 6). Thus it is that thinking and writing about the 'field' also embraces a social relationship. Existing between the Self of the anthropologist and the other Selves about whom s/he thinks, this relationship contextualises every anthropological account of other people's lives.

Patently, there are a number of conceptual problems and moral issues involved in translating between cultures. Eloquently described by Campbell, ultimately these stem from anthropology's embeddedness in social relationships. In introducing his account of living amongst the Wayapi people of Brazil he puts forward a strong case for reflexivity:

> I want to look at the relation between us and them . . . at the possibilities and difficulties of mutual comprehension between me and the people I stayed with. If I emphasize that ethnographic interpretations of other peoples are founded on this relation, where the grounds of our interest in them are just as much part of the questions as the peculiarities of what they say and what they do, this avoids, or at least tries to minimize, the obscuring effects of the conventional hypostasis that makes the people named in the title of the essay, the paper, or the book, into an object, susceptible of description and observation, so obliterating the 'us' side of the relation and turning the enterprise from a fluid indeterminate effort of understanding towards a petrified lump of observed fact. (1989: 11)

As Campbell argues, it is this very emotional and intellectual tacking between Self and other Selves, between the present of encountering Others and the present of writing about that encounter which sustains the vitality and viability which anthropological accounts can have.

In summary, then, the contemporary focus upon reflexivity in anthropology centres on the relationship between cultures through the methodological and theoretical issues raised by the individual anthropologist's encounter with individual Others in the 'field'. In doing so it makes a radical break both with the clutch of scientistic myths which have long shrouded anthropology in a cloak of social *science* and the see-and-tell, humorous fieldwork stories (Barley, 1986). It readily acknowledges the fact that anthropology is 'the study of one human being by another human being' and that that particular self-other relationship must be accounted for (Okely, 1975: 172). This shift in focus means that the 'specificity and individuality of the observer' and the inherent subjectivity of the research process can both be harnessed to theoretical endeavours (1975: 172). Released from the yoke of proving objectivity or establishing detachment, anthropology is free creatively to explore the nature of the relationship between Self and Other both at the inter and intra-personal level of fieldwork practice and that of the written text. And this holds out no less a theoretical promise than any of the intellectual strides made in earlier generations. It foretells, in effect, of an ethnography of ethnography. To this end, as Okely argues, reflexivity can and should be extensively incorporated into anthropological practice: 'the anthropologist's past is relevant only in so far as it relates to the anthropological enterprise, which includes the choice of area and study, the experience of fieldwork, research, analysis and writing' (Okely, 1992: 1).

This book is unashamedly reflexive and follows through such a programme. Clearly, a particular and personal commitment to the study of childhood informed the genesis of the project, in the manner I have already briefly described. No less, it patterned the process of the research. It prompted the questions I asked, the actions I took and the way in which children, parents, teachers and health professionals responded to me. Similarly, it shapes the style and content of this final written account. I am suggesting, then, that the knowledge and understanding of children's lives which I gained, and which I write about in this book, developed in and through my relationships with them and with the other adults who shared their lives. In this chapter I explore some of the methodological issues raised during these encounters and consider how these helped shape the understanding of childhood identities which I reached.[2]

In Search of the Self: Anthropology at Home
The ritual and teasing warnings given to initiand graduate researchers against 'going native', traditionally delivered on the

eve of departures for the field, are issued against the backdrop of a mythology of generations of encounters with the Other. These tales from the field – termed by Clifford as 'fables of rapport' – ironically affirm, through their retelling, the conceptual gulf between anthropologist and informant, between the Self and Other (1988: 40). Traditionally, they were invoked gently to remind the novice researcher that, whilst communication and relationships are very much part of doing the job over there, the main task of the anthropologist over here is to analyse, or in Campbell's (1989) phrasing, to diagnose. However, with the move towards a more reflexive research methodology gaining credence, increasing attention has been given to the experiential aspects of fieldwork and to anecdotes as a valuable source of data. This has challenged the traditional dichotomy between anthropologists and the people they study, forcing a more critical consideration of just how the Other is recognised as different and, conversely, how the Self of the anthropologist is accredited by the others whose lives s/he shares.

It is in the unpicking of this traditional dualism that anthropology 'at home' has had a particular role to play (Jackson, 1987). For instance, many anthropologists working in their own cultures have been brought up sharply by what Cheater describes as the 'disparate expectations of citizenship and profession' (1987: 165). The demands of these different identities become glaringly, at times painfully, clear when, for example, the anthropologist cannot retreat behind the roles of stranger or cultural incompetent to avoid or overcome a moral dilemma (McDonald, 1987). Furthermore, unable to leave the 'field', even when fieldwork is over, anthropologists working in their own cultures must continue to face up to the political, moral and ethical difficulties which can arise through this mixing of social roles (Cheater, 1987). On a more positive note, anthropology at home also offers particular research opportunities. Here I shall consider just two which arise from the recasting of the traditional role of the anthropologist as stranger.

The constitution of Otherness – and therefore also of Selfhood – is difficult to bound, contain and conceive of for an anthropologist working at home. It is all the more so when, as Young (1990) describes, the Self and Other are one and the same, both object and subject of study. In his study of police society in England, Young indicates the personal and professional

problems which can arise. Nevertheless it was through exploring, both experientially and intellectually, the overlap between
these arenas that Young's comprehension of police society was
enhanced. Having been a policeman for many years he took
time out to do a first degree in anthropology and then returned
to the force. Later, he completed a PhD in anthropology while
remaining employed as a policeman. It is precisely this personal
movement, in terms of his own biography, within and across
the symbolic boundaries of police society, which becomes central
to the account he provides of it. Like many other anthropologists
describing their work 'over there' from a position 'here', Young
interprets his movement out of and back into police society as
a rite of passage which provided him with a keener insight into
the structure of society (Turner, 1974a). However, for him, this
movement wrought a profound personal, as well as intellectual,
change. The policeman who returned from student life had
not only a new perspective on the future but found his past
shattered. What was more disturbing, he had to live daily, as a
new kind of policeman, with this radically revised version of
his own Self:

> I had no preparation to contend with the changes which
> the field experience created in me. That which had been
> so familiar to me and accepted almost without thinking now
> took on a new and almost bizarre aspect . . . personal trans-
> itions made across physical and psychic boundaries during
> the subjectivity of the field situation can produce disjunc-
> ture; indeed they can paralyse. (1990: 61)

Young's response was not one of stasis. In reassembling his own
biography as an insider anthropologist, personal anthropology
became an essential research tool:

> I feel the subjective account must of necessity become part
> of the ethnography in which I play all of the parts. I am
> the institutional member as well as the marginal moving
> player. I am the anthropologist and the field of study.
> (1990: 62–3)

The compelling account of police society he provides is thus
framed by the stranger to his own Self that he became in a
situation of great familiarity. The conflicting demands he experienced led him to play the role of what Mascarenhas-Keyes
(1987) has termed, the 'multiple-native'. In contrast to the concept of 'marginal native', which stresses the traditional, partial
integration of anthropologists into the communities they study,

the anthropologist as 'multiple-native' experiences an exclusive inclusion into its many different and often conflicting domains. Young's account of police society, for example, is filtered through the different lenses of being a British male, a British citizen, a British policeman and a British anthropologist and, in the text, he reflects on both the difficulties and insights gained from such a combination.

If geography is no longer the only guarantor of the stranger role for anthropologists studying their own cultures, then is it still the only way to achieve the framework of strangeness which underpins the 'distanciation' process integral to anthropological understanding (Jackson, 1987: 14)? For Ardener (1987) this is definitely not the case because, as he argues, the strange or 're-mote' lands of anthropological enquiry are also near at hand. Thus, as Hockey's (1990) study of elderly people in the north-east of England shows, the narrowing of biographical distance can offer the experience of cultural and cognitive dissonance, akin to that traditionally arising from comparative study made possible by geographical distance. For an anthropologist work-ing at home it defamiliarises the familiar, offering a peculiar opportunity to re-examine that which one thought well-known. In deliberately harnessing biography to research, Hockey creates a comparative framework within which to situate her anthropological understandings. Personal experiences of three deaths had left her literally bereaved of a perspective from which to understand these events. It was through her ethno-graphic fieldwork that she obtained one. In her account of car-ing for elderly and dying residents in a residential home, we follow the growth of her own understanding:

> Through learning the skills and taking on the tasks of a care aid for a period of nine months, I encountered the confusions and the pitfalls of performing hitherto familiar tasks such as bedmaking and bathing, table-laying and toileting, in an unfamiliar role, responsible for elderly and often incapable strangers rather than youthful relatives. These experiences were common to each novice care worker, uncomfortable but fleeting. For the fieldworker these experiences are material to be grasped, stored and sifted through. With every blunder and hesitation the gap between personal assumptions and the priorities of the in-stitution widens. Through careful reflection each can be made to stand and be known in sharp contrast to the other.

In this way a critical lack of fit comes to arise, by virtue of
the fieldworker's deliberate and self-conscious cultivation
of a sense of personal disorientation. (1990: 18)

This lack of fit, between what one thought one knew and what,
as an anthropologist at home, one gets to know anew, exempli-
fies the 'event-rich' quality characteristic of all 'remote spaces'
which sustains anthropological accounts, be they located in Oxford, the Cameroons or the Hebrides (Ardener, 1987).

These two examples have indicated the potential which a reflexive approach to research can have for anthropologists working in their own culture. Biography is intimately and inevitably
entwined with the research process; it cannot be left conveniently 'at home' while the professional assumes the leading role.
It must therefore be set to work. Thus, whilst it is clear that a
most personal and emotional experience directly prompted the
research on childhood which this book recounts, I wish now to
explore some more subtle, but no less significant, aspects of
Self-involvement in the research process. It will be shown how,
from the generation of ideas through to the writing of texts,
particular themes predominate and are threaded through the
hitherto unacknowledged influences, unvoiced disputes and unarticulated biographies in my personal history. These are reflexively recaptured to show how they have inclined me towards a
particular comprehension of childhood and of the social world
of children. I have not merely studied children: I have been a
child and borne children. Like Young (1990), I have played all
the parts of my field study through three different contexts of
childhood – my own, other children's and my own children's
childhood. In doing so I too have learnt to see from different
vantage points that which I thought I knew. The personification
of children and understanding of childhood, which I present
through the following chapters, is thus contextualised by these
three very different personal experiences and shaped by the
interplay of the themes they embrace.

Being a Child: 1954–1965

Memories of my own childhood are brief and fleeting; a series
of images spark off others. I remember my first day at school,
peering tearfully at playtime through the wire-netting fence
which cut me off as a school child from the world of the home
and the street. I remember the boy who got a wax crayon stuck
up his nose, the girl who rubbed plasticine in her hair. I remem-

ber, too, the pain and incomprehension which I, and others, daily experienced as one small girl chose those who were to be her friends. Her great power over us was matched only by our own bewilderment at it. At home my memories coalesce around our house and garden where I played, often alone, but sometimes with my sister or a visiting friend, where the Wendy House, located in the darkest corner of the garden, seemed frightening in its distance from the house. Holidays – always sunny – focus on sandy beaches and wet campsites when tiptoeing through the grass I had to avoid, shuddering with revulsion, the slugs which had come out to graze. Strung between home life and school life, memories of my childhood weave in this way an intricate web within which I locate my Self.

But such conscious memories combine with others belonging to a family lore. This fixes a mythology of experience for me as tales of my childhood are re-told. Thus, my childhood is constituted both through my own experience and the experiences of those who were part of it. As I have matured, I have grown into these other constructions of myself. I have become part of them and they have become part of my Self as different people's memories have been collectively reworked into a history of my childhood. Steedman (1986) describes this process in the introduction to her own autobiographical account:

> We all return to memories and dreams . . . again, and again; the story we tell of our own life is reshaped around them. But the point doesn't lie there, back in the past, back in the lost time at which they happened; the only point lies in interpretation. The past is re-used through the agency of social information, and that interpretation of it can only be made with what people know of the social world and their place within it. (1986: 5)

In this passage Steedman makes clear a distinction between lived childhood and accounts of childhood. She emphasises not only that childhood, like a story, is culturally constructed but that the form it assumes is shaped in the moment of narration. Thus it is that the teller of the tale becomes intimately part of that tale, reflecting the manner in which the anthropologist's Self is entwined with the selves which s/he accounts for. Memories of childhood arise out of the relationship between stories and voices, Selves and Others. Thus, whilst recalled childhood is a story which I tell myself, and which others tell for me, as my personal history will reveal I too have had a part to play in shaping accounts of childhood for other children.

Looking at Children: 1977–1983

In 1977, having left both my childhood and adolescence behind, newly graduated from Durham University, I embarked on my doctoral research. Taking up residence in a small north-eastern village, my aim was to study the culture of childhood. In my undergraduate work I had explored, through books written for children, differences in the cultural perception of childhood between the 1860s and the 1960s. This time I wanted to explore children's own perspective on the world, to see them as 'people to be studied in their own right' (Hardman, 1973: 87). I wanted, in effect, to understand children's points of view of a childhood which, in Western societies, has defined them as culturally Other than adults (Hockey and James, 1993; see also Chapter 3). During fieldwork, I delighted in this Otherness. Through the creative and evocative voices of children I explored children's cabalistic use of language and nicknames, their reinterpretation of spaces in the village, their dress and bodily style, the ways in which they teased and insulted one another. I sought to reveal their articulate and demanding participation in the socialisation process which, in more theoretical accounts of it, denies them such a vocal presence (see Chapter 3).

Thus it was that in my doctoral dissertation, I described my experiences of fieldwork with children and young people in terms of learning how to be a child again. My own adolescence, only recently discarded and yet already but half-remembered, came to me anew as I talked and listened to the children. But, experienced as an adult, it was not a childish encounter. Nor, in retrospect, was it the authentic account of childhood I had hoped for. Whilst children's stories and voices permeate the pages of my thesis and resound through the text, that text was ultimately mine: a story told by me in an attempt to make sense of the Other, through the childhoods which were daily unfolding for me. As Okely has pointed out, in her account of girls' boarding schools:

> In the study of childhood a temporal split between participation and observation is special and in some instances unavoidable, because children cannot articulate their experiences in the language of adults. Only after childhood can it be thus expressed. (1978: 111)

There is, then, an inherent paradox in the study of children and childhood. Centring on the balance between agency and structure – a rephrasing of the old problematic of the relationship between the individual and society (Cohen, 1992) – it wrestles with a number of conflicting issues. How can a voice be given to children in a culture (adult society) where the authority of their perspective on the world may be, at worst, denied or disbelieved or, at the very least, trivialised or ignored? How can children's voices – their jokes, their games, their insults – capture a cultural context (childhood, children's society) which children themselves gradually disown over time? How might a culture (childhood) be depicted which lies within a wider adult culture to which time alone gives access? All these themes run through my autobiographical dealings with childhood.

For example, from the emotional and intellectual distance which maturity brings, my post-graduate work now seems strangely divorced from any ethnographic reality while, at the same time, curiously appearing to rely heavily upon it. In part, this can be explained as a function of doing anthropology at home. As an undergraduate student at Durham University I had embarked upon a joint degree course in sociology and social anthropology but, mid-stream, a year's absence due to illness gave me time for reflection. It saw my return to social anthropology with an altered vision, both literally and metaphorically, as gradually I was seduced away from sociology by the inspired teaching of one particular lecturer, who later became my supervisor. Thus it was that as a graduate student, steeped in anthropology, I yearned for the exotic Otherness which is its promise. Following Douglas's call 'to break through the spiky, verbal hedges that arbitrarily insulate one set of human experiences (ours) from another set (theirs)', I sought to recreate, in a small British village, the Others which anthropologists more usually encounter (1973: 26). This agenda, at that time implicit and unarticulated, was accomplished through 'exoticising' the familiar world of childhood. In the manner described by Just, I worked hard to 'render it momentarily strange and bizarre' in order to understand it more fully (1978: 85). However, in doing so, I did not really 'bring the argument back from tribal ethnography to ourselves' at all (Douglas, 1973: 15). I simply rewrote it. Ironically, too, in endeavouring to give children a loud and active voice – by deconstructing their Otherness and attributing them with agency – I compounded their difference, through over-emphasising their separation from the world of adults (Munday, 1979).

My early anthropological account of childhood is thus also distanced from an ethnographic context through its more over-riding concern to critique socialisation theory. Looking with the eyes of a child, as it were for the second time, I had come to see quite clearly that cultural knowledge is acquired by children through an active, and not a passive, process of socialisation. But, in arguing this case, through a model of the separate and oppositional culture of childhood, I inadvertently displaced children's own part in the process of socialisation. At a theoretical level one universalising explanation (the plasticity of children) was quietly replaced by another (the separateness of childhood). Remaining deaf to the disquieting voices in my head and ignoring the prompts from my supervisor, in the end, I failed to give children their voice. I told their story for them. The story of childhood which comprises my thesis is but a different version of the socially and culturally constructed world of childhood. As I later came to realise, through constructing childhood as so divorced from the adult world, children themselves became spatially and temporally stranded as culturally Other. As a heuristic device it simply will not do:

> The casting of children into a timeless culture of childhood was a crucial step towards incorporating children within the discourses of social scientists – and indeed an under-standable reaction to the past obscurity of children – but claims to authenticity were . . . misplaced. This 'time capsule' model of childhood ironically reflects and con-tributes to the very universalization of childhood which it is attempting to deconstruct. (James and Prout, 1990b: 230)

Having Children: 1982–1993

My third encounter with children came through the birth and care of my sons. The decision to have children had been taken while completing my Ph.D. and having a child signalled my rite of passage into motherhood. As a parent, I was quickly con-fronted with the competing ideologies of childhood articulated by nurses and health visitors, by my own extended family, and by my friends who were also mothers. They all 'knew' what babies needed, what children wanted, what I as a mother should do. Often through my own failures to conform to these expecta-tions of needs and oughts, (which stirred memories of my own failure to be a this or that sort of child), I began to see how my children's childhood was being culturally defined. They were learning to be 'children' through confronting and negotiating the definitions of childhood given to them by me, as their mother, by their father, their teachers, their grandparents and their friends; through the books they learnt to read, the television programmes they watched and the advertisements they knowingly enjoyed. I began to see, through this mothering experience, that although children do actively carve out their own childhoods they do so within and between relatively fluid cultural constructions of what that 'childhood' could or should entail. It is this process of negotiation which this book explores.

In Search of the Self and Others: 1988–1992

By 1988, then, the themes which had run through my biographical dealings with children since the late 1970s were becoming knitted together into a more intricate pattern. Still keen to explore the child's perspective on the world, I now sought to discover what, from that perspective, distinguishes the Self from other selves, be they child or adult. Moreover, I wished to explore how such differences are culturally framed for children by concepts of childhood, socially contextualised and individually played out through their everyday experiences. The transition from research idea to viable project was facilitated by the granting of a three-year Post-doctoral Fellowship from the British Academy and was begun in the autumn of 1988. Continuing with the theme of reflexivity in this section I explore how, through the methodologies I adopted and the experience of encountering yet more children, my comprehension of the sociocultural world of childhood was to become further refined.

In setting up the project I had a number of aims which reflected aspects of my earlier research experience. For instance, I decided that, in contrast to my previous work which had specifically excluded children's experience at school, I would this time work almost exclusively in that context. In part, this reflected a personal wish to maintain some separation between my domestic and work life. The intensity of my earlier participant observation research had permitted no such boundaries to be drawn. Working this time from the experience and daily reality of parenthood, I felt it necessary to maintain some boundaries between my own children's lives and those other children with whom I would be in daily contact.

But more epistemological issues overlaid these practical considerations. First, I wanted to explore just how the 'culture of
childhood', with which I was already so familiar as a context
of children's socialisation, intersected with the children's wider
socialising experiences at home and school. This would rectify
the major omission in my earlier work. Second, the eleven years
intervening between the two projects had witnessed a prolifera-
tion of interest in ethnographies of childhood and, although
published ethnographic accounts of childhood were still few in
number, there was now a more ready acceptance of the child's
perspective on the world (see Chapter 3). This had seemed quite
radical in the 1970s. The study of childhood was no longer
regarded as only the study of socialisation or child development.
With inputs from anthropology, sociology and education it had
become one in which children could be studied in their own
right (James and Prout, 1990a). In 1977 I had deliberately
avoided contexts where adults predominated powerfully over
children in attempting to follow through such a perspective.
By 1988, I was released from the necessity of establishing this
conceptual space. I felt free to tackle the paradox of the relationship between the seemingly independent culture of childhood
and the social interdependency of children's and adult's lives.
Third, working this time in an urban rather than rural context,
schools were the easiest place to seek out children, for it is here
that children largely socialise with one another. Thus the location of my research was obvious.

Another decision concerned which age groups of children
to work with. Unconsciously perhaps I chose to work with children of ages comparable with those of my own children. At
the same time, however, I wished to locate more precisely when
children begin to participate in the 'culture of childhood'. My
earlier work had witnessed their withdrawal from it; now I
wished to observe its beginnings. A further consideration was
the growing recognition within the social sciences of the temporality of childhood, a key issue in childhood ethnographies
(James and Prout, 1990b). Discussion centred on the cultural
construction of childhood through the age-grades of the school
system and on children's own experiences of its various points
of transition (Bernardi, 1985; Measor and Woods, 1984; Woods,
1987). My past encounters with children had already alerted
me to the importance of age, along with gender, in children's
experiences of childhood. They were two aspects of identity

which children used to differentiate one from another. In the light of my current focus on the signification of difference, it was obvious that age would have to be regarded as an important cultural, as well as cognitive or developmental, variable (cf. Bloch, 1985). Whilst clearly a longitudinal study of one particular group of children was impractical, the process of social maturation could nevertheless be captured in snap-shot form by working with children who were at different social and developmental stages. I chose therefore to follow through the cycle of a school year, moving at key points of transition between different age groups of children. Beginning with those three-year-olds who had made the transition from home to nursery and were about to enter 'big school', I would leave with the nine-year-olds as they transferred to Middle school.

The school where most of my fieldwork was done was large, with approximately 400 on the roll. Situated in the middle of an estate in the centre of a large English town, Hilltop School had extensive grounds, with tarmaced and grass areas where the children could play. It boasted a new nursery unit attached to its older main building and the Middle school which it fed was a couple of streets away. As a Lower school, it catered for children between the ages of three to nine years, drawing its pupils across a broad social range but from a fairly limited locality. About 60 per cent of the children lived in council houses or rented accommodation and it was estimated that approximately 18 per cent of the children came from lone parent households or from families where parents had remarried.[3] Its ethnic mix was low – about 4 per cent – with this composed largely of children from an Afro-Caribbean or Chinese background, with some children being of mixed race. Describing it as 'not a middle-class school' the Head told me that, whilst parental involvement was high when the children first started school, it tended to drop off as the children grew older. Keen to encourage more links between home and school, the year before I joined, the Head had initiated home visits by the staff. These took place before a new child's entry into school. The school also had a Hearing Impaired Unit which, in the past, had facilitated the integration of children with a hearing disability into this ordinary school. With declining numbers of children with hearing difficulties, and the growing acceptance of children with special needs into other mainstream schools, the Unit was destined to close. During the time I was at Hilltop School there was only one child making use of this facility. However, the Head was keen to promote the integration of other children with special needs and was developing specialist resources for children with speech and language difficulties. Hilltop was, therefore, an 'ordinary' school, but was one which offered a diversity of children with whom I might begin to explore some of the issues I had identified at the outset of my research.

There were, however, two major difficulties associated with the project. The first related to the age of children I had opted to work with; the second to the sensitive nature of the issues I wished to explore. In practical terms, I could not ask such young children to philosophise or speak abstractly about the nature of friendship. Ethically, I would and could not discuss with them their reasons for disliking or excluding other children or raise issues about stigma and prejudice. Intellectually, I did not wish to define, a priori, what children might find different or unusual about other children or to make assumptions about its significance in terms of their patterns of friendship. Having chosen to be a participant observer, I would only be able to wait, watch and listen, as the children played out such issues and emotions through their daily encounters with one another. As my first day at school approached, I began to feel uneasy and ill-prepared for the task at hand.

It was these anxieties about the potential pitfalls and difficulties of the project which encouraged me to explore other avenues of research. I decided to make contact with the parents of children who, although attending ordinary schools, had defined their children as having particular kinds of special needs through membership of local Self-Help groups. I reasoned that by talking to these parents, and hopefully to their children, I would get some sense and feel of the social and emotional problems such children faced. As it turned out, these interviews provided me with not only valuable insights into children's experiences of being with other children but also of the ways in which the concept of childhood itself is given substance by the limits and boundaries which adults draw. The accounts of childhood the parents provided led me to reflect on the ways in which the concepts of 'childhood' they embodied were revealed to the children themselves and whether, in turn, this shaped children's own understanding of the Self. These preliminary observations fed into my later participant observation research in the school – for example, sensitising me to subtle nuances in children's classification of bodies and behaviour, making me more keenly aware of children's appropriation of adult language and categories or their experience of those classifications – and also, necessarily, contributes to the analysis presented here (see Chapter 3).

In essence, therefore, the research project followed two pathways to the same goal of exploring childhood identities. But the intersections I was able to construct between these different strands were instructive. They made me consider more carefully the meanings of the concepts which I was addressing. It is these which are explored in the next section.

Identity, Personhood and the Researcher

Broadly, the research upon which I had embarked sought to discover boundaries of social identity. I wished to explore not only the limits of the cultural and defining space of childhood, through which children come to know themselves as children, but also those finer lines of social discrimination used by children themselves to sort out those who belong and those who do not. Furthermore, I wished to know from whence these conceptual boundaries came, how they were erected and subsequently dissolved and the ambiguities which are engendered through their emplacement. Subsequent chapters detail these processes in their ethnographic instances as I trace out the shifting pattern of children's friendships and social relations. However, even at the outset it is possible to indicate the dynamics of this social process of identifying, or more correctly, personifying, by considering how the children saw me. This changed through time and space, as we got to know one another. It also changed through the time of childhood itself, as I moved to work with children of different ages. Thus, it is that through my experience of and feelings about being given an identity by children, the background to the processes by which personhood and social identity is ascribed, achieved or lost during childhood can already begin to be sketched in.

As a tall woman, mid-30s, my presence in a nursery class of three and four-year-old children could hardly pass unnoticed. Yet the children were well used to adult women, other than their teachers, being in the nursery. Mothers often came in to help out, trainee nursery nurses worked there intermittently and the dinner ladies appeared daily to supervise their meals. What did the children make of me? Being anxious to divest

myself of the status and power of 'teacher', I made it plain
to each new age group of children that they should call me
'Allison'. Although the three and four-year-old children did
gradually accustom themselves to this, at first they seemed con-
fused by my ambiguity. At times, through their questions and
comments, they appeared to be classing me as some kind of
equal: 'Are you in big school?'; 'Shall I hit you?'; 'You're late!';
'What is your mother called?' At other times, I was clearly more
like an adult, yet not really a teacher: 'Hey, lady', they would call
out. By the end of the term my ambiguity was beginning to be
resolved as, increasingly, they took me by the hand or asked to
sit on my lap and chatted confidingly with me. Four-year-old
Carol was by this time quite clear where I fitted in, as she reveals
in her conversation with Vera:

    VERA: (to me) Miss . . .
    CAROL: She's not Miss . . . She's Alice in Wonderland.
    CAROL: (to me) You're not a teacher. We don't call you
              teacher, do we. You're Alice in Wonderland.[4]

Moving to work with children of six and seven-years-old my
ambiguity seemed to diminish. They understood that I was writing a book about children and, although some children still
called me 'Miss', after I had known them for some time, those
with whom I most often talked usually called me Allison. On
one occasion they delighted in teasing me with the nickname,
'Mrs Bookwriter'. However, their inclusion of me into their
activities varied both spatially and temporally. In the vastness
of the playground, where the children mixed with other children of different ages and classes, I would more often revert
to the status of 'Miss'. Indeed, being on good terms with 'Miss',
seemed for some children to be a weapon in their status armoury
as they introduced me to friends in other classes. By contrast,
others, particularly the footballing boys, cared not to know me
in this context although after the bell had rung they would
resume their banter with me. Still others might call on me to
settle an argument or to intervene on their behalf; in these instances my greater authority as an adult 'Miss', would replace
my ambiguity as 'Allison'.

    The eight and nine-year-old children were less fickle in their
designation of my identity. For some, particularly the girls, I
was a confidante and friend. I was someone with whom they
could talk and, when I left the school, they wrote notes to thank
me for playing that role in the cards that they had made for

me. Others were more circumspect and maintained my adult status as a barrier between us; some vacillated in their attributions, making me the butt of jokes between themselves. Thus it would seem that increasing age permits, for some, the solidifying of their personhood as social identity becomes less context-dependent.

However, identity is not just attributed; it can be negotiated and managed as Goffman (1968) has amply explored. This too I was made conscious of during fieldwork. Like the mothers who came to help, from time to time I heard the six and seven-year-old children read, checked their spellings, supervised painting and sewing sessions and helped clear the desks at playtimes. As I did so the children chatted with me and I listened, as do other mothers, to their complaints, delights and banter. But, in my professional role, I listened more intently, attributing perhaps more significance to their casual callousness or persistent teasing. In this role of classroom helper the children regarded me most often. But in that I did not always behave as a mother, chastising or imposing upon them, I could also become subject to their jokes and teasing.

At times I consciously assumed the role of 'book writer', setting the children small tasks to do such as drawing, writing or taping conversations for me. Through their participation in these different activities, the children revealed other aspects of their social world to me. For many, such occasions represented a chance to escape from the routines of classroom life and in these contexts I was on more equal terms. The children took more notice of me; the girls would comment favourably on my ear rings, the boys might try to guess my age. Physically removed from the classroom, sitting together in the library or outside in the passage way, my adult status was diminished and, on occasion, the children would test the limits of my identity as an equal: at what point would I revert to my adult social identity and reassert my prescribed authority? Just what would I allow them to say or do? For others, particularly the girls of eight and nine-years-old, these occasions became ones when I was drawn more closely into their social lives. They told me of social alliances reforged, squabbles recently played out and more serious breaches in their friendships. In this way I became not only privy to the volatile and changing nature of their relationships but, at times, was used strategically by them. As with their own friends they tailored their conversations with me, choosing when and what to emphasise, which details of their lives to reveal, which to conceal. At times of heightened dispute among particular groups of children, sharing this intimacy with them was disturbing. It recalled for me aspects of my own childhood which I had conveniently forgotten, classing as 'childish' tiffs the very real struggles for power which they in fact were (see also Attwood, 1989). It made me anxious, both on behalf of the children with whom I worked and my own children to whom I returned each day. Thus it was that through such private conversations I was made to share in, rather than simply observe, the emotional context of childhood and the processes of social exclusion which children employ. Keeping trust and confidentiality, as different groups of girls used me in this way, was both painful and distressing.

These different identities, which I assumed and which the children imposed upon me, permitted me a partial and differential access to the children's social world. But, at the same time, I remained objectively an adult and had to behave as one. This the children also saw and it filtered their relationships with me. I was a woman, a researcher, a Dr., and a mother of two children. As an adult, the children sometimes invested me with particular powers over them to arbitrate in disputes and to relax or reaffirm school rules or wider social conventions. This I was reluctant to do and tried to circumvent but, belonging to the category of 'responsible adult', was forced on occasion to do. As a citizen anthropologist (Cheater, 1987) I could do no other. I was made to balance the conflicting demands of my personal and professional identities. Moreover, my desire to get to know the children better, to be a kind of friend, had to be reconciled with the willingness of the school staff to have me in their midst and to include me so generously in their professional and social lives.

In turn, my status as an academic, from time to time, required proof. The unobtrusive participant observation which I wished to pursue lacked any of the outward signs of 'scientific' research in progress: I had no forms, no markers, no clipboards. Gladly, and with relief, the teachers noted that I was not as serious, nor as formal, as they had at first feared. They were also grateful that I was not over-familiar with the children, that I maintained some kind of distance. One teacher recounted, with horror, her experience of a young researcher who spent her playtimes on the swings with the children, playing their games of chase and chance. The children would return to their classes high-spirited and reluctant to 'settle'. Her active presence in the children's social world collapsed too many of the child-adult boundaries of identity around which relations within schools are so delicately strung. On the other hand, although the teachers appreciated the extra pair of hands that I provided, concern was at times expressed about whether I was actually doing anything at all. Many of the research strategies which I used, and which will be discussed more fully later, were developed in response to these expressed concerns. I employed them as external signs, to signify work in progress, to reaffirm my identity as 'book writer'.

At the end of each day I left the school and assumed yet another identity. I returned to being a wife and mother, often hearing in my children's chatter affirmation of the research I was carrying out through the context of other children's childhoods. In the school this identity had no place. While my name and age were of significance to the children, relating memories of my own childhood raised no flickers of interest. Similarly, comments to them about my own children evoked few responses and if, as occasionally happened, I met the children outside the context of the school, they were often embarrassed or reluctant to acknowledge me. My identity, for them, was bound to their school context. For over a year, then, I teetered continually along these different boundaries of my own identity. My adult certainty of Self was ruptured as I was made experientially aware of the processes I had set out to study through shifts in the temporal and spatial framing of my own identity.

Identity and Personhood during Childhood

That an understanding of identity is one of the more fundamental tasks of social anthropology can be seen in the disciplinary shift from the study of social groups (1920s–1960s) to that of categories (1960s–1980s) and more recently still to that of movements (1990s). As Ardener depicts it, whether it is spoken of as 'ethnicity', 'identity' or in terms of the more fluid concept of 'belonging' (Cohen, 1982) the job is the same. It is to explore the 'apparent paradox of the continuity between social space and individuals that constitute it'; to understand how 'they are defined by the space and are nevertheless the defining consciousness of that space' (Ardener, 1987: 39).

In addressing it in this volume, I take as my starting point Cohen's (1986) observation that the 'compelling need to declare identity is social as well as psychological' and that it is the experience of belonging – whether to a culture or to a smaller unit such as a household – which allows people to mark out their 'sense of similarity to and difference from other people' (1986: ix). To belong, thus, both presupposes sociality – the being-social – and is constituted by it. However, whilst a collective cultural wisdom marks out conceptual boundaries – broadly differentiating 'us' from 'them' – it also forms more private individualised identities (Cohen, 1992). This latter point is particularly pertinent to the concerns of this volume.

First, it highlights some important theoretical issues about the constitution of 'the child' in society and children's experience of belonging to the category 'children'; second, it makes clear that 'learning culture', which is what childhood socialisation is ultimately about, is done by individuals through their experience of collectivities. Both these issues are central to the concerns of this volume. It will be shown, for instance, that whilst the concept of 'childhood' may give to individual children an identity as 'child', the experiential process of 'being a child' is not so easily categorised or contained. And yet, although no two children's experiences, no two accounts of childhood are the same, they nevertheless share in and are shaped by a commonality called 'childhood'. This interplay between categorical and individual identities will be shown to both contextualise the experiences of childhood which children have, and their re-telling.

This process can be briefly illustrated through considering how the concept of numerical age works to define childhood in Western cultures. The setting of specific age limits to the activities of all children, which denote levels of intellectual achievement in relation to age, prescribe their participation in particular social spaces while proscribing others. This means that those children whose actions take place outside the limits set for 'childhood' become pathologised. The 'gifted' child, like the 'backward' child, shares in a qualified childhood (Freeman, J., 1979). In a similar way, the Western ideology of childhood as a period of happiness and innocence works to exclude those for whom it is not (Ennew, 1986; Holt, 1975). As adults, then, we stereotype children and remain strangely reluctant, despite mounting evidence, to acknowledge, for example, the crucial differentiating roles which class, gender, health or ethnicity can play in shaping children's experience of and participation in the social world. Children are regarded, first and foremost, as 'children', a reflection perhaps of the persistence of the ideological hegemony of body-based theories of child development (Hockey and James, 1993). The experiential process of being a child becomes elided.

A corollary of this is that children become imbued with the quality of Otherness. This is effected through the social structuring of ideologies of childhood which are played out through the life-course of individual children. For example, in Britain, state institutions such as schools and the legal system combine with child-centred commodities and markets to constrain and limit the everyday activities of the young. In doing so, 'childhood' differentiates and separates children off from the rest of society. The 'culture of childhood' – the games, language and concepts used by children to map out the time and space allotted to them, their being-in-the-world – becomes, in turn, a symbol of their exclusion, a marker of their identities as children (Opies, [1959] 1977; 1969). Thus, for example, children's nicknaming practices and verbal games are understood by adults to be a sign of children's childishness, the slings and arrows, sticks and stones of being a normal child. In this way the power and influence which these names can have in children's lives may be belittled by their adult caretakers (James, 1979a). The form which childhood takes is therefore prescribed by its conceptual separation from the world of adults and the autonomy of the 'culture of childhood' so vividly depicted by the Opies is, ironically, a function of its dependence on the adult world. In a complex Western society such as Britain this is itself rapidly changing, however, and, as Schwarz (1976) has observed, may make identity temporally, rather than simply spatially, grounded, and render it responsive to fashionable changes and shifting cultural values. Tracking these shifts is as integral to the process of becoming a child as to any account of that becoming.

Childhood is also locked into a relationship with adulthood in another way. For each individual, the time of childhood is of limited duration. It ends in the Otherness of adolescence and, later, of adulthood. Being a child in a complex Western society thus presages its own opposite, with the social and experiential process through which this discontinuity (Benedict, 1955) is managed being variously glossed over with terms such as 'maturing' or 'growing up'. Thus childhood is, simultaneously, the cultural space within which children learn not only what they were but also what they are not and what they will become.

No longer babies, nor yet adult, children must, at the same time, discover what it means to be a 'child' in British society. These meanings too are temporally as well as spatially grounded.

This volume is therefore concerned to ask not only about children's identities but also about their personhood. It explores how children become socialised, become persons in the world as they socialise as persons in the world. The latter aspect is less often considered for, through their constructed Otherness, children's status in British society is as non-persons, relegated to a social, economic and political marginalisation (Carrithers, Collins and Lukes, 1985; Hockey and James, 1993). Children are regarded as people in the process of becoming, rather than being: a distinction which both circumscribes interpretations of children's social lives and, through providing the grounds for particular social policies on their behalf, impinges more directly upon their own lived experiences.

For example, while any casual observer in the streets, parks and playgrounds of Western industrial societies would find it hard to deny children's active social presence, the idea that children have the conceptual status of 'persons' seems far more radical. Children are children: of the same species certainly but still not quite fully human. As Marcel Mauss ([1938] 1979) observed, although consciousness of the Self is a human universal, social recognition of the Self varies in relation to jural rights and moral responsibilities. Thus it is that not all individuals in a society will have the social significance of their identities confirmed by acquiring personhood (La Fontaine, 1985). They will remain marginalised or excluded on the basis of their age, sex or ritual status.

For example, the persisting reluctance to grant children the status of persons in British society is the culmination, during the nineteenth century, of a progressive social and ideological marginalisation which accompanied the development of the concept of childhood (Hockey and James, 1993; see also Chapter 3). Nineteenth-century philanthropic and benevolent acts on behalf of the child effectively set children apart from the adult world and put a final seal upon the category of child. This cultural process is most obvious in the history of child labour reforms. Whilst the nineteenth-century Factory Acts spared children from the many exploitative practices they had endured in cotton mills and mines, this legislation at the same time gradually took from children any right to work. In turn, children's absence from adult work-space became a definitional criterion of the social status, child, a conceptual grounding upon which the Education Acts rapidly began to build. What these reforms did not do, however, was to eradicate entirely the labour done by children. Instead, it was driven underground, which perpetuated, if not exacerbated, its exploitative aspect (Fyfe, 1989). That concepts of 'personhood' are intimately entwined with concepts of 'work' in Western industrialised societies (Kohli, 1988) means, contemporarily therefore, that children, who by definition are non-workers, are also non-persons (Hockey and James, 1993).

Personifying Children

What I have to say in this volume starts from these theoretical perspectives on identity and personhood. The Western idea of childhood 'as a period of lack of responsibility with rights to protection and training but not to autonomy' means that the beings which children are, are continually set apart from the persons they will become (Ennew, 1986). In consequence children's individual identities are transformed and homogenised through their categorisation as children, with their individuality, their Selfhood, often made secondary to their status as children. This process occurs no less in academic accounts (see Chapter 3), than it does in the course of everyday life where laws and cultural norms dictate what children can or cannot be. Just as 'other cultures' become subject to generalisations, 'the child' has often been used as a generalised identity through which to depict the lives of individual children (Campbell, 1989) It is in contrast to such perspectives that this volume is written (to adapt Geertz (1983) 'from the [child's] point of view' to (adapting Cohen) 'find the 'self-conscious [children] who are submerged beneath' the generalised category of children (1990: 2). Such an approach does not mean that anthropology is being replaced by social psychology. Rather, it means that anthropological approaches to childhood may help to restore to children their conscious humanity.

The idea of personifying children, the aim of this volume, captures this mood. It hints at the emphasis placed here on reflexivity for, in its very ambiguity, it elides any distinction between Self and Other. First, through its use as a transitive verb, personifying children suggests that children are members of a marginal social category, beings who lack the status attribution of a 'person'. They are in a position to be personified by an Other, be that another child or an adult anthropologist. This highlights the ambiguities of children's assumed structural dependency and categorical passivity. Second, and in radical contrast, personifying can be regarded as an adjective, used to describe children: children who personify. In this sense, children are positioned as active members of the social world who attribute personhood to themselves and to Others. This stresses their participatory presence in the process of learning about social identity. Forming a bridge between these positions, third, personifying children describes the process of doing ethnographic research with children and of writing about that research. Following Hardman's (1973) proposals for an anthropology of childhood, this involves seeing children as 'active in the construction and determination of their own social lives, the lives of those around them and the societies in which they live' (Prout and James, 1990: 8). It also acknowledges the ways in which the cultural construction of Western childhood works to deny them this attribution. Personifying children thus encapsulates my own desire to grasp the horns of this conceptual dilemma, one which children themselves face daily in their everyday encounters.

Although making no claims to novelty, the style in which the argument of this book is presented reflects a genuine desire to move away from ethnographic authority (Clifford, 1988) while not rejecting the 'burden of authorship' (Geertz, 1988). For this reason my account – my interpretation of children's activities, of parents' comments, of teachers' observations – is placed alongside theirs. My analysis of the children's conversations is accompanied by those conversations. In this way, the polyphonic voices of children of different ages, their parents, their teachers and their doctors, permeate the text, recalling and reinstating, as Clifford (1988) notes, the role of the privileged informant by whom Malinowski (1922) laid so much store. For children, in particular, such a role is indeed a privilege in that traditional accounts of childhood tend to mute, mimic or misrepresent their words. Extracts from tape transcripts, rhymes, jokes and snatched phrases thus literally indent the formal analysis in the text as, stylistically, children's words (and those of adults talking about children) are separated from my words, just as their understanding of the world is distanced from my own. In this way I try to evoke and give space for the many and varied voices of which this account is composed.

Adopting such a polyphonic style, however, entertains certain risks. In particular, criticism can be levelled against the use of apt illustration or memorable anecdotes for, in the end, of course, ethnographic authority remains with me, the author. I have the power to select some rather than other voices: 'quotations are always staged by the quoter and tend to serve merely as examples or confirming testimonies' (Clifford, 1988: 50). However, in the context of the centrality of Otherness to this volume this risk is worth taking. Children's understanding of the relationship between Self and Other, of being constituted as Other by other Selves, and the part this plays in their becoming social, constitutes the core of what I wish to say. In the light of this, to write as if Otherness were unproblematic would seem strange.

As Cohen observes, the history of social anthropology has been that of distancing 'self' from 'other' through perpetuating 'the absence of self-conscious selves from our accounts' (1990: 6). Elsewhere he reminds us, that while a collective cultural wisdom marks out conceptual boundaries, broadly differentiating 'us' from 'them' – the English from the Welsh, ethnographers from informants, teachers from pupils, parents from children – these, simultaneously, mask a set of disparate, more private identities (1986). Thus, he argues

> (a) that we should not confuse the appearance of conformity with the uniformity of selves; and (b) that we must not go on writing ethnography in a manner which ignores self-consciousness for to do so is to misrepresent people. We cannot do justice to societies if we cannot do it to individuals. (1990: 11)

For these reasons, then, I have opted to unpack the generalised category of children not only through what I say but by the way in which I write about it. In brief, I began with a personal crisis, translated by an initial imaginative act. Later, I pursued my thoughts further through participant observation fieldwork and interviews, endeavouring to discover and unravel some of the meanings which children variously attach to the body's appearance and gender, to social skills and behaviour, in the making and breaking of friendship. The following chapters explore some of these ideas, showing how children's concepts of self, identity and personhood begin to take on particular forms and meanings as they grow older. But, in turn, this raises conceptual questions about the nature of childhood in Western society which, necessarily, feed back into my interpretation of what children think and feel about the process of growing up and making friends. In the very act, then, of thinking and writing about the Other (children), the Self (the I) becomes involved in its creation (Clifford, 1988; Geertz, 1988). The account of childhood I present in the following chapters can only ever be one version; it is my interpretation of the many childhoods which the children I worked with lived and experienced.

Notes

1. A previous encounter, no doubt also shaping my research ideas, was an illness which I had at 19 years of age which left me blind in one eye.
2. In turn, these are, of course, framed by Western constructions of childhood such as those discussed in Chapter 3.
3. That this figure may seem rather low, reflects the differential experience for children of social factors such as divorce and poverty through the life course. As Qvortrup (1990) has shown, statistical information does not usually take into account this variation in experience. Single-parent households may not be as common an experience for children under nine years of age as they are for older children.
4. This intriguing literary reference by this four-year-old girl reflects less her familiarity with the classics of English literature than her early sociality, in which such verbal skills as punning and rhyming are highly valued (see Chapter 5).

TWO

Accounting for Children

Narrating Difference

In his discussion of conversation in the city Rapport (1987) shows how varied and various are the meanings which emerge through talk, despite the apparent consensus of meanings upon which conversations are predicated. He writes that 'language may be revealed as hosting a multitude of voices in situational agreements and oppositions, overlapping, colliding and contradicting' (1987: 140). The following two chapters trace out such a kaleidoscope of voices by exploring the variety of accounts of childhood which are given of and to children in contemporary British society. It is alongside these that my own account of childhood must be situated and by these which children's own accounts of childhood are contextualised.

I begin with a particularly dramatic account offered by one woman as, seated one evening with other women around a low coffee table, experiences of child-rearing were exchanged. For each woman, the childhood of one of their children had been particularly problematic and it was to share this experience that the women had chosen to gather together. Each had a story to tell about the everyday difficulties and feelings involved in caring for a child with asthma or eczema or the problems they had encountered on discovering their child was dyslexic:

> She was like a wild animal . . . normal things like brushing her hair or cleaning her teeth – that didn't matter. Just getting through a day with her . . . doing that. We took it in turns to go out because I couldn't cope with the stares and the comments. Not always . . . because I think it came through ignorance about the illness but the lack of compassion. I couldn't cope with it on top of everything else. I don't think it was the right thing that we did but obviously you do what you think was best at the time, but we used to hide away like hermits.

In this account is a densely textured vision of a particular

childhood – Phillipa's. It is not, however, Phillipa's experience
of it but her mother's memory of what life was like when her
daughter was not yet two years old. As a reconstruction of the
past it is both emotive and evocative, condensing in one brief
paragraph, past and present feelings about the strain her daughter's condition placed on 'normal' family life. Neither is it a
childhood which rings with familiarity. It presents a radical
contrast to the safe, happy and protected childhood which has
become sentimentalised in the particularity of its dominant
Western ideological form (see Chapter 3). As portrayed by her
mother, Phillipa was like a wild animal at eighteen months old,
rendering abnormal the normality of daily mothering routines.
The object of stares rather than fond gazes, her mother recalls
her early life as taking place in a twilight zone outside the
boundaries of normal childhood.

Yet Phillipa's condition was not uncommon. She had chronic
eczema. Neither was this a singular account. Many comparable
stories of childhood were recounted for me during other interviews, carried out at the start of my research. Envisaged as a
pilot study for my later participant observation research among
children in schools, these slim biographies allowed me to identify
significant areas for future exploration and themes which could
be followed through. As active members of self-help groups for
asthma, eczema, dyslexia, diabetes, epilepsy and food allergies,
these women with whom I talked laid out for me at different
times some of the problems their children had at 'being children', at participating in their own childhoods.[1] Thus, while
some of the other narratives might lack the vivid imagery and
textual immediacy of Phillipa's mother's story, they are none
the less confirming both of its themes and its emotive style and
framing.

Through these personal narratives of childhood, this chapter
begins to explore the process of accounting for childhood and,
in doing so, addresses some of the issues raised by anthropological work within the field of conversational analysis and
the ethnography of speaking (Bauman and Sherzer, 1974;
Gumperz and Hymes, 1972; Rapport, 1987). The cultural and
psychological settings of the interviews, the implicit and explicit
purposes of the conversations I held with these mothers, and
the tone and manner of delivery which their 'talk' embodies are
all important features of the accounts the women gave, for, as
Hymes has argued, '*how* something is said is part of *what* is said'

(1971: 59). For instance, that these mothers volunteered to talk with me is indicated by a particularity of purpose, paralleling the particularity of tone and style patterning the conversations which I was later to hold with the children (see Chapters 4–7). That all were members of self-help groups, sharing in the norms and illness-meanings of those groups, also gives a distinctive framing to the messages about childhood which these women offered to me. In accounting for their accounts, then, I place considerable importance on these dimensions to our conversations.

These narratives also reflect on and contextualise the feelings which these mothers had about caring for a child with special needs of different kinds.[2] Through the commonality and/or diversity of the images and metaphors which they choose to use in their descriptions can be seen cultural similarities and, at times, important differences between their individual experiences. A common narrational structure scripts a specific cultural performance, designed both to instruct as well as to inform me, a willing and eager listener. Later, a change of tone and content in our conversation might register a shared sympathy and temporary intimacy as I, a mother myself, listened and responded to their experiences (Graham, 1984). This chapter asks, therefore, what particular images of childhood are presented in these women's accounts and how are these representations sustained and enlivened through their delivery? In later chapters, I shall ask the same of the children's conversations with me: what kind of accounts of themselves, what social identities, do children provide through their skilled cultural performances? As narratives of the past, these accounts clearly work as rationalisations in the present. Through this interpretive process they offer a perspective on childhood which derives from a most personal and individual experience. At the same time, however, it is clear that these accounts of childhood are also eminently *social* constructions, contextualised by the parents' participation in local self-help groups, by their belonging to a particular social class, a particular locality and a particular nation. In this sense, as a collection, the women's stories also reveal some common cultural boundaries to the category 'children' and the idea of 'childhood' through, as I shall suggest, their embrace of evaluations of what 'normal' childhood should be like. What this chapter explores, then, is the way in which these stories implicitly acknowledge but differently incorporate some notion of 'normal' childhood. Embedded deep within British culture, this is used by the mothers both to understand and to contextualise their own children's various and varied childhoods. Whether constituted through or shaped in contrast to it, some notion of 'normal' childhood provides an implicit framework, which lends to their accounts an emotive and evocative power (Armstrong, 1983; Vosey, 1975).

In coming to terms with their children's childhood the parents' stories draw on a number of subtly different and, at times, competing discourses of childhood. These range from those centred around specific medical or educational definitions of 'normality' in relation to child health and levels of attainment through to more diffuse cultural concepts of 'normal' family life or ideals of a happy childhood. The accounts reveal, therefore, that the seeming 'homogeneity' of the cultural category 'child', which informs and is informed by a dominant cultural construction of childhood, is refined and qualified through the heterogeneity of everyday social experiences. At the same time, however, the power which the stereotype of a 'normal' childhood has – played out daily through the school, the media or the doctor's surgery – continues to temper and, as it were, normalise or homogenise that varied experience. Thus, it is through exploring these biographical narratives that this chapter can begin to address the central theme of the book: the personhood of children. Here it is pursued through examining variation, rather than consistency, in the categorical identity of 'child'. In this way, the experience of 'being a child' which shapes a child's identity and sense of Self becomes highlighted through the intensity and emotion of these children's particular difficulties.

The women's accounts also provide insight into how, again through reference to unconscious ideals of 'normal' childhood and the 'normal' child, the socialising contexts of the family, the medical world and the school system might begin to frame children's own ideas about Otherness, Selfhood and social identity. Although embracing varied perceptions of what constitutes significant differences in both the social and physical body, these competing discourses are revealed as powerful forces in children's lives. They shape a child's participatory presence in the culture of childhood and permit the realisation that cultural classifications of 'difference' can lead to the devaluation of personhood (Booth and Statham, 1982). A further value of these narratives lies, therefore, in what they might indicate about the wider framing of children's social identities and personhood through the cultural context of childhood, a process to be explored in detail in the chapters which follow.

Reflexivity and Account-giving

Rapport argues that 'in the personalising of language may be found not just the construction of individual identities but also that of larger social entities in which individual speakers locate themselves' (1987: 155). In the gaps and emphases of these parents' accounts can be seen just such a process of identifying. Particular kinds of childhood are being spoken of through the particularities of certain children's childhoods. Questions must be asked, then, about the nature of these constructions: what themes are highlighted, which downplayed and what is excluded altogether from these accounts of parenting? Consideration must also be given to the self-selected nature of the sample. Why did these particular parents, rather than others, offer to speak with me?[3] What does this add to the understanding of childhood which their accounts provide?

Most of the mothers, and some fathers, clearly felt that they had a tale to tell. They had something important and significant to contribute to my research and were willing to speak with me. Often their participation was phrased in terms of the benefit which a discussion of their experiences might bring for other children. In this sense, as in my later conversations with children at school, I was a vehicle for a more public expression of identity. However, it was also clear that in many, although not all instances, I was not the first person to hear their stories. Mainly, but not exclusively, articulate middle-class parents offered stories which were well-rehearsed. In some instances, it was clear that the past had been extensively recounted, reworked and gone over. Possibly, this reflects their participation in self-help groups where hearing other people's experiences provides the comfort, therapy and practical knowledge sought out by new members. It may, too, reflect the more personal and private process of self-revelation by which parents endeavour to make some coherence between past events and present lives. The chaotic, often traumatic, events of the past may be conceptually ordered through acts of repetitive narration and, in this sense, talking with me was an ongoing part of this process (Graham, 1984). Family crises resulting from illness or debilitation can be made to take on a purposive direction through talk which, in

the moment of their occurrence, may seem devastatingly arbit-
rary. Thus, in coming to terms with their own children's childhoods, these tales had often been told. The group of women
who met with me to share their experiences asked of each other:
'What story do you have to tell? Are you going to tell your story?'
A fieldwork note, jotted down at the time, records my own feelings about that evening when, as a researcher, I too was enabled
to re-tell my son's story:

> Ryan (Maureen's son) has dyslexia and his dyslexia has
> obviously been a source of interest for all the family. Maur-
> een's tale is well-rehearsed, told with Chris (his elder sister
> who is also present) filling in the missing bits. She helps
> recount the family's discovery of Ryan's dyslexia. This nar-
> rative reconstruction of biographical events is interesting
> to focus on for each [woman] has a drama to unfold. The
> symptoms, the event, the diagnosis, the coping. Does it
> become less traumatic, more distant, the more often one
> tells the tale?

Further insight into this process of constructing accounts is
provided in the next example. Part of a longer interview, it
stresses the particularity of the childhood being presented to me.
An active participant in her local dyslexia group, the mother sat
with me, her mother, and her two children around a large
dining-table. The father, seated in an armchair in another part
of the room, while listening to our conversation, distanced
himself from participation in it. Throughout our lengthy discussion, it was the mother who took control over both its course and
content. Following a harrowing description of her daughter's
experiences at a local primary school, of her struggles with
spelling and mathematics, the extract shows the mother seeking
confirmation, from the other family members present, of the
distress and difficulty dyslexia can cause:

> MOTHER: Now Paula's confidence at eight had gone.
> Hadn't it? You weren't confident in yourself. Do
> you remember what you said to me? You thought
> you were . . .
>
> JAMES: (breaking in) Thick.

Here the mother encourages her daughter to participate in the
construction of the account, to get the story right and to affirm
the family's view of the past. Interrogatives prompt particular
perspectives in this shared and familial story, for it is James, her
elder brother, who fills in the missing word. It is an understand-

ing of a past event, confirmed again through its re-telling in the present.

Later in our conversation Paula tries to contradict some details of her mother's account of specialist dyslexic teaching:

MOTHER: You recognise the letter and the sound it makes and you slowly build it up. Now also they've got to learn the alphabet frontwards, backwards, from the middle, you name it.

PAULA: (challengingly) I didn't do that.

ALLISON: Did you have a song? [i.e. as an aid to learning]

MOTHER: No songs. Now, this is what you do, see.

In her wish to emphasise the considerable impact which dyslexia has had on her daughter's experience of childhood, the mother exaggerates the specialist learning which she had to become involved in: learning the alphabet frontwards, backwards, from the middle. Her daughter's corrective, 'I didn't do that' is brushed aside; its literality detracts from the pace and power of the unfolding narrative. As the interview progressed, and I learnt of the battles fought with education authorities and the familial distress dyslexia had caused, the mother's purpose in talking with me became clear. Committed to the wider acknowledgement of dyslexia as an educational special need, my research represented another channel of communication. She had helped to mobilise extra teaching resources for local dyslexic children and had conducted many campaigns on their behalf. This is how she described her successful dealing with one school:

Mr Smith took over as head. And I went in the day he took over and said: 'I'm Mrs Jones, Paula's mother, and I shall be removing my child twice a week [for dyslexia lessons]', and he said: 'Do you think it does any good?' And I said: 'Yes'. And as time progressed he went round to dyslexia.

The account of Paula's childhood revealed to me through conversation with her mother has, then, to be read through this particular framing. Paula's feelings of social isolation at school, for instance, are interpreted by her mother as indicative of the wider and encompassing nature of being dyslexic. Problems in her relations with teaching staff are seen as a manifestation of their refusal to acknowledge Paula's dyslexia; her lack of friends is attributed to the humiliating experience of always being bottom of the class. Another mother of a dyslexic child herself recognised this process of easy attribution:

I think that's the problem. With not having a normal child

we tend to think and see everything that she does as perhaps related.

However, noting the strong framing of Paula's mother's account in no way diminishes its pertinence (Bertaux, 1981). Neither does it discredit the experiences it recounts. Many parents of children with dyslexia confirmed, through parallel examples, the personal and educational difficulties it created for their children. What it does do, however, is underline the socially constructed nature of childhood. It alerts us to the implicit structuring of any account of children's lives, whether given by health professionals, teachers, parents or anthropologists and, through this, to the representations of childhood which children themselves encounter in their daily lives. Thus, the process of accounting for children cannot be regarded unproblematically as simply a matter of recall or report. It is an interpretive process which draws on particular discourses of childhood to make sense of and order the progress of individual children's lives. It must therefore be reflexively recounted.

Constructions of Normal and Different Childhoods

As Armstrong (1983) has observed, twentieth-century medical knowledge witnessed the growing objectification of the child and a new way of seeing childhood. No longer merely an object of clinical gaze the idea of the 'normal child' emerged as a by-product of the introduction of child-health surveys and clinics during the 1940s. First located within the body of the child, through the identification and prevention of specific diseases or disorders, this perception of 'normality' later extended to the social space surrounding the child. Medicine forged links with the fields of education and welfare to identify problems external to, but nevertheless detrimental to, the child's body, such as poor housing and feckless parenting. In turn, this became part of an increased community surveillance of the child. This constant questioning of variations in and the limits to normality meant that, in time, all children came to share in the risk of being different. As Armstrong notes, discrete distinctions between normality and abnormality became increasingly difficult to sustain.

For the mothers with whom I talked it was precisely the elusive nature of such definitions which, ironically, enhanced their classificatory power. Through using subtly different stereotypes of 'normality' and 'abnormality', drawn from different discourses, parents were enabled to contextualise the idiosyncrasies of their own children's conditions. That is to say, through distancing *their* child from objectified images of *the* child, they were able to categorise and homogenise that which their children were not. This occurred in two distinct ways. Some parents located the individuality or particularity of their own children's childhood through comparison with a stereotype of 'normal' childhood; others did so through contrast to it.

In terms of the official classification 'child with special needs', most of the children whom I heard of and talked with would not fulfil its criteria.[4] All the children attended 'ordinary' rather than 'special' schools and yet, apparent in their parents' stories, was a perception that these children had particular and special needs which were different from those commonly identified as 'children's needs' (Woodhead, 1990). Some of these 'needs', for instance, related to medication and treatment regimes; other 'needs' had precipitated the restriction or, conversely, the encouragement of particular abilities or activities. The question occurs, then, what is 'special' about 'special needs', and from whose perspective are these being defined (Booth and Statham, 1982; Booth and Swann, 1987)? For many of the parents with whom I talked this critique, whilst unstated, none the less seemed to form the backdrop against which they thought about and interpreted their own child's experiences. No less important, however, in shaping their understanding of their child's condition were prevailing definitions of 'needs' and 'normality' emanating from the world of medicine. As Bryan Turner has argued:

> The way in which an individual interprets or understands their disorders will depend, not upon the individual whim or fancy, but significantly upon the classifications of illness which are available within a culture and by reference to general cultural values concerning appropriate behaviour. (1987: 215–6)

What these parents narratives reveal, then, is the process through which they sought out and got to know the conceptual limits and boundaries of differing definitions of childhood through the minutiae of their daily social interactions with educational and health professionals.

While together the stories depict a shifting categorisation of children's needs and experiences the cultural terrain of childhood mapped out through these accounts is oriented in two main directions: one inclines towards some notion of normality, the other leans to that of difference. Although most of the narratives are patterned with similar themes – the drama and discovery of a specific problem, followed later by the highlighting of particular times of crisis, present difficulties and strategies of daily care – there are, none the less, subtle differences in where the emphases are placed. These vary in relation to whether the parents's image of their child is of a child who is (a) differently *normal* or (b) normally *different*. While in some instances, which classification is used might be understood as an unequivocal response to a particular illness or disease, this was not always the case. There was no one-to-one correlation between disease and parental classification of their child. Instead, what the accounts clearly reveal is the significance of the parents' experiential encounters with childhood professionals such as doctors, health visitors and teachers in shaping and indeed changing their perceptions of their child's condition (see Davis, 1982). This echoes Turner's observation that:

> medical professionals have become the moral guardians of contemporary society, because they have a legitimate domination of the categorisation of normality and deviance. (1987: 217)

However, what also becomes clear from these narratives is the challenge to this domination offered by some parents in their personal quest for a more acceptable and, in their opinion, more accurate classification of their child.

The Differently Normal Child

There have been a number of sociological studies, as well as more personal accounts, of the impact on family life of having a disabled or chronically sick child (see Philip and Duckworth, 1982), of which Vosey's (1975) study of parenting is perhaps the most well-known. In it she shows how parents work hard to 'normalise' family life, to down-play or even deny the significant differences which their child's different needs make to family life. Responding to the moral ideology of parenting, the families found ways to align their own experiences with those of 'normal' families, thereby distancing themselves from the idea of the 'disabled family'. Although most of the children whose parents I talked with were not profoundly disabled, like those in Vosey's study, the rhetoric of some of the parents' stories is remarkably similar. It stresses the essential 'normality' of daily life.

For many of these parents recognition and acceptance of their children's condition had been precipitated by the dramatic enactment of the disease: an asthmatic attack or an epileptic seizure. A mother recalls the events leading up to her son's first asthma attack:

It was a Friday night, 11.00 at night, and I could hear there was something wrong and I phoned up the emergency doctor and they said get him to casualty straight away so we took him down there. We arrived with all the drunks from the town. It was awful and they locked us in one of the side rooms in the end and put him on a nebuliser and he seemed OK. So they sent us away and he hadn't been home a couple of hours when he was wheezing again . . . I didn't know what it was so I sat up with him till 9.00 when the doctors opened. The doctor put him on a nebuliser again and he said, 'I don't know quite what's wrong myself . . . I'll have to send him to hospital . . . there's something wrong.' And he was diagnosed as asthmatic.

From that point on, like the parents Vosey interviewed, she worked hard to 'normalise' her son's physical condition. The identification of such turning-points is common in many parents' narratives. It fixes the time when they felt able to accept their child's condition and to acknowledge it as but a different version of normal childhood. A founder member of a swimming club for children with asthma, for example, described herself as being, 'six years ago . . . the neurotic mother of a neurotic child'. After a period of time, during which she refused to accept that her child's 'chestiness' should be diagnosed as 'asthma', a conversation with her doctor encouraged her to adopt a more positive attitude. The setting-up of a swimming club represented, for her, the 'normalising' of her child's condition and was expressive of her wish that her son should not 'have a chip on his shoulder' about being asthmatic.

Classed by the medical professions as being 'different' – that is, as having particular and special medical needs – many of the children with asthma, epilepsy and diabetes were seen, nevertheless, by their parents as being essentially 'normal' children. Having conditions whose effects could usually be managed through medication, they felt strongly that their children could and should take a place alongside ordinary children. Reflecting a ready concurrence with prevailing medical assessments of conditions, such as asthma, diabetes and epilepsy, they felt that their children's Otherness could be effectively controlled and contained.

This legitimation by the medical professions of their child's condition, as being different but as being within the bounds of normality, is reflected in the attitudes towards doctors expressed in the parents' stories. They are described as being both extremely helpful and sympathetic to children's problems:

> Our doctor's very good. When Patrick was in hospital with asthma he came up a couple of days afterwards just to ask how he was and we hadn't called for him or anything. He's very very good indeed.

> The doctors are fantastic. I've only got to ring and they're here. I got to the stage when he was three and half that I daren't ring the doctors. I thought, 'Oh God, they'll say: Not you again.' But Dr Phillips he's been there a long time – he's retired virtually now – and he said: 'Look, Mrs Tanner, don't ever worry about ringing us because whenever you ring you always need us.' Dr Hughes has a check on him every two months. He's excellent.

A normalising strategy common to a number of the narratives is the evocation of stereotypes of 'abnormality'. The extremes which they represent enables parents to distance themselves and their child from the stigmatised and unwanted categorical identity of being different. The mother of a girl with epilepsy described how, in this way, the family reiterated their daughter's essential 'normality' to themselves:

> You're very lucky if you get through life without anything and we try to accept it that way. We say, 'You've got epilepsy but you could have been worse off.'

A mother of a girl with cerebral palsy adopted a similar strategy. She was able to 'normalise' her daughter's condition through comparison with those she felt to be more 'different' than she. Remarking that, in comparison to a mental handicap, 'with a physical handicap you know what you're up against', she went on to describe in more detail her feelings about her daughter's condition:

> It can't get worse and it won't get better but it will appear to get better because she will be able to do more. But something like cystic fibrosis or muscular dystrophy, that would crucify me.

In this way, the differences in bodily conditions which their own children exhibit come to be understood by parents as but a normal variation of childhood.

In shoring up this interpretation of their children's classification as but differently normal, many parents played down the constraints which their child's condition placed upon family life. For example, although mentioning the disruption caused by the often sudden and dramatic hospitalisation of children with asthma or the difficulties of taking children with eczema on foreign holidays, they chose to represent family life to me as everyday, commonplace, as essentially unremarkable. One mother of two asthmatic children describes her family's 'normal' life:

> It imposes a routine. It's a normal life three times a day. Three times for Robin and three times for Alice plus ventolin when necessary and when they are bad other things as well. I have had to nebulise her four times a day. I take her away from school, nebulise her and back she goes again . . . They take it for granted.

Through incorporating medication regimes into the pattern of daily living, asthma is kept firmly in the background. For this family it is an explicit strategy as the next extract shows:

> FATHER: Monday, I had a holiday and we took them to the park to play football and they were going up and down like mad things, weren't they? Had she had a ventolin before?
>
> MOTHER: No, she had a ventolin half way through . . . but that was a dubious one. She was getting out of breath, but we had run a long way. Although I don't want to overgive a drug I don't want her to get frightened. I did give her one there because I wanted her to enjoy the rest of the running around, but she wasn't in a proper asthma attack.

While houses might have to be kept dust-free, pets might have to be forbidden, and visits to other people's houses, school outings or guide-camps restricted or even forbidden, in their accounts, parents minimised the disturbance which these differences made to normal family life. They preferred, instead, to highlight those events in which their children could freely participate.

Offered to me, then, were accounts of the normality of these children's childhood, a perception sustained by their parents through a broad rather than a narrow definition of what 'normal' childhood consists of. It is one which embraces, rather than denies, heterogeneity in the experience of childhood.

Making the Transition

Some parents less readily concurred with this view of childhood and felt unable so easily to employ such 'normalising' strategies. They appeared uncertain about the lack of difference their child's difference made. Thus, in some narratives can be seen a progressive conceptual re-framing of a child's 'normality' as, still ill-at-ease with this definition, the parents endeavoured to effect a reconciliation between their own experience of child-rearing and the available cultural stereotypes of a 'normal' childhood. Commonly mentioned in such accounts was the role which 'luck' had played in their lives. Perhaps through its random and capricious qualities, this attribution allowed for *both* the continued expression of uncertainty or anxiety *and* the promise of a positive, more normal outlook. Some parents strongly expressed a feeling that they had been particularly 'lucky' in having received good medical care; others that they had been fortunate in the attitudes teachers had taken towards their children's condition. Still others praised the way their children had stoically accepted regimes of medication and bouts of hospitalisation, commenting how lucky they had been that their son or daughter had offered little resistance and remained cheerful. In comparison with other possible outcomes – indeed, as luck would have it – they felt that their children's experiences and their own as parents might be considered to fall within the range of an acceptable and normal childhood.

In the following extract this process of reconceptualising can clearly be seen as one mother comes to terms with her child's eczema. Although later during the interview she admitted to me that coping with her son's chronic condition is both unremitting and emotionally stressful, in this extract she struggles to perceive it more positively:

> We eat better now because it's made me stop and look at what we're eating. We've benefited from him having it . . . if eczema can be a benefit . . . it really has . . . It's time-consuming because sometimes I might be cooking one thing for him and another for us. I try to cook things we can all have so we've improved our diet. And it's got easier. There's a lot more soya-based products now. It's a problem

because they don't have to always declare ingredients unless it's over a certain amount so it could have had milk added to it. So you are limited. But he has helped us. We always say that.

Her son's condition, exacerbated by eating dairy products, made cooking for the family a daily problem. Here her initial, perhaps unguarded, acknowledgement of these difficulties is followed by their swift reframing in a more positive light.

For another mother, whose daughter had asthma, whose son experienced learning difficulties at school and whose husband had recently left home, the concept of the 'normal' family loomed large in her narrative. Summing up her feelings for me, she concluded that:

> there's so many problems that probably could have been alleviated by having a proper family life.

Other parents, although recognising that their child's condition had wrought some changes in their life-style, were struggling hard to retain a commitment to this 'normal' family life. Like the families in Vosey's study, a mother of a Downs Syndrome child remarked pointedly:

> Just because you have a handicapped child it doesn't make you a handicapped family. Susan doesn't even know she's handicapped.

Thus, some idea of 'normal' family life and 'normal' childhood also permeates these accounts. In this instance it provides an implicit life trajectory from which many parents feel they have been forced to make a deviation and on to whose course they are striving to return.

A Normally Different Childhood

The narratives so far considered have depicted a childhood that is perceived as differently normal. That is to say, while recognising that their children have particular problems, the parents' experience of them has been conceptualised within a framework of normal childhood, an understanding which was facilitated by the medicalisation of these 'differences'. Parental claims for acknowledgement of their child's sickness or disability had been unproblematically affirmed by the medical profession. Assistance, advice and medication had been readily given and had become routinised into a normal way of life. However, it is clear from other accounts that such confirmation of a child's special needs is not always so forthcoming. Some parents described how their children's conditions had been dismissed by health and educational professionals as being but common childhood complaints. The differences their children exhibited were seen as unexceptional, only to be expected, as falling within the normal range; consequently, they had received little or no specialist attention.

Not surprisingly, these parents' stories offer a radical contrast. First, the accounts of their children's childhoods emphasise its difference, rather than its normality. Second, they are shaped by a more homogeneous and restricted conception of 'normal' childhood than the expansive version previously described. Against this the differences which their children exhibit are made to stand out as significant and substantial. Third, vociferous in their claims to the disturbing effects their child's condition had had on family life and the difference it had made to their children's lives, it is ironic that, later in our conversation, these parents none the less went on to detail the intensive and systematic efforts they made to 'normalise' those very differences for the sake of their children. Thus in these parents' accounts can be seen a 'career' of categorisation, shifting between concepts of normal and different childhoods.

This progressive redefinition of normality was made in the face of resistance from medical and educational professionals. Some of these parents felt that their fears for their child had been simply dismissed; they had been made to feel that they were making a fuss. In other instances, parents recalled how they had been accused of seeing a problem that did not exist. Still others felt that their children had been classified, by childhood professionals, as 'not different enough' to warrant any extra attention. Phillipa's mother eloquently describes the feelings of helplessness which were prompted by such responses:

> I used to get annoyed when people told me that it was common because we were living in this small village and every time I went to the skin clinic they said, 'Oh, its very common', and I was dying to meet someone. It was horrendous for the only way she could pass water (because of her sore and cracked skin) . . . you had to run a shallow bath and sit her in it. That sounds nothing but if every time a young child wants to go to the loo you have to run a bath . . . The doctor had said she's bound to grow out of it by a year.

Not until she was ten years old did Phillipa's eczema begin to improve. In being a common skin complaint of childhood which tends to disappear with age, in not often being life-threatening, many parents felt that 'having eczema' was seen by GPs as an aspect of 'normal' childhood, an observation confirmed by Orton (1981). The phrase 'it's only eczema' rang with familiarity for them. And yet their own daily experiences of dealing with the intractable soreness and itchiness of their children's skin, sleepless nights and food restrictions, made their children's childhood seem far from normal. In these cases, membership of a self-help group had been crucial. It had helped parents justify their own attribution of difference to their children.

Other parents encountered similar definitional problems which were exacerbated by the lack of any visual bodily clues with which to substantiate a claim for their child's different needs. A mother of a boy with a food allergy observed that:

I used to get a lot of staring because he really was quite hyperactive and he would scream for hours straight off and throw a tantrum in the street. I had to hit him just to get him to breathe more than anything else. There was nothing obviously wrong with him. And people just didn't understand and it's much more difficult if it happens in the middle of the street rather than in the privacy of your own home.

Parents belonging to the Food Allergy and Dyslexic groups had shared the common experience of continually failing to get the help that they felt their children needed from medical and educational professionals. Those who had been successful told of the energy and perseverance it required. Many parents of dyslexic children angrily recounted to me the disbelief and scepticism which greeted their first voicing of a fear that their child was not progressing 'normally'. In most cases a long-drawn-out battle, lasting several years, had ensued before their worries were taken notice of:

I knew Justin was different fairly early on. He didn't play with educational toys in a standard way but I knew he wasn't dim . . . At the age of six we knew things weren't going as they should because he could recognise twenty words and count to thirteen, after a year at school and two years at nursery . . . then two years later things weren't much better and he still didn't make progress . . . It dragged on again until he was about ten or eleven.

Throughout this period it was Justin's parents who had initiated

contact with educational psychologists and special-needs professionals, meetings which were on the whole unhelpful:

> It was all put down to attitude. And I can remember one of
> them saying to me 'Oh, he'll be perfectly alright. Some kids
> have it, some haven't.'

It is clear that these different interpretations of Justin's ability –
parental and professional – derive from different ideologies of
childhood. The professionals conceived Justin's reading to fall
within the broad range of 'normal' ability for all children. Working from a model of *the* child', they regarded him as being
'barely average'. Their judgement that there was nothing
'wrong' with Justin was made in the light of the statistical spread
of levels of academic attainment in the child population. By
contrast, in their struggle for an acknowledgement of difference, Justin's parents employed a specific rather than a generalised notion of normality. This derived from their familiarity
with him as '*their* child'. It was a conception of childhood based
on relationships of kin (my child), rather than category status
(the child). Compared to the promise shown in other aspects of
his educational development and accomplishments, Justin's
reading was judged by his parents to be abnormal:

> We knew Justin was bright. I don't think that was just
> parental pride. I'd been an infant teacher and had got
> enough experience to know that he was unusual but the
> educational psychologist told us that he was barely average
> in intelligence. He told us politely that we were being
> over-ambitious, that if my husband was a brick-layer and I
> worked in a shop there would be no problem.

Like parents of children with food allergies and those with
eczema, it was the continual dashing of their own expectations
of a 'normal' childhood for their child which led Justin's parents
doggedly to pursue, and eventually achieve, an alternative
classification. At the age of twelve Justin was finally assessed as
dyslexic and as having a non-verbal IQ of 142.

For a boy with a slight ambulatory problem, a different kind
of normality was construed. Health professionals worked from
a model of child development to classify his unusual gait as
'normal'. The consultant told his mother that the problem would
right itself, that it was just a matter of time. It was his age. It was
nothing to worry about. The mother regarded this assessment
as both inadequate and dismissive of the tendency to fall over
and trip up which her son daily exhibited. This example is,

again, revealing of subtly different discourses of childhood. The mother's account is a coherent narrative about her son's significant difference which reflects her personal struggle for recognition by those in power – doctors and teachers – of the particularity of her son's difficulties. In essence, it was a struggle against a more generalising model of the kinds of difficulties facing all growing children. Thus, in her story she emphasises Timmy's difference from other children through aligning her feelings, if not her experiences, with those of a mother of a disabled child:

> Timmy was terribly long in the body. He didn't sit up until he was nearly nine months old, and didn't start crawling till nearly a year. I was dying for him to go and get a toy. I'd get him something and he would get angry because it wasn't the right thing. So it wasn't an easy time. I was desperate for him to get into anything. Like the mother of a disabled child, I would love him to get up to pranks. I'd love him to get into a cupboard on his own and throw all the saucepans out or something.

A third and perhaps more telling illustration of the ways in which concepts of 'normal childhood' are used as classificatory tools centres on a failure to diagnose coeliac disease. In the mother's opinion it was her working-class and lone-parent status which had, initially, led the health visitor to classify her son as 'failing to thrive'. She recalled to me how, at first, she had concurred with this definition, had accepted that she might be 'putting it on to him' due to the stress and worry of a recent marriage break-up. Accused by the health visitor of underfeeding her son, she defended her self, saying: 'I was giving him all the right things which were of course all the wrong things' to eat. Following general dietary advice on the feeding of children she had been giving him brown bread and weetabix, thus exacerbating rather than ameliorating the effects of coeliac disease.[5] Her narrative graphically relates how on the verge of her son being taken into care, she created a disturbance in the doctor's surgery. Only then were her opinions taken note of. Her child was finally hospitalised and diagnosed as coeliac. In the mother's opinion it was an implicit knowledge of the correlations of social class, poverty and poor health which had combined to produce a normative model of *the* child which the health professionals used in their judgements of *her* child. Failure to thrive, while an infrequent occurrence, would not be thought an unduly abnormal outcome for a child from such social circumstances.

Other parent members of the Food Allergy group echoed similar experiences of professional disbelief, arising from the still ambivalent attitudes expressed within medical circles about the relationship between diet and health. Recalling their children's early childhoods, between six and ten years previously, these accounts reflect the greater scepticism of this period. One mother, whose daughter later turned out to have coeliac disease, was told that she was being 'over anxious' about her daughter; another, whose daughter transpired to have an allergy to milk, that she was making her daughter neurotic through fussing over her feeding. How, she asked me rhetorically, can you make a child neurotic at nought months old?

The competing discourses which work to define a child's childhood can again be seen in these latter examples. According to the professionals, working from a dominant textbook perspective on the feeding and mothering of children, in general, children tolerate wheat, milk and food additives in their diets. Thus, they reasoned, the child's problem must lie more with its mothering. Against this version the mothers insisted, time and again, on the specificity and particularity of their own child's difference, on his or her dietary abnormality in the context of a normal mothering relationship. As the mothers recalled, it was only through pushing for a confrontation of these competing discourses that a satisfactory diagnosis of their child's condition was finally achieved. Their response to the implicit critique of their mothering was to fight all the more vehemently on their child's behalf.

Given the complex and often emotionally stressful encounters many parents had had with different professional groups, it is not surprising that, in their accounts, this group of parents gave greater emphasis to the difficulties which arose in caring for their children. They emphasised, rather than minimised, the differences their child's condition had made to the pattern of 'normal' family life and stressed, rather than dismissed, the problems which their children had encountered. It was, after all, precisely these differences which the parents had used in their armoury against professional disbelief. In their narratives, therefore, it is only after making this position clear to me, that the parents then went on to describe the 'normalising' strategies that they too used to minimise disruption in

everyday life. Thus, a mother of a child with eczema remarked
with feeling:

> It's hard work. A child with eczema is hard work because
> they make demands upon you a normal child wouldn't.

I was told of demands made on parent's time; time needed to
apply creams before and after bathing; time in hospital; time to
cook different types of food; and time spent awake with children
scratching during the night. Unlike descriptions of the accommodation of medication and care regimes within the normal
pattern of daily life, typical of the other set of accounts, these
narratives emphasise life's extraordinary aspects. Details were
given, for example, about the extra budgetary demands their
children's condition made on the family purse: in the case of
children with eczema, it might be money for special cotton cloth-
ing and for the extra washing needed because of the ointment
and creams daily applied to the child's body; for a child with
dyslexia, the cost of the purchase of computer equipment and
of special lessons was mentioned. Extra emotional demands may
also be made, on levels of patience, tolerance and understanding. A teenager remembers her childhood:

> Even in your sleep you don't stop scratching . . . it's a terrible
> noise and the worst of it is if you're in the lounge and every-
> one's watching TV and you're scratching. Mum and Dad
> would say: 'I know you've got to scratch but can't you do it
> more quietly.' I mean I used to scratch my feet with a fork
> and sit on the floor and rub my hands up and down on the
> carpet.

In these accounts, therefore, greater emphasis is given to the
significant difference being different makes and in one instance
the very stability of the family network was portrayed as being
placed at risk through the demands a child with eczema can
make upon the family:

> Every grandma wants their granddaughter to look nice and
> I was always scratching. I looked awful. I also had it in
> my hair so you can't brush your hair sometimes, a scabby
> mouth. I couldn't wear nice short frilly skirts, the back of
> my knees were sore. She lived in Scotland so we didn't see
> her a lot but when we did see her once I ended up in tears.
> She said: 'Oh she's scratching and there's skin all over.' I
> should have thought: 'Well, if I'm going to scratch and
> make a mess I'll put a newspaper down and scratch on
> that.' When you're eleven you don't think like that. You

think: 'Well it's only skin, it will hoover up.' And she just
blew her top and everyone else was in tears.
The implicit normality of family life – 'every grandmother wants
their granddaughter to look nice' – is here offered as a way of
coming to understand the rift which occurred in that particular
family. It is the invocation of a cultural stereotype of normal
childhood which provides an explanatory context for these felt
differences.

But, having firmly established in their accounts the difference
their children's difference makes, these parents went on to stress
how they also, nevertheless, tried to normalise family life as far
as possible. They did so for the sake of their children. The
mother of a dyslexic boy cites humour as one strategy they as a
family adopted:

> There was one teacher who, in the family situation, was
> known as the Bitch and we would all refer to her as the
> Bitch and we would say: 'Oh dear, what has the Bitch done
> today?' . . . to show that we were supporting him or we
> taught him how to make a joke out of it.

A young woman, remembering back to her childhood eczema,
recalls her own experience of being on the receiving end of
such a strategy:

> I used to have coal tar bandages at home. They used to put
> them on and leave them on for a week soaked in tar. It was
> a joke. Mum said, when I was in hospital, 'I didn't have to
> ask where you were. I could smell you.' This coal tar, drift-
> ing down the ward. But you had to joke about it. Mum'd
> say, 'Lizzie's been in the lounge scratching, you can see the
> skin.' I'd say, 'It wasn't me, it wasn't me.' But I couldn't
> get away with it as no one else used to scratch.

Having had to battle with the child-care professionals for recognition of 'difference' in their children, these parents then
vigorously followed, somewhat ironically, the paths of integra-
tion/normalisation adopted by those parents whose children
were more readily classed as having particular needs. One
mother recounted how she had twice changed her dyslexic
daughter's school, eventually moving her to a private school,
to try and help her progress 'normally'. Another told me of
the efforts she had made to cook party food for her son's
birthday without the aid of chocolate, dairy products, food
colourings or additives. She remembers thinking that his party
would be 'really grim' because of his food allergy. In the

event, and through her ingenuity, it turned out to be a great success.

Running through all these narratives, therefore, there are two distinct modes of accounting for children. The first depicts parents and professionals in agreement; both concur with the classification of the child as different, but as still essentially belonging to the category of 'normal' children. This perspective affirms variation in the forms which childhood can take and the parents are encouraged to think of their children positively: they are not really any different from other children. The second mode of accounting for children, by contrast, reveals competing definitions of the child. While professional judgement of a child's difficulties is once again framed by a heterogeneous conceptualisation of childhood, the resultant categorisation is a less positive identity for any individual child. From the parents' perspective, it implicitly stigmatises their own child: in the case of eczema, the child may be offered little help to cope with his or her visibly different skin; in the case of dyslexia the child may be seen as simply intellectually dull or as the offspring of fussy or pushy parents; the child with a food intolerance may be dismissed as socially difficult, spoilt or ill-tempered. Such negative social identities were, unsurprisingly, rejected by parents on their children's behalf and they worked hard to achieve alternative categorical identities for them.

A thin and shifting defining line thus separates ideas of childhood normality from those of different or special childhoods. Through the subtleties of claim and counter-claim put forward by parents and professionals, categorical social identities for particular children are accepted, negotiated or changed and in this process of attribution membership of self-help groups often played a significant role (Robinson and Henry, 1977). For some whose children had been unequivocally diagnosed as different and for whom help was readily forthcoming, the self-help group offered another way of coming to terms with – of normalising – their child's condition, as one woman describes:

> It's a good idea for people with young babies who've never had any problem with skin and all of a sudden they've got this baby with eczema.

However, she goes on to warn of a potentially darker, less positive, aspect:

> I still think that some people take it too far. You can almost

cut yourself off and say, well, we are different and so we'll
act differently.

Another woman who, by comparison, had received little help
from the medical professional in coping with her son's eczema,
viewed her membership of the self-help group in a somewhat
different light. For her it offered a positive categorical identity
for her son, which was elsewhere rarely, if ever, affirmed:

> I felt very much on my own and then we joined the Eczema
> Society and that was useful. We weren't sure whether we
> were doing the right things. There wasn't anyone else to
> turn to.

Such a perspective confirms Robinson and Henry's observation
that self-help groups are 'one way of undermining or, at least,
counterbalancing the power of the established professions
(1977: 124).

The Constructing of Children's Childhoods

In different ways these narrative accounts of particular children's childhoods have revealed some of the processes through
which ideas of childhood are socially constructed in and through
everyday life. They have shown how, as Goffman (1968) suggests, stigmatising categorisation is the product of social relationships rather than an intrinsic aspect of particular individuals
or certain physical or mental attributes. It is a social process,
fluid, dynamic and open to negotiation. In this sense, then, these
narrative accounts of childhood have also demonstrated that
the consciousness of a child's childhood as being normal or
different is pragmatically, rather than definitively, acquired
through the specificities of social encounters and the passage of
time itself (Turner, 1987: 215).

But what of the child's own developing consciousness of the
Self? What might this ongoing construction of their own childhood mean to children themselves? How do children take on
cultural ideas about health and sickness? What factors might
contribute to children's recognition of the significance of difference? As Davis has shown, 'children [do] not overtly voice doubts
about their own normality' (1982:26). Three themes predominate in the accounts. In general, parents thought that the medicalisation of the social world, the pattern of family life and the
process of schooling were all important contributory factors to
their child's well-being and sense of Self. It was through their
experience of these different socialising contexts that, according

to their parents, children developed and refined their sense of Self and Other.

The first potential source of knowledge for children, identified by the parents, was the processes through which disease and illness categories are culturally constituted. Temporally and spatially specific, ideas about health and illness map out systems of classification which children must both learn about and learn to live with and, in this respect, my conversations with the parents of children with asthma were particularly instructive about how this process might take place. It was they who responded overwhelmingly to my request for interviews both locally and nationally. Partly this can be attributed to the nature of the condition; its often dramatic manifestations, its potential life-threatening consequences, its seeming irrational patterning. It is extremely frightening for parents to witness their children gasping for air, an experience which perhaps benefits from the distancing which re-telling brings.

However, the historical construction of asthma as a disease (Gabbay, 1982), and its relationship to constructions of childhood, may also have had a part to play in prompting their willingness to talk with me. Prior to the development of appropriate drugs – especially the development of inhalers which children can use by themselves – the treatment of asthmatics was difficult. According to one GP – himself a sufferer – there was a tendency in the past not to label a child as asthmatic. As there was little effective treatment, labelling a child as asthmatic was, as he put it, to 'condemn them to an invalid life'. Children were therefore more often described as 'chesty' or 'wheezy' and encouraged to 'struggle on' or 'to fight it'. Now that asthma attacks can be quickly and effectively controlled with the right cocktail of drugs, diagnosing a child as asthmatic has radically different social consequences. I was told, 'you must get them labelled as quickly as possible' so that children can receive the appropriate treatment to enable them to lead 'normal' lives.

But it would seem that a wider cultural awareness about asthma lags behind these medical advances. Asthmatic children may still be stigmatised as 'delicate' and 'weedy', leading, in a few instances, to medication being withheld and to teasing. Some children had been urged to get a 'grip on themselves', to carry on as normal: that is, to be like a normal child. While in most schools a child's medicine is kept in the school office and administered by the staff on the parent's behalf, I was told of one school where this did not occur. Here a boy with asthma was forced to hide his inhaler in the cloakroom and, at lunchtime, secretly to retreat to take his medicine. Even within the medical profession itself the recognition of asthma as a 'real' disease, rather than as a relatively normal condition of childhood, has yet to be fully accomplished. Thus it was that one role of the local self-help group appeared to be conspiratorial. Ideas about how to handle a GP reluctant to prescribe medication were swopped by parents, for, in their opinion, it was this which would provide the most obvious route back to 'normal family life'.

The accounts given by parents of dyslexic children provide a comparable example. In this case, as I have already suggested, the social construction of the condition and, hence of the child for whom it becomes an identifying attribute, is revealed in the battle against the deep-seated prejudices which link social class with levels of academic attainment. I was told, quite firmly, that the main problem for the parents of dyslexic children locally was that 'the Education Office doesn't believe in dyslexia'. In using the word belief this mother underlined the negotiable and socially constructed character of this condition. For parents of dyslexic children obtaining recognition for their child's difference was therefore always difficult, often traumatic, and only occasionally successful. For children themselves, caught up in these webs of belief differently spun between parents and professionals, categorical markers of identity may become disturbingly ambiguous and a locus for the Self correspondingly difficult to find.

The second theme in parents' accounts of the social construction of childhood, of significance for the way children come to see themselves and others, is the manner in which wider cultural ideas about illness or difference are mediated through the family's day-to-day social interactions. All the parents, for instance, believed that they bore a tremendous responsibility for their children's self-image. They understood their own attitudes to have direct and powerful consequences for their children's developing sense of Self. The family unit was regarded as an extremely important element in enabling children to develop a strong and positive self-image. A mother and teacher of dyslexic children summed up her thoughts by saying:

I think the child copes as well as the parents cope.

Self-esteem is visualised by her as the critical factor in the child with special needs growing up 'normally':

I would think the child will get on with other children in proportion to their own level of self-esteem and their own level of self-esteem is very much governed by what parents have done.

Many parents voiced similar feelings, expressing to me their concern that what they did or did not do, said or should not have said, might have had an adverse effect on their child's sense of his/her own worth:

It's a terrific nuisance and a worry to us of course but we try to make light of them because if we didn't it would have an adverse affect on her . . . They show no fear of the doctor nor the hospital and I think that's because of the attitude we try and show to them. If they saw we were worried they are going to say, 'Well, Mummy and Daddy are worried.'

Many parents also feared the psychological damage which might accrue to their children as a consequence of their own 'wrong' or 'inappropriate' reactions. Telling her story of the gradual discovery of her son's dyslexia, one mother commented:

I can see it all now . . . I just wish I had known at the time.

Even after her son had been finally assessed as dyslexic she admits making what, with hindsight, she believes to be yet another mistake with disastrous results:

We mishandled things from then on because we, the adults, sat and looked at him and then we told him that he had problems and that this is what we would do about it . . . and the school mishandled it . . . He didn't improve because he was very negative about the extra lessons, feeling different and just before Easter he had a complete freak-out and he did all but throw his desk at her (his teacher) and rushed out and said he wasn't going back.

Overlaying such 'populist' psychologising, evidenced in parents' critiques and observations about their own behaviour, the wider cultural construction of the child as moving towards independence works to sustain the negativity which many parents attached to the idea of being 'over-protective'. Reinforced through other common cultural wisdoms such as 'a child must learn to stand on its own two feet', must learn 'to fight its own battles', 'to stand up for itself' parents believed that the admission of difference would risk denying their child a normal passage to adulthood. Phrases such as 'we're determined we won't be over-protective' or 'I feel that I tend to over-protect her' recur time and again in the interviews. Thus, one mother was adamant in her defence of the carefully calculated attitude they had chosen:

> We just pass it (asthma) off by saying there's a lot worse things you can have. OK, it's inconvenient but it's going to be alright. We don't want him to think that he's worse than he really is.

Another mother observed:

> I know people who don't discipline their children because if you tell them off they start scratching. I've tried very hard not to do that because that can cause another problem.

A third possible source of influences on children's feelings about themselves and their own attitudes to and understanding of their condition was seen by many parents to stem from the process of schooling. They judged the teaching staff of the schools their sons and daughters attended to bear a heavy responsibility for the way their children had come to see themselves. This was not just in terms of the school as a context where children meet with one another, but also in terms of pedagogical practice itself. This was understood to be particularly important for younger children, most of whom would have yet to question the school's authority and legitimacy.

In general, parents thought most teachers were 'very good' with their children and 'understanding' about their child's condition. Sympathetic teachers were judged to be those who would show tolerance to a child scratching in class, who would permit asthmatic children to take control of their own medication or turn a blind eye to a dyslexic child cheating in spelling tests. Only a few teachers were accused of being unhelpful or dismissive of children's particular needs. But, over and above such instances of the way personal style might affect relationships between teacher and pupil, it is clear that the process of teaching itself structures the experience of being different for many children. Children readily picked up on the implicit meanings and subtle distinctions which are imparted through its praxis. Thus these parents and their children saw that the rhythm and discipline of the 'hidden curriculum' of schools makes its own demands upon nonconformity, creating particular tensions and problems for the 'different' child (Holly, 1974).

School rules were a case in point. Transgression of them represents an offence against the social and moral order of the school where, in primary schools particularly, rules are often framed within an ideology of parity. Thus, despite the rhetoric of child-centred education – that every child is different and should be treated as such – in practice an ordered and rule-bound uniformity is more commonly promoted, under the guise of the equality of opportunity. For children with special needs of various kinds this conceptual slippage may serve to compound their difficulties at school, as was made clear to me in some parents' narratives. One mother instanced a school rule that soft slippers should be worn indoors. This created problems for her boy who had to wear orthopaedic boots. Another mother told me how the school insisted that, despite a cold and biting wind, her asthmatic daughter should go outside at playtime, under the rubric, 'If we do it for one we'd have to do it for all'. When in these ways children are continually made to break the rules, their difference must slowly and surely become subtly underlined. Listening to my conversation with her mother, Susan described to me how this happens:

> It takes me about five minutes to do my spinner [inhaler for asthma] and I'm always late starting my dinner and Mr S. shouts at me.

The disciplined order of the primary school invariably means that children have to move about the school in a crocodile, holding hands with a partner. This choosing of partners is a tense moment, for no child wants to be left out (see Chapter 5). For the child with severe eczema such moments may become even more highly charged; who wants to hold a hand that is rough, scratchy and liable to bleed? One woman recalls how, in her own childhood, this difference was actually compounded by the teaching staff who always made her pair up with a boy who also had severe eczema:

> It was just a small primary school and when we were going for walks in a crocodile we always used to be at the end . . . We had to wait behind in the cloakroom . . . and as we filed out of the cloakroom you had to wait till the last two and then you were at the end.

A little thing, maybe, but it had remained in her memory for more than twenty years.

The use of supply teachers was cited as particularly problematic by some families. Children with asthma may, when feeling ill, not like to ask a stranger if they can leave the class should their condition begin to deteriorate. Children with eczema may fidget and seem inattentive, those with dyslexia appear stupid. The invisibility of many of these conditions means that supply teachers are often simply ignorant of the existence of a problem. Alice, confirming her mother's story, describes one such occasion:

> At my school, you know, these stand-in teachers. When I couldn't do my work I walked up to her and she practically shouted it across the room, how she explained it and everybody was staring.

Irene recounts similar feelings in her description of how, as a child, she coped with the itchiness of an eczematic skin:

> although you could go out of the room [to scratch or apply creams], everybody knew what you were going out for.

Examples proliferate. A professional working with children with special needs told me that the child who really stands out in a class is the one with a poor short-term memory, a feature often associated with dyslexia. This is the child who is always at the teacher's desk, who is always taking up the teacher's time. Being only able to remember one instruction at a time, such a child may become regarded as a nuisance. S/he may later be referred for behavioural problems rather than as having a specific learning difficulty. Other children in the class, noticing this demanding pattern of behaviour, may adopt the teacher's definition and exclude this 'nuisance' from their games. For the dyslexic child many common pedagogic practices – spelling tests, reading aloud, memory games and written work – merely serve to underline perceptions of their own status as class dunce. Alice's mother describes this process:

> The teacher goes, red pen, red pen . . . they are totally destroyed . . . the child's story and their confidence. You do that every day, five days a week, forty weeks a year. The child's confidence is smashed to the ground.

The parents' accounts of their children's childhoods are not therefore simply narratives of facts and events. They are primarily interpretations, presenting particular points of view, designed to persuade. Not only do they depict in differing ways the many subtle means by which a child's childhood is constructed through processes of negotiation with medical and educational professionals, they also sketch in the bare outlines of how children experience this external construction of themselves. They show that the child's consciousness of being significantly different or, conversely, of being like other children, is poised precariously between the competing definitions of his or her own childhood emanating from the home, the school and the wider society.

Rarely, however, do these parental accounts depict the child as having an active part in this negotiating process, of being involved in the process of Self-discovery. Indeed, on the few occasions when children took an active role in the interview alongside their parents, their participation was implicitly but carefully structured by the adults present. Their voices intersperse the conversation as confirmations or markers in a narrative, defined, for the most part, by the style and concerns of an adult conversation. From the perspective of their parents this tacit agreement and passive dependence upon adult constructions of their own Selves appears unproblematic. Using the interview as a public vehicle for their more private worries about their children or as a channel for a wider public airing of the difficulties all parents potentially face in relation to the caring professions, their children's input was minimised. In this way, then, parental accounts of their children's childhoods confirm and reproduce a specific and particular ideology of childhood. It is this wider social construction of childhood for children which the next chapter explores.

Notes

1. I did thirteen taped interviews with parents and their children, and a further taped group interview with four women. In the course of gathering this material I also gave talks at local self-help group meetings about the nature of the project. On these occasions I spoke more informally with parent members and with health professionals associated with these groups. Through other contacts I also had brief conversations with children, and parents of children, with psoriasis, diabetes, coeliac disease, and cerebral palsy and with members of a Gingerbread group, a self-help group for single parents and their children. Thanks are due to all these people and organisations (see Preface).
2. In a few interviews fathers also participated, contributing a good deal to our mutual discussions. However, in general it was the mothers who offered to talk with me. This reflects more general cultural assumptions about motherhood and women as carers (see Hockey and James, 1993).
3. This is a pertinent question, for some of the self-help groups to whom I wrote did not reply to my initial letter requesting assistance with the project. In this sense, those that did reply can be seen as having a more active interest in my research. But the exact nature of interest or perspective was not certain in many cases.
4. These were defined by the Warnock Report of 1978.
5. People with coeliac disease must follow a gluten-free diet, gluten being found mostly in wheat-based products.

THREE

Accounts of Childhood

Reflexivity and Reflections

Images of childhood, evoked through visual and verbal representations of children, commonly pepper the news and entertain-
ment media of Western societies. These provide a particular
way of seeing children and are illustrative of the cultural lens
through which childhood in these contexts is ideally understood
as a reassuring familiarity. The naked baby advertising nappies
is recalled in the blonde-haired blue-eyed young girl who helps
her mother in televised domesticity. Both these images contrast
starkly with the photographs of 'lost childhood' portrayed in
the story of the abused or homeless boy and whose picture
appeals for aid and charity from the black and white pages of
the Western press. Such images, through their positive affirmation or negative and emotive denial, offer a visual account of
what childhood should be like in a contemporary Western
society such as Britain. Thus it is that through verbal accounts
and visual representations of many individual children, one
dominating model of childhood emerges and is daily construed
for the adult and child viewer. As Giddens has argued,
self-identity is 'a reflexively organised endeavour . . . which
consists in the sustaining of coherent, yet continually revised
biographical narratives' through the complexities of modern
social life (1991: 5).

The theme of reflexivity, traced out through personal re-
collection, parents' accounts and theoretical critique in the
previous chapters, continues here, then, through an exploration
of the more generalised process of the representation of childhood. It addresses first the notion of representation as mirrored
reflections. This is developed through exploring evocations of
the child which, while offering individual children images of
and for the Self may, at the same time, embrace a subtle
distortion in and through the everyday lives of children. In
this way, I continue to map out themes in the social construction

of childhood identities for children. Second, this chapter reflects on the process of image-making, by delineating the conceptual and theoretical space within which my own following account of children's lives can be contextualised. The subjects of childhood and children have been extensively studied by historians, developmental psychologists, medical specialists, sociological theorists, and educationalists. Childhood, in providing sources of adult identity, has also long been the traditional province of film-makers and novelists and has furnished the starting-point of autobiographical memory. Through acknowledging Geertz's observation that 'anthropological writings are themselves interpretations, and second and third order ones to boot' (1975: 15), I am reminded, therefore, that the account of childhood I shall offer is not authoritative. It is just one kind of childhood heard from. This raises, then, the possibility of other, alternative visions of childhood, confirming the suggestion already made that childhood is not solely to be understood as the condition of biological immaturity. More accurately, my account of childhood is one of its envisagements: a cultural phrasing of that biological condition which arises in and through particular social and cultural processes. This chapter asks, therefore, what themes predominate in different accounts of childhood, and within the images of children which are common currency in a Western society such as Britain? How might these have filtered my own understanding of children and what shifts in perspective might a social anthropological account contribute to these well-established representations of children's lives? Finally, how might an ideology of childhood feed and sustain children's own image and Self-identity?

In taking this step back from my own ethnography to explore the process of representing childhood, this chapter addresses Malinowksi's (1922) point that the ethnographer does not arrive empty minded in the field. S/he brings to his or her study a set of 'foreshadowed problems', hypotheses-in-the-making and hunches to be followed and reflected upon. Malinowski considered these to be derived from pre-fieldwork theoretical study and, forming the 'main endowment of a scientific thinker', to lend a theoretical rigour to more qualitative encounters with Others during fieldwork (1922: 8–9). What Malinowski did not see, however, was that such book-work was, like the ethnographer's personal anthropology, something which would later have to be reflexively recounted. For instance, questions can be asked as to why certain topics arouse an immediate interest on a merely idle reading; what memories are evoked, what thoughts let loose, in the dialogue engaging reader with text; what relationship with the past informs the shape and content of the researcher's present reading? These questions beg answers for it is in theoretical study that research themes become illuminated, key words begin to signify new ideas, thoughts start to crystallise and research schemes are hatched. Problems are therefore complexly, rather than simply, foreshadowed in an ethnographer's thinking.

Making Representations

Contemporary anthropological theory has drawn attention to the gulf between the collective cultural representations offered by people about themselves and social anthropological analysis of them (Clifford, 1988; Clifford and Marcus, 1986; Geertz, 1975). This difference was, until recently, often subtly elided in ethnographic accounts. Its recent acknowledgement recalls Geertz's perceptive comment that, despite the appearance of greater endeavour or mystical insight, what ethnographers do is both more prosaic and more imaginative: 'the ethnographer "inscribes" social discourse; he [sic] *writes it down*' (Geertz, 1975: 19). Thus the ethnographer both literally and metaphorically constructs an account. Processes of representation constitute, therefore, the very core of ethnography.

For instance, it is clear that it is precisely through the effort of 'thick description', characteristic of good ethnographic writing, that events are portrayed, experiences captured and the sense of person or place brought vividly to mind. A well-written ethnography can speak volumes for what a particular culture is like. But through this evocation of images, anthropology therefore also *makes* representations. An ethnographic account does not just assemble 'facts'; instead, through arranging them, it presents a particular interpretation of the social world, it invites a particular understanding. The juxtaposition of ethnographic details, the selection of events to report and the re-stating of dominant themes in the text are, for example, at one and the same time the literary devices and the methodological means by which anthropology seeks to persuade. But, in that same moment, interpretive anthropology also deals in representations. It explores ideologies − for example, in this account the idea of childhood and concept of 'the child' in relation to notions of 'identity' and 'personhood' – as 'structures of signification' within and about a particular cultural context (Geertz, 1975). It is with these that anthropologists make sense of what people do. Thus it is that the material stuff which anthropologists write about are symbols that stand in for, act as if, appear to be, fill in or substitute for. They are ideas, rather than facts, about the social world. In short, what is now being more readily acknowledged is the extent to which ethnographic writing inevitably reflects a particular point of view from a particular point of view.

Contextualising all this activity is yet another aspect of the process of representation which has recently been scrutinised critically by Rapport (1991): the act of ethnographic writing, of putting pen to paper. He argues that the process which transforms the jotted note or scribbled comment of the fieldwork diary into the final polished report involves the conceptual dusting and ordering of a reality, first but hastily and chaotically noted down in the 'field'. That the events, places and persons who people an ethnographer's fieldnotes, must eventually become represented through linear 'words on a page' Rapport sees as problematic. Tidying up fieldnotes, in the process of writing them up, risks losing the 'very ambiguity and duality which is their special life' and from which anthropological understanding draws its strength (1991: 13). Care must be taken, then, against substituting the 'subtlety of equivocation' by a positivistic 'demand for singularity of focus, limitation and precision' during the very literal process of making the final marks on a page (1991: 13). Although this process of representing Others with words has always been part and parcel of anthropological practice, lately it has begun to take on rather more significance. Through the realisation that the way one writes, as much as what one writes, subtly shapes the meaning and comprehension of what one has written, anthropology has come face-to-face with its own subjectivity.

These theoretical shifts in understanding the process, and not just the products, of ethnographic work reflect the legacy of an earlier paradigm shift in social anthropology. No mere deviation or siding, the movement from a functionalist to a semantic enquiry was a complete change of direction. It is seen by Crick (1976) as a radical epistemological break with the past. No longer was reality conceived to be 'out there', easily accessible, observable, countable, graspable and factual in the Durkeimian tradition of social facts as things. Instead, reality, its substance more dissolved and diluted, was to be variously and vicariously understood and interpreted. It was to be found writ small in the Balinese cockfight (Geertz, 1975), dancing on the Gypsy's washing-line (Okely, 1983) and paced out along the pilgrim's path (Turner, 1974a).

Of most importance in this vision of 'human beings as meaning makers' was the rehabilitation of the study of language in social life and the move towards seeing language as a source of and for cultural meanings (Crick, 1976: 3). In time, it placed the wordy nature of anthropological accounts under scrutiny. Just as 'social facts' had been displaced by 'interpretations', so the authorial authority of the ethnographer's words became usurped. Clifford and Marcus summarise these changes as follows:

> No longer a marginal, or occulted dimension, writing has emerged as central to what anthropologists do both in the field and thereafter. The fact that it has not until recently been portrayed or seriously discussed reflects the persistence of an ideology claiming transparency of representation and immediacy of experience. Writing reduced to method: keeping good field notes, making accurate maps, 'writing up' results. (1986: 2)

However, this belated admission of the literal literary quality of anthropology does not mean, as some have feared, that anthropology necessarily and irrevocably enters the genre of fiction (Carrithers, 1988). There is, as Geertz points out, a deal of difference between 'making things out' (anthropology) and 'making things up' (novels) (1988: 140). The former is descriptive, 'a rendering of the actual, a vitality phrased' (Geertz, 1988: 143). The latter, while often realist in style, is, however, no mirror for reality; fictional realism involves its deliberate reworking (Martin, 1981). However, despite this crucial difference, both the anthropologist and novelist *are* involved in processes of representation. Albeit of different kinds, they both demonstrate ways in which one person, a Self, can re-present Others, many selves.

Explicit recognition and acknowledgement of ethnographic writing as a process of representation is becoming increasingly important for more practical reasons too. First, because the Others represented in the writings of social scientists are often those who are denied social and or political power, careful consideration must be given to the ways in which representations are made on their behalf, to the ethics involved in writing as much as in research methodologies (Paine, 1985). Second, and perhaps more pragmatically, because the Others anthropologists have traditionally written about are beginning to challenge or rewrite our representations of themselves (Marcus and Fisher, 1986). Although anthropologists working in their own cultures have long had this experience (McDonald, 1987) this 'ethnography in reverse' is now beginning to oblige all anthropologists to develop a greater sensitivity to the written word (Marcus and Fisher, 1986: 37).

With respect to the study of children, the first of these conditions already applies. In time, so might the second. If, as I show below, children in contemporary Western cultures are not conceived of as persons – if they have no central or active social role and if their words carry no effective power in the social world – then, inevitably, they must rely on others to represent them, to make representations on their behalf. They are therefore vulnerable to, and often at the mercy of, the very representations which others (usually adults) impose on them and the constructions of their lives that others make (Boyden, 1990).

The Social Construction of Childhood

The recent conceptual shifts within social anthropology have been paralleled in the movement towards seeing childhood as a cultural representation of the early years of life, rather than as an unproblematic description of them. It was a suggestion which first gained widespread notoriety in the French historian Phillipe Ariès's bold claim that in 'medieval society the idea of childhood did not exist' (1973: 125). He argued that the concept of childhood emerged in European societies between the fifteenth and eighteenth centuries and that, prior to this development, children were regarded as miniature adults. Once past infancy, children were not accorded particular social significance in the mediaeval world and participated in society alongside, not separate from, its adult members. From a twentieth-century Western perspective, with its child-specific laws and institutions setting the child apart as a special kind of human being – 'a mixture of expensive nuisance, fragile treasure, slave and super-pet' (Holt, 1975: 22) – this claim seemed radical indeed. However, although serious challenges were issued to Ariès's thesis, as the 'facts' of the case were teased out and debated by historians and social scientists alike – (see, for example, De Mause, 1976; Pollock, 1983; Wilson, 1980) – his claim was not entirely rejected. Instead, what eventually emerged was the more sober, but no less important, statement that the childhood characteristic of modern Western societies is an historically specific institutional form. It is just one among many possible ways of seeing and classifying children.

This simple point – that the concept of childhood constitutes a referential frame of and for children's lives – has wide ramifications for the understanding of childhood and for the study of children. For example, it enables the history of Western childhood to be charted not just as a series of unproblematic and welcome social reforms, but, more searchingly, in terms of a set of changing ideas about the child (Hockey and James, 1993). It becomes possible to see how, in successive intellectual generations, the child's 'nature' has become essentialised as a critical aspect of childhood. Differently delineated over time, the debate as to what this might consist of has encompassed a wide diversity of opinion. From the Puritan emphasis upon original sin, through Rousseau's depiction of the child's inherent innocence, to Locke's *tabula rasa*, there runs a complex stream of ideas about what children are like and what childhood is (Boas, 1966; Coveney, 1957). Accompanying each new, philosophical construction of childhood were changes in society's more prosaic and everyday dealings with children as, in the home, the classroom or the street, new social, educational and reformatory regimes were introduced to curb, control and order the activities of children (Plumb, 1975). By the late nineteenth and early twentieth centuries these changing attitudinal tides had culminated in both the conceptual, and literal, marginalisation of children from adult social spaces (Hockey and James, 1993). Ironically depicted in terms of an increasing child-centredness, through its concern for child-protection and saving (Hendrick, 1990), this social marginalisation was effected through particular child-rearing practices (Ehrenreich and English, 1979), and particular institutional settings (Pinchbeck and Hewitt, 1969; 1973) in response to particular ideas about child psychology and development (Bradley, 1986).

The lesson to be drawn from this complex historiography is clear: ideas about children directly impinge upon the experience of childhood which children themselves have. However, although seeming obvious, this relationship was rarely given critical attention before the 1970s. Its importance can be illustrated in the example of the increasing globalisation of Western childhood which, through a continuing failure to acknowledge the socially constructed nature of childhood, has sometimes had devastating and demoralising effects for children themselves. Envisaged as 'a kind of walled garden in which children, being small and weak, are protected from the harsh ness of the world outside' (Holt, 1975: 22), this culturally and historically specific Western idea of childhood has been, and continues to be, exported to cultures in the South.[1] Here it chimes badly for the many children whose daily experience is of the devastating effects of famine, war and poverty. In relation to social policies, such as those proposed under the UN Convention on the Rights of the Child, Boyden observes, for example that, 'the consolidation of a universal standard for children can have the effect of penalizing, or even criminalizing, the childhoods of the poor', often for the simple reason that poor families are unable to reach this standard (1990: 202). Thus, for instance, the export of the Western ideal of schooling and education may mean that children, from families where their labour makes a significant contribution to income, may suffer rather than benefit from their withdrawal from the world of work into that of school.

Ennew (1986) notes similar discontinuities. She argues that the world of conspicuous Western consumption is often displayed in Southern contexts through portraying childhood as a period of happiness and security, with parental love being signified by the purchase of commodities:

> These images are most frequently received by the poor through the medium of television, for even the poorest shack in a shanty town, lacking water and sewage, may still have an illegal electricity supply and a television set. The images which flicker in the windowless huts are almost universally drawn from Western contexts or from the indigenous Western-influenced middle class. This happiness is unobtainable, yet it may be the only available knowledge of life outside the slum. The sense of cultural deprivation and lack of personal worth is reinforced by the information that they are failing even in the basic roles of parent and children. (1986: 23)

Drawn from cultures where children's social status and roles are radically different from those of their Western counterparts, these examples demonstrate, unequivocally, that an appreciation and understanding of children's own experience of the world must involve, first and most importantly, unpacking the *ideas* which shape the contextual practices and perceptions of childhood as it daily unfolds for children. Childhood cannot be regarded, simply and unproblematically, as the universal biological condition of immaturity which all children pass through. Instead, it must be more critically depicted as embracing particular cultural perceptions and statements about that temporal biological condition. It is these which shape the life experiences of members of the social category 'children' through providing a culturally specific rendering of the early years of life.

This stress on the ideological aspects and cultural relativity of concepts of childhood considerably complicates the process of writing about children, forcing consideration of both what is written and styles of writing. It means taking seriously Geertz's point that 'becoming human is becoming individual and we become individual under the guidance of cultural patterns, historically created systems of meanings in terms of which we give form, order, point and direction to our lives.' (1975: 52). The form which childhood takes in any culture or historical period is shaped, then, by the articulation of these systems of meanings through the lives of its individual child members and their adult caretakers. In turn, this means acknowledging that writers and social theorists of childhood are also not immune from this process. On the contrary, as I shall show, the forms within and with which children are and have been traditionally represented have played a significant part in giving voice and shape to particular experiences of children and particular re-representations of childhood. In this chapter I shall therefore ask, of particular accounts of childhood, what meanings style their form of inscription? What ideas about childhood do they implicitly incorporate? What is the relationship between texts produced about children and the socio-historical context of their production? The writer, enmeshed in language – whether historian, social scientist or novelist – is inevitably enmeshed in ideology and, as professional pedlars of words, such persons are involved in its re-creation.

However, in presenting these diverse accounts it is not my intention to provide an exhaustive documentation of the ways in which childhood has been variously described or analysed. This has been done fully elsewhere (James and Prout, 1990a; Jenks, 1982; McKay, 1973; Quicke, 1985; Rafky, 1973). Rather, by working through some selected writings about children, relevant to the questions which this book addresses, I shall indicate the common features and repetitive themes threaded through the childhoods they depict. In this way my own following account of children's lives can be more reflexively contextualised.

In discussing these different genres of writing about childhood it will become clear that, although each embodies a relatively discrete discourse – a way of speaking about children which is subtly accented – there are none the less significant areas of overlap. Together, these can be taken to constitute a dominant ide(a)ology of childhood; that is, they form a particular and persuasive representation of children, which both stands in for and helps perpetuate a particular conception of 'the child'. In the Western tradition this representation of childhood is as a time in the life-course, prescribed by ideals of happiness and sexual innocence, 'a period of lack of responsibility, with rights to protection and training, but not to autonomy' (Ennew, 1986: 21). It is this set of ideas which allows us, as adults, to attribute to individual children an overarching categorical identity, one which both specifies and justifies children's marginal position within Western societies and denial of their personhood (Carrithers, Collins and Lukes, 1985; Hockey and James, 1993). And, as later chapters reveal, these same ideas also shape children's growing consciousness of Self as they encounter them writ large in mundane and everyday social interactions.

Accounting for Children's Socialisation

A first genre of representation – socialisation – stems largely from sociology. This firmly locates the problem of childrens' identities as a temporal and structural phenomenon, through centring on the process by which 'the social' and the 'individual' come to mesh together. The process of socialisation is identified as the mechanism through which this occurs: that is, through which 'individuals become members of society' (Musgrave, 1987: 1). Although socialisation is acknowledged to continue throughout life (Mayer, 1970), childhood is still commonly perceived to be its most critical period.

However, within the traditions of this literature, although

childhood is represented, children rarely appear as themselves. Instead, they are depicted as symbolic embodiments of culture, literally objectified in the process of cultural reproduction. Rarely do traditional accounts of socialisation present children as knowing subjects. These visions of children and childhood (Bradley, 1986), the consequence of a functionalist perspective predominating in the social sciences until the mid-1960s, suggest that children learn and later come to embody a society's cultural schemes through a kind of 'grafting process' (Tonkin, 1982: 245). Thus, although certain that socialisation takes place, many writers have remained strangely coy when it comes to detailing its precise mechanisms. Social behaviour is said to be 'inculcated' or, more mysteriously, 'acquired', as social processes creep up secretly upon a passive and unwary child:

> At a time when positivism gripped the social sciences it offered a 'scientific' explanation for the process whereby children learnt to participate in society. Within structuralist functionalist accounts of society, 'the individual' was slotted into a finite number of social roles. Socialisation, therefore, was the mechanism whereby these roles came to be replicated in successive generations. The theory purported to explain the ways in which children gradually acquire knowledge of these roles. (Prout and James, 1990: 12)

Sometimes socialisation works well, and the child becomes social; sometimes it fails and deviance sets in (Mackay, 1973). In this sense, traditional socialisation theory is a strange mixture of psychology and sociology (Rafky, 1973) in which children themselves are primarily construed as the passive objects, rather than active subjects, of socialising processes. It is also a theoretical position within which the biological aspects of childhood are often implicitly accredited with a determining role.

One consequence of this perspective was that, through an insistence on socialisation as an essentially normative process, children's own views, thoughts and ideas about growing up were rarely documented. Even less often were they theoretically accounted for. It was assumed that, necessarily, they would be congruent with, rather than antithetical to, society's — that is adults' — aims and aspirations. In this way, therefore, the theoretical marginalisation of the child inherent in accounts of socialisation unquestioningly mirrored children's own everyday social experiences of limited participation in and access to adult society.

However, in somewhat contradictory mood, traditional social-isation theory at the same time embraces a concept of the child as Other, as different. Through its implicit and uncritical accept-ance of the dominant developmental approach provided by psychology, sociological accounts of child socialisation rest on an implicit notion of childhood as a 'presocial period of differ-ence, a biologically determined stage on the path to full human status i.e. adulthood' (Prout and James, 1990: 10). Thus, within this genre the child is depicted as not yet fully human, as more subject to and dependent upon some essential 'nature' than adults and as making little active contribution to a predomin-antly adult social world. This view of the child thus also both sustained, and was sustained by, a wider Western ideology of childhood which sets children apart from adult members of society in everyday life.

An uneasy reconciliation of these oppositional representa-tions of the child, inherent within socialisation theory, was effected through a third and dominating emphasis on the tem-poral aspects of childhood. Being construed as but a transient condition of marginality, it is the future, rather than present, which assumes the greatest significance for childhood. Most traditional socialisation accounts, together with those of devel-opmental psychology upon which they relied, wholeheartedly embrace a perspective that:

> It is children rather than 'fate', 'gods' or 'demons' who will most likely endure to shape and participate in any future social world; they are the 'next generation', 'the guardians of the future' on whose shoulders time itself sits. (James and Prout, 1990b)

Children's experiences are therefore to be gauged largely in terms of their future outcome, that is as adults in society, rather than in terms of their meanings for children in the present.

In this way, socialisation theory uncritically re-presented the Western idea that children as children are without a socially significant personhood. Only in terms of future adulthood is childhood seen to assume an importance. It is not surprising, therefore, that children themselves do not people accounts of socialisation, for, from the perspective of dominant adulthood, childhood's significance lies mainly in its representation of a personal 'past':

> Childhood is frequently represented in the 'past' as some-thing to be remembered, as a time to look back upon

during later life. It is the older people who remark to the younger that 'school days are the best days of your life'. This constitution of childhood as memorabilia is, however, double-edged; there is a darker side. Childhood, in con-temporary western societies, is also popularly regarded as the potential antecedent for adult neurosis . . . This means, therefore, that in such representations childhood becomes important with respect to the future. (James and Prout, 1990b: 225)

Accounting for Culture

Clearly, traditional socialisation theory was located within the parameters of a very old debate: culture versus nature. It is one which constitutes the core of Western perceptions of child-hood, for questions continue to be asked about the extent to which culture or biology directs the passage to maturity for the growing child (Macbeth, 1989). In the earlier work on childhood carried out by the culture and personality school of social anthropology this had been an explicit focus. Flourishing in the United States during the 1920s–1940s, theorists had argued against the universalising tendencies of the then new disciplines of psychology and psychoanalysis (Honigman, 1976) and had worked to convince their dissenters of the determining role which culture has over nature's course.

Unlike the later and more cautious accounts of socialisation, therefore, the culture and personality studies readily embraced the notion of childhood as a culturally relative representation of the period of biological immaturity. Mead, for example, took issue with the psychologist Stanley Hall who had character-ised adolescence as a 'the period in which idealism flowered and rebellion against authority waxed strong, a period during which difficulties and conflicts were absolutely inevitable' ([1928] 1963: 10). Through her work among adolescent girls in Samoa, she strove to demonstrate that this was not always and everywhere the case. As Benedict later commented, adoles-cence:

> is in our tradition a physiological state as definitely charac-terised by domestic explosions and rebellion as typhoid is marked by fever. There is no question of the facts. They are common in America. The question is rather of their inevitability. (1935: 22)

In her own work, Benedict was committed rather more to an

idea of cultural determinism found within the Durkheimian tradition, than to that suggested by psychoanalytic approaches (Morris, 1984: 4). She believed that the great emphasis placed in American child-rearing practices on the difference between children and adults in terms of their status roles and physical capabilities reinforced other sets of binary oppositions in the child-adult relationship: non-responsibility: responsibility, submissiveness: dominance, sexlessness: sexuality. Citing the Amazonian Indians as a comparative example, she showed that such discontinuities were not inevitable. Of this cultural context, she wrote that a child 'is continuously conditioned to responsible social participation while at the same time the tasks that are expected of it are adapted to its capacity' (1955: 24). By contrast, the American child is praised just 'because the parents feel well disposed, regardless of whether the task is well done by adult standards' (1955: 24). Thus, an explicit intention was to demonstrate the infinite plasticity of human kind and, through observing and analysing the child-rearing practices of different cultures, the culture and personality writers found ample evidence to support their claims.

Again in contrast to socialisation theorists, the culture and personality writers regarded children as valuable informants. Mead acknowledges this in the appendix to her book about Samoan adolescents:

Quantitative data represents the barest skeleton of the material which was gathered through months of observation of the individuals and of groups alone, in their households and at play. From these observations, the bulk of the conclusions are drawn concerning the attitudes of the children towards their families and towards each other, their religious interests or the lack of them, and the details of their sex lives. This information cannot be reduced to tables of statistical statements. Naturally in many cases it was not as full as in others. In some cases it was necessary to pursue a more extensive enquiry in order to understand some baffling aspect of the child's behaviour. In all cases the investigation was pursued until I felt that I understood the girl's motivation and the degree to which her family group and affiliation in her age group explained her attitudes. ([1928] 1969: 210)

However, despite the often vivid accounts of children's lives which these writers presented and their professional encounters with children through fieldwork practice, they too did not emphasise children's subjectivity. Their overriding concern was to consider the process and outcome of cultural reproduction, rather than children's own understandings of cultural processes. Ironically, therefore, despite an explicit emphasis on cultural relativism, the representations of childhood offered by the culture and personality school of social anthropology turn out, like those of socialisation theory, to be embedded within a Western ideological construction of children. They too envisaged the child primarily as an agent of cultural reproduction, as having a social significance more in terms of the future than the present. In this respect children's activities and experiences were unproblematically cited to illustrate aspects of their growing, and more culturally significant, adult sociality. Summing up her later New Guinea work, Mead acknowledged her intentions with respect to the study of children as follows:

> I watched the Manus baby, the Manus child, the Manus adolescent, in an attempt to understand the way in which each of these was becoming a Manus adult. (Mead, [1930] 1968: 16)

The recent controversy surrounding Freeman's critique of Mead's work, which sparked off both popular and academic debate in the United States and Britain, shows the power and persistence of such Western representations of childhood (Firth, 1983; Freeman, 1983; 1984; Glick, 1983). Freeman's objection to Mead's Samoan work fundamentally centres on her insistence on childhood's cultural relativity. Quite simply, Mead's argument that children were less at the mercy of their biological and psychological development than is commonly thought is at odds with Freeman's wish to establish that the 'genetic and exogenetic are distinct but interacting parts of a single system' (1983: 299). The notoriety this debate has assumed can be seen as a function of the questions about childhood it raises. It poses the perennial question of whether the form which childhood assumes for any child is predominantly shaped by nature or nurture or the product of them both?

Traditional social scientific accounts of children and childhood have therefore spoken loudly of Western conceptions of childhood. They have rehearsed in their specific research foci more general social and philosophical concerns about children's position in society with respect to social and biological immaturity.

Contemporarily, these remain pertinent issues for many social scientists interested in childhood. In Whiting and Edward's recent re-study of six cultures, for example, their express intention was to explore the ways in which cultural processes interact with a child's biological and cognitive development. In their words this was in order to investigate the 'universals that govern interpersonal behaviour and the extent to which these patterns are influenced by culture' (1988: 10). Hendry's interesting work on child-rearing, although concerned more with cultural specificity than its diversity, voices a similar intent. She wishes to explore how Japanese children become Japanese through identifying the 'salient features of the system of classification' underlying the child-rearing practices of Japanese parents (1986: 153). She begins from the following premise:

A child in any society learns to perceive the world through language, spoken and unspoken, through ritual enacted, indeed, through the total symbolic system which structures and constrains that world. Thus, the essentially biological being gradually becomes a member of society sharing a system of classification with other members, with whom he or she learns to communicate and interact in a meaningful way. This process is part of socialisation. (1986: 2)

This dominance of a socialisation perspective in social scientific thinking about childhood, as well as in more populist writings about children's lives, has left a peculiar legacy. It has meant that, despite a wealth of literature about children's physical, psychological, cognitive and intellectual development, there is still relatively little knowledge of:

how small children shape themselves by the actual, successive physical encounters of their lives, in what shapes they perceive power and authority, how soon they internalise specific expectations of social action, how far their milieu successively blocks, or creates, or enables them to become people with certain capacities. (Tonkin, 1982: 25)

In part, this void in the study of childhood reflects the more general contemporary theoretical tension within the social sciences: what weight or emphasis should be given to the role of social structure as opposed to that of human agency? Thus, for instance, while the culture and personality school was able to illustrate the synchronic differences between cultures, the more difficult question of explaining differences within a single culture could not be so readily answered by their material.

Like those of traditional socialisation theorists, their representations of childhood provided a general, structural explanation of how cultural knowledge was reproduced in successive generations. It could not, however, explain its more subtle changes, its dissonant elements nor the very different responses individual children might have to similar socialising processes. Moreover, in implicitly incorporating an ideology of childhood which denies children an active social role, greater emphasis was placed on child-rearing practices than on children's own activities. Thus individualised accounts of childhood which might have more easily emphasised children's human agency were effectively written out of that tradition. Ironically, therefore, although the childhood which children experience is regarded as central to any discussion of the reproduction of cultural knowledge, how children receive and make use of that knowledge remains relatively uncharted.

The Medicalised Child

In the example of research into children's health and illness can be seen the powerful model for the study of childhood which socialisation perspectives have provided. Just as the biological basis of childhood came to dominate and legitimate perspectives on socialisation, so too it permeated accounts of child health. As Armstrong notes in his discussion of the development of medical knowledge in Britain during the twentieth century, the child became 'construed as precariously normal' (1983: 27). A vigil on childhood was variously kept through the increased institutionalisation of child health – welfare clinics, the child-guidance service and population surveys – to guard against an individual child slipping into any one of a number of qualified childhoods, described through disease, sickness or ill treatment:

> Nervous children, delicate children, neuropathic children, maladjusted children, difficult children, over-sensitive children and unstable children were all essentially inventions of a new way of seeing childhood. (1983: 15)

The legacy of this construction of child health is that children who are sick or disabled are doubly marginalised. Not only do they, as children, share in childhood's conceptual isolation from the adult world but, through disablement or disease, find their social personhood subject to further qualification. As Wedell and Roberts report, despite the recommendations of the

Warnock report (1978) which emphasised the desirability of moving away from seeing children in relation to handicap categories, much research continues to define children in this manner, rather than 'in terms of the nature of their problems' (1982: 21). As in the adult world, children with disabilities may often find that the 'handicapped identity is seen as a central organizing factor around which explanations of the person are constructed' (Thomas, 1982: 18). For children, Western emphases placed upon the biological basis of childhood compound this classification problem. Thus, while there is a vast and disparate body of literature and research concerning children with specific disabilities, there is no 'overall perspective of what it means to be a child with disablement' (Philip and Duckworth, 1982: 9). This means that little is known about a possible commonality of experience shared by children with disabilities of whatever kind.

The persistence of an ideology of childhood, which denies children an active social presence and articulate voice, means that, just as in traditional socialisation accounts, relatively little research has explored what the experience of disability or sickness is like from the child's point of view. Accounts such as those by Hegarty and Pocklington (1981) or Booth and Statham (1982), which are focused on the integration of children with special needs into mainstream schools, are welcome exceptions, but more research is needed into exploring the quality and substance of the social relationships engaged in by children with special needs of any kinds.[2] Thomas, for example, writes that the experience of handicap is a social learning process in which the 'nuances and meanings of identity are assimilated' (1982: 39). Echoing the vagueness with which the process of socialisation is traditionally described, such an observation only explains what happens. We need also to ask how such learning occurs and what social consequences it has from the perspective of the different child.

One outstanding account, which bucks this trend, can be found in Bluebond-Langer's (1978) work, *The Private Worlds of Dying Children*. In this account children are revealed as knowing and watchful commentators about the progress of their own disease (cancer) who actively manage adult perceptions of themselves. We are led to see a mutual dance of pretence, orchestrated by the children, who know that they are dying. Feigning ignorance of their impending deaths, they deflect the concealing strategies which their adult care-takers use with them. Through this account we see, then, not only the child's perspective on illness and death but how children confront the ideologies of childhood which adults impose on them:

> These avoidance and distancing strategies, like all other tactics used for maintaining mutual pretence, harboured the possibility of ending mutual pretence. If the staff or the parents avoided the children's rooms too much, the children sensed it was because the adults were uncomfortable about their condition and 'afraid that the subject of his prognosis might come up'. 'No one comes to see me any more. I'm dying and I look bad.' 'They don't make me get needles no more. Roberta didn't come for two days.' Similarly, the children's avoidance of adults, through the various strategies for inhibiting conversation, aroused the staff's suspicions that the children knew, but were not telling. 'She knows. She just doesn't want to talk about it.' 'He yells so I can have an excuse for leaving.'
>
> As with crying, the children risked being deserted for the action, but they also reinforced the adults' belief that the children were normal. Normal children let off steam. They resist passivity. The leukemics' yelling and screaming was seen as fighting, as throwing off passivity, as living and not dying. (1978: 207)

Bluebond-Langer's seminal account thus starts from a perspective which is radically different to those representations of childhood which make children the objects, rather than subjects, of socialisation practices. For Bluebond-Langer children are 'wilful, purposeful individuals capable of creating their own world as well as acting in the world of others' (1978: 7). They are very much in charge of their own subjectivities. Working as a social anthropologist, using participant observation, Bluebond-Langer's work is a landmark in the study of childhood in its account of health and illness from a child's perspective.

Social Anthropology and Children

The shift towards a more interpretive approach to understanding social life, begun during the 1960s, offered a widespread challenge to the orthodoxies of socialisation theory and created a space for children as social actors. This took place within sociology through work on symbolic interactionism, sub-cultures and age stratification, in education through school ethnographies and in developmental psychology through a radical critique of the work of Piaget (Prout and James, 1990). Within social anthropology Charlotte Hardman (1973) was one of the first to argue for a child-centred approach through proposing that children could be seen as a muted group in society: children, she argued, had been more spoken about than spoken to. Through its traditional emphasis upon the ethnographic method, she suggested that anthropology had the potential to articulate children's views. They could be seen as 'people to be studied in their own right and not just as receptacles of adult teaching' (1973: 87).

Out of these convergent interdisciplinary concerns an emergent paradigm for the study of childhood can be identified (Prout and James, 1990). Essentially, it begins with a construction of the child as an active participating presence in the social world, rather than as a mere passive spectator, and envisages children as having some part in determining the shape which their own lives take. The real promise of the ethnographic approach which it advocates lies in allowing children to have a 'direct voice and participation in the production of sociological data' and for them to be 'seen as active in the construction and determination of their own social lives, the lives of those around them and of the societies in which they live' (Prout and James, 1990: 8). Recent examples of such research within anthropology would be Solberg's (1990) vivid depiction of Norwegian children's use of domestic space, Reynolds (1985; 1989) work with children in Zimbabwe; within the field of education, Davies (1982) and Pollard (1985), and within medical anthropology Bluebond-Langer (1978); Bluebond-Langer, Perkel and Goertzel (1991) and Prout (1989).

However, while such studies represent a welcome advance in social scientific thinking about children, like other genres of writing about childhood, they cannot be seen as ideologically neutral or unproblematic. They, too, both reflect and help create a particular climate of opinion about childhood. But what such child-centred approaches might offer is a way of reflecting on, first, the socially constructed nature of children's lives and, second, on the ways in which those lives are inscribed or theorised.

Briggs's (1982; 1986) discussions of Inuit childhood provide just one insightful illustration of the theoretical issues such a child-centred approach potentially raises. Through her compelling accounts of child life we are brought to see children as active participants in the reproduction of culture. We are led, through detailed descriptions of children's interactions with adults, to appreciate how it is that an Inuit child learns about Inuit society. Briggs observes, for example, that Inuit children are not expected to ask questions and accept answers. Instead, they are encouraged 'to observe closely, to reason and to find solutions independently' (1986: 7). It is an active process of Self-instruction which is often put to the test:

> Inuit children are continually tested in all spheres of competence. When travelling in a complex maze of fjords, cul de sacs, and bays, or in the middle of a trackless stretch of snow-covered tundra, some adult will ask: 'Where are we?' 'Have you ever been here before?' 'In what direction is the town?' 'How shall we pass through that cliff?' and if a child does not know the answer, amusement is very likely to be the response. (1986: 7)

In her writings, therefore, Briggs not only presents us with a radically different conception of childhood to the familiar urban and Western construct, she also writes from a different perspective. Her representation of Inuit children's socialisation captures the experience from the perspective of an Inuit child. Thus, in contrast to the silent passivity of the child in traditional accounts of socialisation or its marginality in accounts of child-rearing, Briggs brings children's subjectivity into focus. The account of socialisation she provides makes children's participation and developing understanding and experience of social life, the main, rather than secondary, aim of a study of how Inuit culture is perpetuated over time.

Moreover, the socialisation process which Briggs describes starts from an Inuit perspective on the place of the child in society. This embodies particular cultural ideas concerning the nature of human cognition:

> *Isuma* refers to 'consciousness, thought, reason, memory, will' – to cerebral processes in general and the possession of *isuma* is a major criterion of maturity. (1986: 5)

Isuma is thought to grow naturally with the child, so that child-rearing involves providing contexts and contents from which the child may learn. According to the Inuit, a child cannot be forced to learn before s/he is ready. For this reason, scolding or anger, while perhaps giving momentary vent to an adult's feelings, are not seen as educative devices. An Inuit child will learn when s/he

is ready. Consequently, learning begins with the child's own willingness to participate and imitate, rather than in response to
adult pressure. For the Inuit, social knowledge is thought to be
encouraged in its development through play and in Briggs's
detailed analysis of the games adults play with children – games
of the body and of the emotions – we see the processes through
which children come to know Inuit culture. At the same time we
are also led to an understanding of an Inuit conception of childhood. For instance, noting that a sense of one's own vulnerability is essential to a nomadic life-style, Briggs describes the
games by which this idea is introduced to children:

> an adult pretends to envy some possession of the child's and
> suggests to the child: 'Why don't you die so I can have it?' In
> another game, the child is asked repeatedly: 'Are you lov-
> able? You *are*? Are you really? Are you more lovable than
> your brother? Is he more lovable than you?' and so on. The
> message – which is delivered with great consistency in
> many contexts and in many forms – is that if one is not
> loved, one runs the risk of being left behind: emotionally
> or physically abandoned or killed. (1982: 1221)

It is therefore both in and through Briggs's accounts of children
at play with adults that the Inuit understanding of children's
subjectivity is revealed. In this way the 'child-rearing' practices
which, from an ethnocentric Western perspective might appear
both dangerous and permissive, become instead comprehens-
ible as the 'child-learning' contexts which the Inuit themselves
consider them to be. The games played between adults and
children are complex in their emotional structure and, according to Briggs, provide valuable participatory lessons in learning
to expect the unexpected:

> In sum, a game may have multiple meanings at the same
> time, as well as different meanings on different occasions
> or in the hands of different players. So the child has to try
> to make sense out of, and figure out how to respond to,
> motivations which may appear to be, or may really be,
> contradictory and changeable. Finally, s/he must make
> sense out of his or her responses, which may be just as
> mixed as the motives of the adult players. For example, a
> child may enjoy being loved and played with, be pleased
> at surviving a test, anxious about being injured, and angry
> at being assaulted, all at the same time. (1986: 15)

Briggs's work is instructive. In working from a perspective of the child as a significant participant in society – the Inuit view – she is able to detail *how* the child learns, not just that he or she learns, the order of Inuit society. This, as Tonkin has observed, is precisely what is lacking in most traditional accounts of socialisation. While anthropologists have variously enquired about rites of passage, structures of cosmology and the 'conditions which make people think as they do' they have consistently failed to explore 'how these effects operate through people' as a key element of the socialisation process (Tonkin, 1982: 254). Briggs's account of child-rearing among the Inuit goes a long way towards rectifying this omission.

The Culture of Childhood

In a radical contrast to the conceptual eliding of accounts of children's social life and perspectives on the world in traditional social scientific writings about childhood, writers within other genres have long made these a central focus. Scholars, such as the Opies ([1959] 1977; 1969) and Rutherford (1971) have, for example, provided detailed documentation of children's rhymes and street games, while biographers and novelists have introduced to their readers the subtle intricacies of children's social and power relations. However, the perspectives on childhood which these represent are, like those emanating from the researches of social scientists, also subject to particularised ideological framings.

For example, the Opies' seminal collections, begun during the 1950s, catalogue the cabalistic rhymes and naming practices which children use, and explore the structure and rules of the games they play. In doing so the Opies give credit to children as an active social presence in the world and provide a most vital and vibrant account of childhood. Their twin volumes on language and games reveal the importance placed by children on particular aspects of their social relationships through the documentation of their fighting lore, teasing rhymes, codes of honour, skipping games, and those structured play-forms of chase and combat.

However, despite the considerable achievement of bringing the significance of children's own language and traditions to adult notice, the Opies' representation of childhood turns out, ironically, to help perpetuate the conceptual marginality of children. This is a function of the uncritical incorporation of the Western ideology of childhood into the accounts of child-life they provide. Untheorised, this means that the childhood lore and language which they discuss is open to be read only as a sign of children's marginality and Otherness. In this way, the child-life which can be envisaged through their work becomes typified as a cosy cultural backwater which may be more an adult's, than a child's, dreaming. Indeed, that this conceptual location of childhood is explicit in the framing of their account is made clear in the introduction to the volume on lore and language. Here, childhood is represented as a secret and protected world:

> The folklorist and anthropologist can, without travelling a mile from his door, examine a thriving unselfconscious culture (the world 'culture' is used here deliberately) which is as unnoticed by the sophisticated world and quite as little affected by it, as is the culture of some dwindling aboriginal tribe living out its helpless existence in the hinterland of a native reserve. ([1959] 1977: 22).

Through deliberately drawing parallels between children and exotic savages at repeated points within the text, children are represented in a conceptual isolation from the social world of adults. They are literally and metaphorically reserved, set apart and exoticised. And in their distance from the adult world they are portrayed as reluctant to reveal the traditions of childhood which bind one child to another. Curiously, therefore, despite the magnitude of the Opies' achievement in redressing the balance between adult and child perspectives on the social world, the ideological framing of their work resurrects the Otherness of children.

Their work also points to a further temporal location of childhood: the past. This has long been a feature of literary representations of childhood. However, in the process of representing children's own individual experiences of childhood as significant to a personal and idiosyncratic past through biography and autobiography, or as central to the timeless time of fictional accounts, these child-centred constructions of childhood seem to become ever more firmly distanced from the central social, economic and political institutions of everyday life. It is therefore a subtle irony that through the traditional relegation of children's own experiences to the realm of folklore and myth, memory and imagination, the social marginality of children is perpetuated.

For example, the second half of the twentieth century has

seen the publication of a number of autobiographical representations of childhood. These books centre on their authors'
memories of childhood rather than, as is common in other
kinds of biographical work, using childhood as the opening
sequence in a narrative primarily focused on later adult life.
According to Bromley, the appearance of this genre of commer-
cial autobiographies bears witness to the wider social changes
which, since the Second World War, have seen a partial frag-
mentation of the class structure. In his view, books such as
Rose Gamble's (1979) *Chelsea Childhood* or Winifred Foley's
(1974) *A Child in the Forest* are written by people who took up
'individualist forms of mobility, distancing them from their
class and locality' (1988: 40). And yet, as he goes on to observe,
they are presented to us as a 'generalized and generational
childhood' (1988: 36):

> Escaping from their childhood, the writers return to it
> almost as anthropologists visiting another country – simpli-
> fying and sentimentalising, or generalising and classifying.
> They are published for their representativeness, or rather,
> for the way in which they are constructed within a particular
> ideology of a representative experience. (1988: 40)

The child that the author was becomes a symbol of and for all
children and all childhoods of that social class and historical
period. Written from the perspective of the present, the past
is reconstructed in its shadow. Thus, the Forest (Foley, 1974)
and the Chelsea (Gamble, 1979) child's experiences of childhood are re-told in the light of and in respect of their future
significance: the authoresses present. In this sense, such autobiographical accounts of childhood share with those written by
social scientists in reproducing the temporal ideological markers
of Western childhood.

   Moreover, as Bromley notes, despite their individualising of
childhood through personal biography, these accounts also participate in generalising and homogenising the category of children, a feature also still prominent in much social scientific
writing on childhood and in everyday perceptions of 'the child'.
That it is possible to talk of 'the child' and to legislate on
behalf of children – for instance, nationally through The Children's Act or globally through the Declaration of the Rights of
the Child – speaks volumes about the continuing denial by
adults of children's subjectivity. Age, gender, class, disability
and ethnicity – all important identity-markers in the adult

world – are often strangely absent as qualifiers of the category 'child', just as in statistical accounting children's experiences of poverty or divorce are regarded, unproblematically, as congruent with those of the 'family' as a whole (Qvortrup, 1990). Thus, although gender and class are acknowledged through these autobiographies, the construction of these accounts as generalisable inevitably softens the contours of the subjectivities they embody. For example, as the dust-jacket summary of *Chelsea Childhood* advises us, it is through one working-class girl's experience of London life during the 1920s that the reader, in the 1980s, can glimpse not only a (blessedly?) past kind of childhood, but also an entire life-style best left behind:

> Rose, known as Rosie, was the fourth child to survive, the pet of her elderly sisters until the arrival of Joey brought a new baby into this astonishingly loyal family. Her father's lofty attitude to employment in the lean years between the wars left the bread-winning to her mother. It was she who provided the six shillings for the rent and the bare necessities for survival, by working as a char. The ingenuity and efforts of the children played a vital part in their hand-to-mouth existence, but there was also fun and adventure for them in their own world – the vivid life of the streets. Here they raced their home-made carts and scooters, pinched road blocks, and played with fag-cards and marbles. And although school echoed to the chants of tables learned by rote, there were also dedicated teachers with books and pictures, crayons and music, to widen the horizons of their urban classes.

Identity and Personhood in Children's Culture

Setting the critiques offered in this chapter alongside the earlier parental narratives about childhood illness offered to me during the pilot project, the task of this book becomes clear. First, its aim is to explain the process and not just the fact of children's developing sociality and cognition as they mature; second, to work from children's own sense and understanding of Self and Other, that is to take account of their own subjectivities; third, to explore how children encounter the representations of that developing Self-awareness through the adults they meet, the books they read, the films they watch[3] and, what will concern me most, the relations they have with other children. Finally, it is to be aware of my own part in both presenting and re-presenting children's accounts of themselves.

Although from the interviews I held with parents I gained many insights into the social construction of childhood as it emerges in and through social action, I learnt only little of the child's experience of being conceptually positioned along a continuum between 'normality' and 'difference'. Seemingly so precarious in its dependency upon the relationships of power, authority and social control exercised by different groups of adults, I was left wondering what were the children's own experiences of it? To what extent did the children share in a self-consciousness of their identities as particular kinds of children? I was offered but few glimpses.

This omission was both a function and a consequence of the interview setting. Through the conduct and context of the very first interview it became clear to me that the parents' interest in their child's condition was to set the framework for any discussion I might want to have. Invited into their homes, I felt bound to pursue my interests on their terms which, while yielding the rich and insightful accounts of childhood discussed above, proved a relatively ineffective way to learn about children's own experiences. In negotiating the interview I had left it open as to whether the children would participate. In some instances the children were absent, while in others, although invited to participate, the children stayed but briefly. Perhaps finding the topic uninteresting, or not wishing to discuss it in so public a manner, they would drift away, reappearing at points through the course of our conversation. On other occasions the children stayed throughout the interview, listening but rarely volunteering information.

On reflection, what these differing strategies clearly reveal is the subtlety of children's social marginalisation in and through their everyday social encounters in a society defined largely by and for its adult members. In these interviews, (which were later to contrast so strongly with those in which children themselves defined the form and content), I was unwittingly drawn into replicating this marginalisation. Thus, the few glimpses which the interviews provide into what it feels like to be a child who is in some way regarded as significantly different must be tempered by the relationships of power and authority which frame the social context of its voicing. In the following extracts, therefore, Alice's confirmation of the difficulty which dyslexia causes must be seen in the context of its utterance in which her mother and grandmother had firmly predefined the tone of the occasion. Is Alice merely acquiescing to her mother's perspective or did the interview and my expressed interest in understanding her viewpoint permit Alice to emerge from the margins to speak about her experiences? The questions are intriguing, the answers elusive.

For example Alice, supporting her mother's claim that the teachers at her rural primary school had been of little help, told disparagingly how she'd been given a 'little professor', a toy for three-year-olds, to help her with her maths. In her account she shows how even a casual remark or careless joke can provide the grounds for the dramatic realisation of stigmatising differences:

> My teacher had wanted somebody to go to the office to get something and I put up my hand and he said, 'No, I want somebody intelligent.'

Later, it became clear how such sarcastic comments merely served to reinforce her feelings of inadequacy, reflecting as they did the opinion which she knew some children also held of her:

> The girl in my village she thinks she is upper class because she has always been good at work and she's always known me and she knows I've had trouble with work and she always treats me . . . like say we are in PE . . . She says: 'That's very good Alice . . . aren't you clever?'

For Alice, then, at primary school it was the other children's opinions about her abilities which were the more pertinent to her self-esteem:

> The teacher's weren't horrid. It was the children. They just didn't want to go around with me and some of the older girls used to tease me . . . Paul had the same problems. Thicko, Dumbo, Dimbo . . . things like that.

Taking a cue from Alice's account, it is clear that, while engaging with the various forms with which childhood is represented and played out in British society, I must also acknowledge the substantial and powerful presence which children's culture has in children's lives. Thus, if as Geertz suggests, interpretive anthropology searches for the 'webs of significance' which people spin then the culture of childhood must constitute an important ethnographic resource (Geertz, 1975: 5). How, then, might it be possible to explore it in a way which can address, rather than simply ignore or implicitly incorporate, the ideological aspects of the Western model of childhood?

One approach would be to think of this culture as a set of 'cultural practices'. The Opies (1969; [1955] 1977) showed how the lore, language and games of childhood persist in time and space, moving between the generations of children who pass into and out of childhood. In this sense, the culture of childhood acts as a conservative force in children's social relationships. At the same time, however, these cultural practices are, again as the Opies have shown, infinitely flexible, providing the form within which new information and styles of speaking can be quickly and easily assimilated. It is this which allows 'mega' and 'wick(ed)' to be the contemporary adjectives of approval, displacing the out of date 'fab', old-fashioned 'smash' and positively antiquarian 'wiz'. Thus, twin themes of conservation and innovation both permeate and help sustain the culture of childhood. However, it would be incorrect to assume, as the Opies do, that the very vibrancy of the culture of childhood ensures its separation from the adult world. On the contrary, like the aboriginal tribe which they cite as a parallel, it is very much contextualised by the outside (adult) world: socially, politically and economically. This will become clear through this volume.

Taking Geertz's point that culture 'consists of socially established structures of meaning', I am suggesting, therefore, that the 'culture of childhood' be regarded, not as an object, a 'thing', but as a context within which children socialise one another as well as socialise with each other (1975: 12). From within this 'culture', children find one way of making some sense of their social encounters with Others – with parents, teachers and other children. In Western societies, the particular form which this culture takes is, however effectively, shaped by adults' wants and desires: we want our children to learn, so we send them to school; we want them to be sociable, so we encourage them to make friends, to play games; we desire them to be protected, so we curtail their activities within a known environment and endeavour to restrict their access to certain types of knowledge. The list is endless. In this way, as Chapter 2 has already shown, children's experience of socialisation is strung between the demands of home and school. But at the same time as adults orchestrate the present of childhood and presence of children, under the banner of what Ennew

(1986) describes as the obligation to be happy, childhood is also constructed as an apprenticeship for the future (see James and Prout, 1990b). It is a future which is both uncertain and unknown and yet towards which children must take on particularised orientations, made manifest to them through the socialisation process. But exactly how children understand and work through this double perspective is rarely made explicit; how do children make sense of the future in their present activities and what do the everyday lives of children tell us about their understanding of what the future holds?

My point about the 'culture of childhood', then, is that it contextualises one important part of children's socialisation experience. In the games and linguistic lore which children share and pass on to one another we may, for example, find Geertz's conceptual systems, in terms of which children 'do such things as signal conspiracies and join them or perceive insults and answer them' (1975: 13). These 'conceptual structures molding formless talents' may be and surely are of the adult world but, and this is the point, they are about the child's understanding of that world (1975: 50). To paraphrase Geertz, they are historically constructed and socially maintained through generations of children, providing one 'link between what [children] are intrinsically capable of becoming and what they actually, one by one, in fact become' (1975: 52).

Following this style of cultural analysis it is possible then to argue that the culture of childhood sets the stage for 'becoming human', although it is just one among many other social contexts through which children begin to acquire a social identity. It does, however, wield considerable symbolic power, demarcating family life at home from life at school and in the playground. It is this, for instance, which allows a nine-year-old girl to privately admit to playing with dolls at home while vehemently denying their importance at school, for, as Pollard has argued, 'child culture . . . acts to provide norms, constraints and expectations which bear upon its members' (1985: 50).

While in one sense, therefore, the culture of childhood is enabling – providing children with a sense of belonging to a group of children – it also constrains the ways in which that sense of belonging is achieved and experienced. Children only gradually get to know and grasp the subtleties of the conceptual structures which inform their experience of the social world; just so, their identities emerge slowly, to be tried and tested out in the company, largely, of other children. In this sense it can be argued that children use the symbols of the adult world – their future – to negotiate a social position and identity in the present. Here then is where the acquisition of a spoiled or damaged identity may start (Goffman, 1968). In short, the culture of childhood is a key area through which to explore the workings of culture as a symbolic system.

The interviews with parents and children provide me with further clues as to how such a focus upon the culture of childhood might be theoretically followed through. Although through my selective and partial discussion of the parents' narrative accounts of children with particular needs it might appear that all differences – whether obvious on the body's surface or only visible in its functioning – were inevitably re-marked on and experienced by children as distressing, this was not the case. Most of the children with whom I spoke were happy and confident with a group of friends and enjoyed their social lives at home and at school. However, most could also recall the sadder times and moments when they had been made to feel different, when they had felt excluded because of the manifest nature of their particular condition. In this way, through their own and their parents' comments, I was led to see the subtlety of stigmatising practices. Rarely overt, it was through the nuances of everyday social interactions at home, at school or in the doctor's clinic that the children experienced feelings of social marginalisation through coming to see them-selves as in some way different.

For instance, time itself often has a significant part to play in this process of classification and the assigning of social iden-tities. A child who falls seriously ill or a disabled child, newly integrated into a class, may be regarded by teachers and children as 'special'. S/he may receive extra attention and consideration, such as, as one paediatrician wryly remarked to me, 'prayers [being] said in assembly.' Indeed the child may become so 'special' that for a while s/he is treated like the class pet. Cards may be drawn by class members and sent during hospitalisation, particular playmates might be assigned to look after and be-friend the 'special' child.   If the illness or condition continues, however, such novelty risks wearing thin. Other children may begin to re-classify the special child as simply 'different'. This was one young woman's experience of the onset of her illness. When first diagnosed, at ten years old, both staff and pupils made a fuss of her. But after a while she stopped being the 'special' focus of attention; she just became 'different', which was far less glamorous. Time, it seems, exerts its own pressures on sympathy and understanding.

From a child's point of view, then, the attribution of 'special-ness' or 'difference', while perhaps being beneficial for a while in terms of both attention and material reward, may become onerous. When the transitory stage of 'specialness' threatens to become a permanent feature, the very individuality which was highlighted through being 'special' may work to handicap rather than augment a child's prestige among other children. Anne describes her experience of this changing regard:

> I think when I first had it they (the other children) said I was teacher's pet because I was always getting attention and things.

But in the end it is better to be the same. Summing up her daughter's attitude to having asthma, one mother described it in the following terms:

> She doesn't want to be different from her friends . . . she likes to think she can do what they can do.

At the level of children's everyday social interaction, then, what semantic resonance does being 'special' or 'different' have? How are the boundaries between normality and differ-ence understood, experienced and used by children and, for those so placed between these extremes, what problems does this position of ambiguity bring with it?

The following chapters explore these issues through develop-ing aspects of Victor Turner's (1974a) work on liminality, mar-ginality and outsiderhood. While liminality and marginality are betwixt-and-between states on the limen of social structures, outsiderhood refers to:

> The condition of being either permanently and by ascrip-tion set outside the structural arrangements of a given social system, or being situationally or temporarily set apart or voluntarily setting oneself apart from the behaviour of status-occupying, role-playing members of that system. (Turner, 1974a: 233)

Marginals are, on the other hand, 'simultaneously members (by ascription, optation, self-definition, or achievement) of two or more groups' but 'unlike ritual liminars, they have no cultural assurance of a final stable resolution of their ambiguity' (1974a: 233).

Thus, although all children necessarily have to negotiate the boundaries between group membership and outsiderhood, in respect of children's culture is this process more difficult for children who have particular or special needs? Being identified as in some way 'different', might they already be considered as 'marginal' to the social group? And is it in their attempts to negotiate the boundaries between membership and outsiderhood, that their 'difference' begins to assume symbolic and stigmatising significance? Might they risk permanent 'outsiderhood' if their attempts to overcome the significance of their differences fail?

Such questions are explored in the following account of experiences of childhood. Drawing extensively on field material, and using the children's own words, I examine these processes of identifying and classifying, of personifying. Through this it will become clear, as Turner observed, that outsiderhood arises out of relationships between people; it is not a fixed or intrinsic quality of the individual. It is therefore subject to flux and change, dynamic, shifting and altering through time and in space. For children this means that, just as any kind of difference may become significant, differences need not necessarily be signified. The important question seems to be just how do all children negotiate a path through this classificatory maze? Sandy identified the problem for me, as she remembers it:

> When you're going through it you don't think it's anything special. You don't think, 'Aren't I being brave' or 'Aren't I working hard.' It's the norm.

At the same time, however, she recalls wondering : 'How is this [eczema] ever going to go, how am I ever going to look normal?' Looking back on her childhood experiences she concludes that it was a matter of negotiating the boundaries between being 'normal' and being 'different', a matter of refusing the ascription of outsiderhood while knowing herself that eczema did make her different in some particularly stigmatising ways:

> There's a fine line. You don't want to be treated differently . . . Oh, I've got two heads or something, you don't want people to say: 'Isn't it a shame.' I'd say: 'Why? Why is it a shame?' I used to hate that. But, on the other hand, you'd want somebody to understand, just a bit and just let you get on with it and not say anything.

And there's the rub. How to achieve 'sameness' when you are marked out as being 'special'? How to prevent marginality spilling over into a more permanent condition of outsiderhood? How is that 'fine line' drawn?

These ideas will be thematically developed through the following ethnographic account of childhood. This is written from and about a particular and explicit construction of childhood which can be briefly delineated as follows. I will explore how children's sociality – that is, the art of being an effective child – develops slowly over the time of childhood and through an individual child's experience of it. In this sense, the 'culture of childhood' is the conceptual space of childhood within which this occurs. It is a space marked out not only by children's perceived Otherness – their difference from the adult world – but also by children's own social practices. Following Geertz, the following chapters will explore, therefore, how it is that children become social and learn to divest themselves of this Otherness while, *at the same time*, participating in that separateness of being a child. A strategic path of exploration will involve, therefore, carefully 'searching out and analysing the symbolic forms – words, images, institutions and behaviours' in terms of which children represent 'themselves to themselves and to one another' (1983: 58).

Baldly and only briefly stated here, I shall search out the shifting conceptual boundary along which a continuum of culturally possible identities is set out. It is with these that children learn to personify one another and, in this case, they can be seen to reflect the Western and urban context within which the research was carried out. This boundary thus prescribes not only the social and emotional space of childhood, but also delimits the context through which children learn about their gross categorical identity as 'children' and their own subjectivity as a child among other children. These 'children among children' identities represent ways of thinking about the Self and about Others which are, as I shall show, actively taken on through the negotiation of particular cultural stereotypes. These set limits to the appearance and presentation of the body, its gender and its behaviour, which may only be revealed in their breach.

In Geertz's (1983) terms, then, these stereotypes of the body and the uses to which it can be put are the 'experience-near' concepts which children use to sort each other out and with which they identify or personify one another. In my representation of childhood these constructions of identity will be grouped together under four 'experience-far' concepts which coexist as balanced but contradictory movements in children's everyday social lives. It will be shown how, tensely poised, cultural ideas of conformity *and* individuality, equality *and* hierarchy frame a range of potential subjectivities for children. They are four 'ways of being' a child which, while being necessarily discourses of and about the adult social world, represent different paths which children can take to come to know each other as persons.

In this way, then, my representation of childhood does not just reveal the possibilities of a social anthropological approach to the study of children. It also illustrates the potential which the study of childhood might have for anthropology (Benthall, 1992). Rather than the marginal activity which it has hitherto appeared to be, the study of children turns out to be central to anthropological thinking. By focusing on children as having an active part in social life it becomes possible to explore, not just what *children* think and do. Wider theoretical issues about the nature of the relationship between the individual and society, between Self and Other, and the semantic range of concepts of selfhood and personhood are also raised. Finally, it permits the supremacy of cognitive over behaviourist accounts to be demonstrably affirmed (Cohen, 1989).

Notes

1. 'South' as used here follows its now common usage as a replacement for terms such as 'developing countries' or 'Third World' countries.

2. There are some notable exceptions to this. Anderson (1973) represents an early engagement with these issues, followed closely by Bluebond-Langer (1978). By the 1980s there were signs of a developing interest in children's experience of illness – Davis (1982) and Prout (1989), for instance – and now, in the 1990s, with the study of childhood becoming more central, the topic is attracting considerable research by sociologists and social anthropologists which can be set alongside the more traditional psychological studies carried out through psychometric testing. Much of this latest research remains, as yet, unpublished or not widely accessible.

3. These aspects of children's experience are critical and, while there is no room to explore them in depth in this book, passing mention is made to television and film in the chapters which follow. While the impact of popular culture upon girls' ideas of the gendered Self has been explored (Frith, 1985; McRobbie, 1978), little comparable work has been done for boys.

FOUR

Embodied Childhood

The Signifying Body

While clearly the social category 'children' has a general and generalising cultural utility, it is frequently qualified in everyday usage. This may occur in order to situate the child more precisely within the life-course – small, little and young children, older, bigger and taller children, for example – or to locate the child in a social context – school children, middle-class children, disruptive children, foster children or mixed-race children. Other ways of similarly qualifying childhood derive from specific cultural models of children's physical and psychological development. Chapter 2, for example, explored how notions of 'normal' childhood are used variously and strategically by parents and professionals to identify children whose bodies are in some way different. Children with special needs of particular kinds have, in this way, come to constitute a sub-group of the larger category 'children', with their difference from other children being mapped out through reference to the biology of their bodies by the adult health and educational professionals they encounter.

Turning away from representations and accounts of childhood, which has been a focus so far, this chapter introduces the theme of embodied childhood. Following Bryan Turner's suggestion that 'the interpellation of persons is, typically, the interpellation of specific bodies' so that 'as embodied consciousness, the body is drenched with symbolic significance' I show how children's perceptions of their own and Other bodies constitute an important source of their, and consequently my, understanding of identity and personhood during childhood (1984: 54–5).

The account of childhood which I begin to lay out here, therefore, both works from and with children's own understandings and ideas about the social world. In this sense children literally embody the childhoods which I describe in this and the chapters that follow. Drawing on material largely, though not exclusively, collected during my participant observation-research work in schools, this chapter starts by asking what significance the body has for children's *own* definitions of the Self and Other in their experience of childhood. A primary focus for this question will be provided by considering the role which cultural stereotypes of the body play in children's social relationships and, in particular, of the conceptual links established by children between body size, shape and appearance, and social identity.

In exploring what meanings the body has for children and how this is signified and mediated in and through their everyday social relations I shall, in the chapters which follow, draw extensively on children's own words and images. These I take at face value. Following Donaldson's (1978) critique of Piaget and in line with recent work within developmental psychology (Richards and Light, 1986), I assume that the children with whom I talked were competent social actors and thinkers. In this sense, the heuristic value of their words and ideas is not seen to be limited by the immaturity of their bodies and minds. Instead, their conversations with me and with each other are seen as key ethnographic contexts within which children's particular and particularising perspective on the significance of the body can be found. Furthermore, in that I rarely asked the children questions, derived from and framed by my own adult concerns, I can more safely assume that the thoughts and concerns which the children brought to our exchanges were meaningful to them, that they were intellectual tasks, ways of reasoning, and modes and forms of expression which, for them, made sense (Garvey, 1984; Tizzard and Hughes, 1984).

To assert that children, in a Western culture such as Britain, are primarily defined by their bodies and use their bodies to signify does not represent a retreat into biological explanations. Rather, it expresses the way in which Western concepts of childhood are predicated upon the particularities of children's physical bodies. The qualities held to be characteristic of childhood, such as sexual innocence, physical and emotional vulnerability, lack of autonomy and physical and social dependency (Ennew, 1986; Holt, 1975; see also Chapter 3) both constitute and are largely constituted by a particular cultural perception of the child's body (Hockey and James, 1993). Thus, for instance, in the historical construction of the category of 'child' it was children's perceived lack of size, age and abilities which gradually came to define their dependence as childish. In turn, this led to the term 'child' becoming restricted in use for the physically immature, rather than the merely socially dependent, and, conversely, of physically dependent people of any age being cared for through infantilising practices (Hockey and James, 1993). Such segregation, between old and young bodies, later institutionalised through the introduction of compulsory schooling and a corresponding exclusion of the child from the work-place, meant that the age of the physical body came to define its social status as either child or adult. Later still, social psychology reinforced these conceptual differences through the influential theories of Freud and Piaget. By demonstrating that children's minds and bodies were in essence different from adults, the already widespread discriminatory social attitudes and practices towards children were confirmed, re-affirmed and perpetuated. Such 'visions of infancy' (Bradley, 1986), while reflecting the varied theoretical concerns of particular researchers, are nevertheless united in their insistence that the distinctiveness of children's bodies and minds is the major definitional criterion of what childhood is and what children should be like.

The age and functioning of the physical body continues to be used as a dominant classifying principle, employed to qualify and further refine the broad and generalised category of child: 'neonatal', 'toddler', and 'preschool' are, for instance, three relatively recent sub-categories used to differentiate between children under four years of age on the basis of the age and abilities of their bodies. Such depictions of the child through an embodied childhood have become increasingly common as the twentieth century has progressed, with children's bodies being used to discriminate between different 'types' of children (Armstrong, 1983). From delicate children to deprived children, from hyperactive to those thought to be gifted or abused, it is the body of the child which serves as one of the most important signifiers and conceptual filters through which any particular child's childhood and social identity is understood.

This emphasis reflects the dominance of the body in offering a definition of the Self and personhood more generally in Western consumer culture. As Featherstone, Hepworth and Turner describe it:

> Self preservation depends upon the preservation of the
> body within a culture in which the body is the passport to all
> that is good in life. Health, youth and beauty, sex, fitness are
> positive attributes which body care can achieve and pre-
> serve. With appearance being taken as a reflex of the self the
> penalties of bodily neglect are a lowering of one's acceptab-
> ility as a person, as well as an indication of laziness, low self-
> esteem and even moral failure. (1991: 186)

This prominence of the body as a location for the Self means
that loss of bodily ability or changes wrought in the body by
the vagaries of age or disease are accompanied by the risk of
losing an acceptable social identity (Hockey and James, 1993).

However, despite the widespread cultural emphasis placed
on 'embodied childhood' in the everyday lives of children in
Western societies, relatively little critical attention has been
given to children's own experience and understanding of the
body as a signifier of identity. Yet this function of the body
has not escaped their notice. No doubt this stems from the fact
that, from the moment of birth, a child's passage to maturity
is marked out through stages of bodily achievement and bodily
control, encouraged and sustained through child-rearing practices:

> The new mother must watch anxiously for the physical
> signs which are the prerequisites for learning more social
> skills: sucking, rolling over, sitting up, crawling, chewing,
> hand to eye coordination, walking, talking, running, jump-
> ing, bowel and bladder control, hopping, climbing, skip-
> ping. Each stage reached and gladly encouraged represents
> movement along the path to being grown up. (Hockey
> and James, 1993: 85)

Such watchful monitoring could not fail to make the body a
potent marker of social status for children.

However, as will become clear, many of the cultural stereotypes of qualified personhood used in the adult world as
markers of a stigmatised identity also resound in the bald
attribution of difference among children (Hockey and James,
1993). Thus, both personal experience of such practices, and a
more generalised cultural knowledge of the body, work to
make the body an important signifier of social identity for
children, a process which has yet to be systematically documented in accounts of childhood. This chapter asks, therefore,
what feelings, attitudes, images and concepts shape and sustain

children's perceptions of having a normal body; how these filter the experience of having a different body; and what significance such perceptions have in children's everyday social relationships?

Richardson's et al.'s (1961) early study of children's attitudes towards physical disability identified which kinds of disabilities children found the more significant, with facial disfigurement and obesity scoring high. Carried out using picture-ranking techniques, this work, along with later replicated studies, does not, however, offer an adequate account of how in their daily interactions and social encounters children actually behave towards one another. As Philip and Duckworth noted (1982), what is required is research which explores how stigma works in and through the complexity of these relations. In this respect more recent sociometric studies (Mannarino, 1980; Zakay, 1985) have underlined the importance of ethnography for exploring children's social relations and attitudes to disability. During the time I spent with the children at school the value of adopting such an approach became abundantly clear. Only rarely could I elicit systematic information about their understanding or attitudes towards the body. Ethical considerations made it difficult to discuss directly children's feelings about and towards bodies which differed in some way from their own. Perforce, and indeed by preference, I waited, listening, until the children talked of it themselves. In this way, it became possible to identify what *children* saw as the body's significant features, rather than what I, as an adult, had beforehand chosen to speak with them about. More importantly, it allowed me to see in what social contexts or through what social encounters their bodies or those of other children proved troublesome or helpful. In this way the signifying role of particular 'different' bodies could be envisaged as flexible, rather than fixed, as emergent rather than predefined. It allowed me to see the body's identifying, rather than identified, potential in children's culture.

Five aspects of the body seemed to have particular significance for children: its height, its shape, its appearance, its gender and its performance. These different bodily features preoccupied the children, often cropping up as conversation topics, as sources of ridicule or distaste, as objects of desire and admiration, as grounds for the beginning or ending of social relations. The frequency with which the children talked about the body thus underlines the corporality of human life of which Turner

speaks, and which sociological analyses must begin to acknowledge: not only does the human body change and become
subject to the effects of disease and time passing, but it is 'also
an effect of cultural historical activity' and a site for the construction of meanings (Turner, 1984: 49).

Body Stereotypes and Social Identities

Stereotypes of the body's shape, size and appearance, its gender
and its performance pepper children's conversations. If as
Taylor argues, stereotypes work to categorise, to 'heighten the
perception of similarities within categories' and 'to sharpen
the perception of difference between categories' then this pro-
liferation of stereotypes of the body underlines its importance
in the conferring of social identity (1981: 84). Further, if such
stereotyping practices flourish, as Rapport (1990a) suggests, in
'edgy' environments, in social contexts experiencing flux and
change or marked by instability, it comes as no surprise to find
them a common currency among children. From the child's
point of view, childhood must appear to have precisely these
characteristics.

   For example, the changing face of childhood for children,
already touched on in previous chapters, means that in a Western culture such as Britain, children should act and behave as
children in the same moment as they must also learn to leave
their childish ways behind them. Similarly, constructions of
childhood, oriented towards the past (through nostalgia and
sentiment) coexist with those focused on the future (through
processes of socialisation and biological maturation) to make
the present of childhood a precarious and unstable context
(James and Prout, 1990b). Children's social identities are thus
changing both in relation to Selfhood and category status.
From the perspective of their present confinement in childhood
the future is that towards which children, as the 'next generation', must learn to take on particular orientations. It is,
however, uncertain and as yet unknown. It lies beyond the
familiar boundaries of childhood in terms both of space –
outside the bars of the playpen, beyond the garden gate, over
the school wall – and time – when I'm a school girl, when I'm
a big boy, when I'm seven, when I go to middle school. From
a small boy's point of view, in the 'beyond' anything might be
possible, as Woods reports:

   So then I went to school someone had done something

wrong and Mrs Brown said she's going to shoot his head
off. I didn't look but when I opened my eyes his head was
still on so I wasn't scared any more. (Woods, 1987: 104)
Or, as a boy of five asked me, 'Is it true you die if a rat looks
you straight in the eye?' Such signs of edginess are common
among children.

Although not bound by geography the cultural world of
Western childhood is also more literally 'edgy'. The time of
childhood exerts a strong constraint on children's activities,
buttressing a set of legal, physical, and social boundaries which
separate children off from the adult world. This makes of
childhood a conceptually marginal domain (see Chapter 3).
Within it children's bodies become confined in designated safe,
but peripheral, spaces: schools, playgroups, playgrounds, gardens, parks, car seats, high chairs, playpens, paddling pools.
Ideally, their social contacts and access to knowledge are similarly restricted: to teachers and school class-mates, family and
close friends, to children's TV, children's games, children's
books, children's lessons, children's films. In this second sense,
the culture of childhood is quite literally poised on the 'edge'.
What stereotypes offer to children, then, is 'a short-cut to
generalities, regularities, uniformities; a source of consistent,
expectable, broad and immediate knowledge of the social world'
to which as children, they have but limited access (Rapport,
1990a: 28). Stereotypes provide a more certain perspective on
the future, on what lies beyond childhood's boundaries, within
a constrained but changing context where tempers are liable
to fray.

Rapport argues also that 'it is through the positing of stereotypical images of difference that individuals and groups garner
their senses of belonging' (1990a: 26). A further value of enquiring into children's use of stereotypes lies, therefore, in their
functionality as cognitive devices. For the child, stereotyping
enables those who do or do not belong to be remarked on or
marked out as different, as Other. It is one way in which
children themselves can strategically or more permanently
attribute a qualified personhood to their contemporaries. For
the anthropologist, stereotypes therefore serve to highlight the
network of fine and criss-crossed lines of discrimination drawn
by children, enabling the process of friendship-making and
friendship-breaking to be plotted and the attribution and
evaluation of different social identities to be mapped out.

The cognitive value of stereotypes for children lies, then, in the bringing of an element of certainty into an uncertain environment. In this sense, stereotypes work as hesitant assertions of facts – 'boys are naughty', 'fat people are ugly', 'girls are nice'. As characterisations, baldly made, they invite confirmation or denial from other children and, in this sense, their usage represents a form of questioning and enquiry, thinly disguised as Rapport has described:

> It is from stereotypical opposition and exaggeration that I come by clarity. More precisely, I know who I am, where I stand, who stands with me, who I stand against. (1990b)

From this it follows that stereotyping may also permit the creation of 'ideal' types for the Self. For children this is clearly the case. Through conceptual opposition to and exaggeration of the differences which other children's bodies exhibit, a child becomes more certain of his or her own body and of the social meanings and social identity which it literally *em*-bodies. Many of these stereotypes (negative) and ideal types (positive) are wisdoms received from the adult world, which means, inevitably, that for some children this self-knowledge about the body – about its size, shape or appearance – may be less than welcome. Sadly, it may affirm their feelings of difference and signal exclusion from, rather than inclusion within, the culture of childhood.

However, as 'groundworks for anticipating the future', field material reveals that stereotypes are not acquired or used unthinkingly by children (Rapport, 1990b). Children do not just passively absorb the stereotypes on offer. Rather, reasons are sought for the source of stereotypes, explanations offered to sustain them in the face of evidence to the contrary and judgements made by children as to their effectiveness or suitability as markers of identity. In the following conversation six-year-old Sylvie and Pat are explaining the rules of Kiss Chase, invoking gender stereotypes as they do so:

ALLISON: Do the boys like playing Kiss Chase?

PAT: The girls have to run and the boys have to try and catch them.

ALLISON: Is it ever the other way round?

PAT: Yeah after they've catched the girls we catch them.

SYLVIE: But they are too fast.

PAT: Girls are slow.

SYLVIE: How could the girl be first . . . because they [the boys] are fast and we are not.

The stereotypes of weak females and strong males are known and articulated by the girls – girls are slow, boys are fast. These stereotypes offer the girls some account of why it is that boys catch girls. But the girls recognise, too, that they do not provide a wholly satisfactory explanation: their own experience in the playground contradicts this cultural stereotype, for some girls do run faster than boys. And some boys run slowly:

SYLVIE: [continues] Because they've got trainers on and we've only got shoes on.

ALLISON: That makes a difference does it.

PAT: Some people have got shoes on . . .

SYLVIE: Some girls can run fast because they've got shoe-laces.

PAT: And if the girls have got trainers they can run fast and if they haven't they can't. So if the boys have got some trainers at home they can run fast.

ALLISON: So it's not just because they are boys or girls, it's because of the shoes is it?

PAT: Yeah.

This logic was later confirmed by Warren who confided to me that 'girls can't run fast' because they don't wear trainers. It is a form of reasoning eloquently described by Rapport: 'she moves between stereotypes, posing one against another, personalising what they purport in her own image' (1990a: 28).

As signs of present or potential identities, of the Self and of Others in the present and in the future, stereotypes of the body are explored by children through a web of significances anchored in its three complimentary aspects. Fixed attributes such as skin colour[1] and gender are, together with transient features such as the appearance, size, smell and feel of the body, refracted through a third more dynamic aspect: the actions and movements involved in the body's performance (see Chapters 5 and 6). Thus, although the next three chapters explore these different aspects of the body separately, in the everyday cut and thrust of children's complaints, arguments and teasing each feature resonates with and through the others. Thus, among children it is not just what kind of body a person has, but what the body does, which has a significant bearing on perceptions of personhood and social identity. The reverse also holds true: a person's social identity and personhood is thought to find expression in the appearance and performance of the body. Such conceptual linkages are not uncommon in the adult world, as Goffman's work on stigma (1968) and more recently Synnott's writing on beauty and appearance (1989) have shown. Among children they are just perhaps more boldly stated.

The Changing Body

The early part of my recent research work was spent in the company of three, four and five-year-old children. As I sat with them, doing jigsaws or playing in the sand, I became aware of how frequently children were bringing me their bodies to examine. I would be shown tiny cuts and abrasions, minute bruises, or minuscule scabs. Rarely were these battle scars of dramatic and obvious injuries, like those proudly displayed by older boys. They were instead but small reminders of the day-to-day knocks which anybody's body takes. Bemused, I would murmur something consoling and, adult-like, dismiss the encounter. On reflection, however, I realise my error: it was not sympathy the children were after, for the change to their bodies had long since occurred. It was my acknowledgement of, or indeed reassurance about, their altered bodies.

This demand for recognition of the scraped knee and bruised shin reflects, I suggest, young children's awareness of the strategic importance of more generalised body changes in relation to social identity and, in particular, its increase in size. This concern no doubt stems from their early socialisation experiences, when corporal growth is used by adults to signify children's growing sociability and potential personhood. Many of the ritualised remarks which adults make about children, for instance, conceptually link future physical size to future social identity. While the statement 'eat up your dinner or you won't grow into a big boy' is literally true, at the same time it contains an implicit and veiled threat which cognitively links a child's social future as a 'big boy' to the present care of the small child's physical body. As a piece of parental rhetoric it has many common echoes: 'Haven't you grown!'; 'Aren't you a big girl!'; 'Be a big boy!'; 'What do you want to be when you're grown up?' The stereotypical import of such statements is clear: the bigger one is, the better one is and the more social – literally the more personable – one becomes. The received emphasis for children is clear. It stresses the importance of the growth and development of the physical body in the present for future social identities.

But, in everyday conversation, physical size is often conceptually intertwined with numerical conceptions of age, as in the approving, 'Isn't he big for his age!' or the concerned, 'Isn't he rather small for his age?' For young children, therefore, 'bigness' may appear to be a rather slippery concept, subtly changing and sliding in everyday speech. During the summer term at Hilltop School, for example, 'big' school was promoted by the nursery staff as the place where the children would be moving to. The children were encouraged to contemplate their futures – when they would be 'too big' for nursery – through being taught the school routines with which, on leaving the nursery, they would have to become familiar. Safe still in the nursery setting, the children were able to practise being 'big' by answering their names during registration at the start of the day and learning the words of the special birthday song, sung during the ritual of Birthday Assembly, which took place weekly in 'big' school and to which, on their birthdays, they would be invited.[2]

Through such social practices the four-year-old children learnt that 'big' school is, undoubtedly, for 'big' people and, in this way, the numerically 'big' (in terms of age) came conceptually to prop up, and was itself given meaning, through conceptions of the physically 'big' (in bodily terms). The following example illustrates how this slippage occurs. During their pre-school visit to the lower school, one small boy anxiously tried to reassure his friend with the comforting phrase, 'We're big now'. Just to check, he turned to me with the questioning statement, 'I'm bigger, ain't I?' But on starting school in September, he soon learnt that he had to grow still bigger; he found himself restricted to the bottom corridor and playground, the spaces for the 'little' children and was not allowed to roam the top corridor and playground where the 'big', that is the older children, were to be found. Thus he learnt that the description, the 'big' playground, was more to do with age than acreage. Five-year-old Arthur and George reveal a similar understanding:

ARTHUR: Your birthday is before mine.

GEORGE: Yeah, I'll be six and I'll be bigger than you then.

ALLISON: You'll be older not bigger.

GEORGE: (unconvinced) Mmm.

The social and cultural relativity of 'bigness' became restated for the older children who moved to the middle school at nine years of age. For some, being among bigger children confirmed their sense of a growing maturity; for others, however, it served as a reminder of just how far they had to go. From a position of prestige and respect in the lower school as the 'big ones', in September they became the inferior 'little ones' once more:

SUZY: You feel more grown up but in some ways you feel more babyish because you're the youngest in the school . . .

ALLISON: Instead of being the oldest?

SUZY: Yeah, because when we were at Hilltop School we could say what we liked and no one would mind because we were older and the biggest . . .

KAY: I feel grown up being around with all the big people.

This uneasy conceptual relationship between physical size, age and identity becomes increasingly stigmatising as children settle into the social world of childhood and familiarise themselves with its concerns. Among four and five-year-olds I rarely heard height discussed but, talking with six and seven-year-old children, it was clear that it had begun to take on a particular significance. My conversation with two seven-year-old boys illustrates this:

JOEL: I know who's the tiniest in our class – Cindy.

ALLISON: Who's the tallest?

JOEL: Me.

CHARLES: Me.

ALLISON: Who's the tallest?

JOEL: The teacher.

CHARLES: I'm taller than him (pointing to Joel). Who's taller than me?

JOEL: Marty's the tallest.

In declaring that Cindy is the 'tiniest', rather than simply the smallest, in the class, Joel greatly exaggerates her difference and, through doing so, signifies the importance placed by children on height. The two boys go on to confirm this through competitive claims to be the tallest: Joel, who is the smaller of the two, tries to save face and status by arguing that the teacher is the tallest, while Charles, ignoring this strategy, points to Joel to confirm his own superiority.

The relationship between concepts of body size and those of social identity may become critical for children whose bodies refuse to grow at an appropriate rate. By the ages of eight and nine-years-old height has become, quite literally, a quantifiable measure of social status and, consequently, also of identity. Children who are significantly smaller than others may find themselves teased through nicknames such as Titch. More rarely, they might be excluded altogether from the social body of children. In the course of our conversation Lilly and her mother offered me a number of examples of the ways in which height is used as a powerful symbolic marker of childhood identity, concluding that:

> although we don't think she's deficient in growth hormones, if you stand her in her class she's always been that much smaller . . . and it becomes patently obvious sometimes and people tend to pat her on the head.

Sometimes Lilly was teased by the other girls at school. Whereas they were able to wear adult-sized clothes, bought from boutiques, Lilly could still fit into clothes and trainers sold in Mothercare, a shop known best for selling babywear. For Lilly, a passion for horse-riding had proved her salvation for, as her mother remarked, 'You don't look small on a horse.'

This pressure for the body to conform begins in early childhood as my conversation with five-year-old Carol clearly demonstrated. She and Lorna are standing back-to-back to assess each other's height:

CAROL: I'm bigger.

ALLISON: Would you like to be tall.

CAROL: Yeah . . . I want to be fifteen.

But while Carol, like many other children, acknowledged the relationship between increasing age and physical size, her desire to be fifteen reveals a more sophisticated appreciation of it. As an additional comment showed she was already aware that an increase in age enlarges access to social space and permits a range of identities, denied to younger children (James, 1986). When asked why she wanted to be fifteen, Carol replied that then she would be able to smoke. Four-year-old Patsy, admiring my ear-rings, made a similar connection between age, size and social identity. She commented, 'I'm not allowed to have ear-rings at this size but when I get bigger and bigger I have ear-rings.' Five-year-old Diana's desire to be seven is similarly structured:

> When I'm about seven I'll be able to go to school by myself – my Mum said.

In this extract it is clear that, for Diana, going to school by herself signalled a future independence and autonomy, presently denied. As she went on to observe, going to school by herself would be nice 'because you don't have to hold your Mum's hand'. Not holding her mother's hand would be a sign of her literal and metaphoric independence : walking *by* herself she would be in control *of* her Self.

That the social independence which ageing brings is consistently mapped on to the increasing size of the physical body is what makes small stature such a negative body stereotype for both young boys and girls. Small size is reminiscent of the previous and only just relinquished state of babyhood and infancy, the time of maximum physical and social dependency when control by children over their own bodies is minimal. Eight-year-old Camilla, usually silent and reserved at school, was moved to eloquence in describing the experiential consequences of this conceptual pairing for me:

> What [i.e. why] I like to be big and what I want to be older is because everyone treats me like I'm a little kid, like a baby. They say, 'Camilla, will you do that?' Like I'm a little baby. And my sister gave me this little toy to play with and, guess what, my mummy picked me up and put me in the chair and she goes, 'I'll feed you in a minute' and I said, 'No, I can feed myself.' And my sister she never gets dragged round like me. Like she always drags me around and shouts at me, like, 'Camilla, you silly little girl. Why have you been in my drawers? Why are you wearing my bra?'

Body behaviours such as dribbling, runny noses and incontinence were all negatively viewed by the children for they, too, belong to that complex of body behaviours stereotypical of young babies. These aspects of the body children of five and six-years-old had not long relinquished nor yet necessarily gained full mastery over. But, already oriented towards their own futures as 'big' children, any bodily signs of a reversion to babyhood became potentially stigmatising and were certainly unwelcome:

Stevie, Bobby and Charles are sitting talking on the mat:

STEVIE: (to Bobby) You've got a runny nose.

BOBBY: You've got a mark on your face.

The observation 'You've got a runny nose' recalls a common parental remark, as, in their caring-control of their children's bodies, a young child's nose is wiped clean (Hockey and James, 1993). By choosing to use this particular phrase, Stevie not only points out Bobby's transient difference – his changed appearancc – but positions himself as an adult-like commentator. He is, momentarily, in a more powerful position. Whether or not this was an explicit intention, Bobby is not slow to recognise its import. Forestalling any doubts about his own maturity, and hence his social identity, he retaliates. He draws attention to Stevie's own sign of potential difference: the mark on his face.

Small but significant instances such as these often occurred in classroom and playground encounters as the children sought out the boundaries of bodily acceptability. Those with poor bladder control were easy targets for teasing and suffered on each occasion of incontinence the temporary loss of an acceptable social identity. Figuratively instanced through having an 'accident', this would literally be seen in the tears of social shame which these children shed. They were perceived by Others to have bodies which resembled those of 'little children'. And, the older the child, the more social stigma such events incurred.

Further evidence that small physical size may contribute to a stigmatised social identity can be found more generally in the insults children use. The adjective 'little' frequently appears as a qualifier of personhood: 'stupid little', 'little twit', 'little nit' and so on. By negatively stereotyping others as 'little', an ideal of 'bigness' for the Self is simultaneously portrayed. Thus it is that the insult 'cry baby' is the one most deeply felt by children. It symbolically reassigns a child to his or her previous and less autonomous social status of baby.

In the following extract Saul and Joseph reveal just how relative positions of power, ranked through age and size, are played out in the course of children's everyday social relationships. In our conversation these two seven-year-old boys drew on negative stereotypes of 'littleness' to demonstrate to me their own more superior social status and personhood. Such is the stigmatising power of small stature as a bodily difference that, as the next extract reveals, the little boy Saul teases loses his social identity completely. In Saul's account, 'he' becomes 'it':

SAUL: I scared a little first year. I was playing with it. I ran up behind it and went 'Aaagh!' and it jumped, didn't it?

JOSEPH: You know this little boy, with the brown coat on and the same hair as me? I just went like this [pretends to strangle him] and he went 'Aagh' and cried.

ALLISON: So what do you call him?

JOSEPH: Cry baby.

ALLISON: Are there lots of cry babies at school?

SAUL: Yeah.

The six and seven-year-old girls also made much symbolic capital out of differences in size. No less significant nor less effective than the boys' explicit physical overpowering of the 'little ones', the girls adopted powerfully controlling roles as their playtime carers (see Chapter 7). A field-note records one such example:

> Veronica, aged six, tells me that she plays with the 'little ones', aged five, in the playground because she can look after them and 'show them Roger Red Hat [a reading book] and things'. One year older, but a few inches taller, she has a sense of her own far greater Self worth and social status.

Further illustration of this cognitive linkage between physical size and social identity is evidenced in an annotated children's picture-story book. This was shown to me by a woman who, as a child of nine or ten years old, had herself been considered small. In offering a perspective on a 1950s childhood, the book reveals the persistence over time of this particular cultural stereotype of the body within children's culture. Entitled *The Very little Girl*[3], it tells a simple story of a girl who was so small that she fitted in her mother's work basket. Then she began to grow. This printed narrative has been added to in a childish hand, thus giving the fictional story a more personal actuality through a child's own experience of being small. The amendments first appear half-way through the story. On the page bearing the sentence 'she was smaller than all the other little girls she played with', is added the statement: 'they would not let her play'. Other qualifications to the story continue to flesh out the feelings that the tale engendered in its child reader.

The denouement of the story is a happy ending. It reads: 'She was no longer a very little girl. She was the same size as the other little girls she played with.' The child author adds, as an afterword, 'and she was very happy'. Thus, the child-authored sub-plot tells a perceptive, perhaps more accurate, story of childhood relations than the fictional account it accompanies. It reveals how, through being small, a child risks social exclusion from the games other children play and, conversely, how through being the same the ideal of childhood happiness might begin to materialise.

In summary, then, the term 'grown up', while primarily used as a metaphor for adult social status, is also more literally a representation of the corporal changes that accompany the move out of childhood into adulthood. It relies for its effectiveness as a marker of social identity on a semantic redundancy, whose significance resonates more loudly as children grow older. Eight and nine-year-old children could be quite ruthless in their teasing as a field-note records:

> Milly is in my group today. She has been crying and tells me that she doesn't like Toby and Mike. They keep finding very small things and saying that she is that size. She is a slight child but not particularly small. Indeed, she's possibly no smaller than Patsy, who doesn't seem to suffer the same treatment.

Why it is that some children manage to effectively resist or negotiate such testing of their identity will be discussed more fully later (see Chapter 5). But one strategy, to be already noted here, is the adoption for the Self, voluntarily and with good humour, of a stigmatised identity. In effect, it means willingly becoming the ideal type of a particular stereotype. One eight-year-old used this to good effect:

> I was sitting with Jerry, [who is much smaller than his contemporaries] and some other boys. During our conversation Jerry casually refers to himself as a 'titchy little boring person'. Grant immediately says, 'No, you're not,' and the others, seeming a little taken aback, quickly concur with assessment.

Through this strategy of self-ascription Jerry cunningly forestalls the controlling power which others might have asserted over him. His overt recognition and cheery acceptance of his own difference defuses, temporarily, its social significance as a stigmatising feature. However, as adolescence approaches, when the ever-strengthening conceptual links between size and social status can make small stature increasingly problematic, such deflecting strategies may be rendered ineffective. Ablon describes the experiences of American children with dwarfism:

> No matter how popular they formerly were, or how attractive or well dressed they are, they may meet a painful and usually unconquerable barrier in the social pressure for conformity when dating begins by other children in their age group. (Ablon, 1990: 884)

Fatties and Thinnies

And yet not all forms of 'bigness' are viewed positively by children. At four and five-years-old, children are already cognisant of another cultural stereotype of the body: to be fat is to have an unacceptable body shape and, potentially, an unacceptable social identity (De Jong, 1980; Ley, 1979). During casual conversation the children often made observations about fat bodies, ranging from the mild and affectionate, 'Fat people are funny,' to the more derogatory 'Fat people look horrible.'

However, again it is clear that the children had not accepted such cultural stereotypes uncritically. They had thought through the practical consequences of being fat, seeking perhaps some satisfactory explanation for the negativity with which fat bodies are culturally perceived. I was told a number of different reasons why it might be particularly problematic to be fat: if you were fat you might bounce, you couldn't walk properly, you couldn't see your new shoes, you couldn't do your shoelaces up. I was also advised that fat boys could not run fast. In the chasing playground games of Tig and Stuck in the Mud, beloved by boys, this would be a distinct disadvantage. Being fat could, thus, quite literally become a social handicap (see Chapters 5 and 6).

'Fat pig' was a common insult used by the children, with even the insult 'pig', standing alone, recalling a set of culturally unacceptable behaviours such as 'pigging oneself' and 'eating like a pig'. In the rhyme which children use to deflect the insults of others, it is the adjective 'fat' which combines with an animal metaphor, to qualify a child's social identity. Used strategically it stigmatises the Other:

> Twinkle twinkle little star
> what you say is what you are
> and if you answer back to me
> you're a great fat chimpanzee.

De Jong's work among adolescents has shown that 'it is not the mere fact that obese people are physically deviant which causes them to be derogated, but that they are assumed to be responsible for their deviant status' (1980: 85). The younger children with whom I spoke had already made this conceptual link between morality and physical shape. For example, when discussing a poem about a fat boy, seven-year-old Lorna announced emphatically that he would get a 'belly ache' and that it would 'serve him right'. Variously, and derisively, I was told that fat people 'eat too much' or that Joe is fat 'because he's greedy and eats three bars of chocolate a day'. As in De Jong's study, fat children were seen to lack self-control and to have a diminishingly acceptable social identity. Similarly, it is this linking of morality to body shape which works in children's perspectives to make the stereotypical 'bully', stereotypically 'fat'. This can be seen in the next conversation when I was discussing a poem about bullying with some six-year-old boys:

ALLISON: So what do you think about him in this picture?

GARETH: He's pulling her hair.

TONY: He's a bully.

GARETH: He's a fat bully.

At this point in our conversation I observed that in the accompanying picture the boy was far from fat, a fact which was dismissed as irrelevant by my six-year-old friends.

ALLISON: He's not fat though.

TONY: He looks like a fat pig.

GARETH: Thin pig. [They all laugh]

The laughter which accompanied the idea of a 'thin' pig is intriguing and suggestive. If the insult 'pig' is applicable to all children who use their bodies inappropriately – who kick, lie, boss or bully – then the lack of self-control which fatness is thought to represent inevitably means that a metaphoric 'pig' (a naughty child) must be fat rather than thin. The suggestion that pigs are thin, whether real or metaphoric, is laughable therefore. Both the pig-child and the fat-child must bear a discredited personhood.

The subtlety of this conceptual interplay between physical appearance, morality and social skills means that thinness is much less of a social handicap than fatness. Thin children, conforming as they do to wider cultural ideals about body shape (Featherstone, Hepworth and Turner, 1991) are less likely to be teased:

> Jeremy shows me a picture in a Mr Men book – it is of a very fat man. He says: 'You shouldn't be fat, you should be skinny.'

However, should thinness be combined with small stature or signs of illness its more positive cultural value may well decrease. Burton's (1975) study of children with cystic fibrosis, for example, suggests that their different appearance – the children were often small for their age, thin and with teeth blackened through treatment with antibiotics – prompted teasing by their well peers: 'They call me Biafran. They just shout it at me and run' (1975: 114). It was a self-consciousness about their bodies which significantly increased with age and public revelation: 'Fear of physical unacceptability or inadequacy was exhibited by a refusal to undress for PT, clinic visits or when buying new clothes' (1975: 177). Myra Bluebond-Langer et al. (1991) noted similar negative feelings about their thin bodies among children with leukaemia.

In their comments about one another's bodies, the children with whom I worked confirmed the existence of this narrow and divisive line separating an approved 'thin' frame from one which is overly 'skinny'. Six-year-old Catherine told me that, 'If you be skinny everybody looks at you and says you're skinnyman.' The ideal is to possess a body which seems, to those who view it, to conform to an average shape and size, to be approximately the same.

In this way these stereo/ideal types of body size and shape furnish children with a conceptual base from which to begin to contemplate their own futures or to 'countenance conceptions of radical change' for, as already suggested, it is the changing body which, in Western cultures, images for children aspects of their developing social identities (Rapport, 1990b). For this reason, some bodily changes, such as the loss of baby teeth or developing muscles, are welcomed by children as signs of their growing maturity: on revisiting a class of six-year-olds after a term's absence, it was the gaps left by missing teeth, rather than pictures painted or stories written, that I was most eagerly shown.

In these ways, therefore, children use the changing size and shape of the body to distinguish between those who are different and those who conform, providing one illustration of the more generalised cultural process through which childhood identities are created and maintained. As depicted schematically in Chapter 3, the culture of childhood provides the context within which conformity (similarity) is competitively fought for through the playing out of hierarchies of individual esteem (difference), a theme which Chapter 5 will develop through further illustrations.

The Gendered Body

The most significant change to the maturing body of the child is, of course, the development of secondary sexual characteristics. For the pre-pubescent children with whom I worked, these changes had yet to occur but this did not mean that the body was therefore seen to be ungendered. On the contrary, as Chapters 6 and 7 will explore, gender is already an integral discriminating feature in the social relationships of young children. Thus, while the youngest children knew that the different sexual organs denoted male and female gender, more subtle aspects of these cultural identities were gradually reflected and refracted through the body as the children grew older. Fatness, for example, was perceived to be more damaging to a girl's identity than a boy's, as two seven-year-old girls explained to me.

ALLISON: Is it worse for girls or boys to be fat?
BARBARA: Girls.
CARRIE: The same.
ALLISON: Why is it worse for girls?
BARBARA: I don't know.
CARRIE: They don't look nice, that's why.
ALLISON: Girls have to look nice, do they?
BARBARA: Yeah.
ALLISON: Why's that then?
CARRIE: For going out with their boyfriends.
BARBARA: If they be fat and they go out with their boyfriends they won't be able to kiss them.
CARRIE: Because their tummy's in the way.

However, although fatness in the present body of the child is seen negatively to prescribe and to qualify a girl's identity, future fatness is viewed more positively. It signals the welcome transition to motherhood and the assumption of a new social identity. Carrie and Barbara explain:

ALLISON: What else would people look like to be nice?

BARBARA: Fat and cuddly.
CARRIE: And when we have a baby.
BARBARA: Yes, ladies look fat when they have a baby.
CARRIE: When you have a baby, they look fat.
BARBARA: Yeah your tummy looks fat and all nice and soft.

The use of stereotypes to furnish an understanding of ideal types for the Self through processes of comparison can be seen clearly here. Carrie's comment – when 'we' have a baby – envisages a future changed body with which she, as a girl, can identify: the body of a mother. Barbara reaffirms the different attitude to this kind of fatness with her own observation that, stereotypically, 'ladies look fat when they have a baby'. The cognitive translation of this general stereotype into a more specific type of ideal for the Self, and the girls' realisation of the relationship which that has to their present and future identities, can be seen in Carrie's somewhat curious statement: 'When you have a baby, they look fat.' Fat boys, on the other hand, had no comforting future envisaged for them. They would simply become fat men.

The body's discrete parts also appeared to have a gendered significance amongst five and six-year-olds, and it was through this that the boys found a more positive declaration of their masculinity. I was told, by a group of proud boys, that 'boys have big muscles'. Girls, in contrast were negatively stereotyped as having 'tiny' muscles. Big muscles represented a positive ideal for themselves, an affirmation of the boys' identities achieved through the processes of opposition and overstatement at work in stereotyping. The adjective 'tiny', used to describe girls' muscles, through its exaggerated aspect, provides a bold, definitive contrast with the ideally large size of the boys'. As Saul explained, 'If you haven't got big muscles then you're weak,' a statement which was later supported by Alec's more practical rationalisation of this masculine stereotype: 'If you have muscles you can punch people back, can't you?' Although the girls concurred with this stereotyping of themselves as weak, they none the less had a subtly different interpretation of the significance of muscle size. Six-year-old girls saw themselves as being 'gentle' and 'kind' in their presumed weakness. For them, it was a positive ideal type of femaleness with which they counterposed, what they viewed negatively, as the stereotypical 'rough' behaviour of boys.

Hair is another body attribute which, from four years old onwards, assumed significance for children as a gendered marker of identity. This may simply reflect their knowledge of the adult social world, which differentiates between men's and women's hairdressers and men's and women's hair-care products, but it may also draw strength from the persistent conservatism of children's culture (see Chapter 6). In many of the drawings which the children did for me hair was often picked out in great detail – a pony tail, a fringe or the fashionable flat-top cut for boys – with its length and colour providing telling identity markers. While the ginger-haired child soon discovers this through the nickname 'Gingernut', more generally, it was hair length which the younger children used in their stereotyping: ideally girls should have long hair (preferably blonde) while boys' hair should be short (preferably dark), as Candy tells Sally:

CANDY: Disgusting . . . ugh . . . I don't like short hair. Girls should have long hair.

Thus it was that six-year-old Sylvie derided her sister's boyfriend for the length of his hair, Neil accused Bob of having 'girl's' hair and Penny arrived, close-cropped and miserable, back to school after the summer holidays. Tearfully she told me that she would like to have very long hair, hair long enough to wear in a pony tail. Kylie Monogue (who at that time was six-year-old girls' current ideal of femininity) was, they assured me, a star: 'she's pretty, she's got nice hair'. Long and blonde and curly, it contrasted with Jason Donovan's dark, short cropped hair (the six-year-old girls' current ideal of masculinity).[4]

This form of gender stereotyping was already evident among the reception-class children of four and five years old. Playing with some jigsaw puzzles, which depicted portraits of men and women from different ethnic groups, I noticed that many of the children found difficulty in assigning gender to them. Particularly problematic was the portrait of a Chinese lady who had short black hair. Toby confidently, but wrongly, remarked, 'He is a man because he's got black hair.' These stereotypes were daily reinforced in the children's mutual conversation, their resonance as gender signifiers sustained through the toys they played with in the classroom. The sticklebrick construction toy contained male and female heads which could be incorporated by the children in their building. The face of the 'male' piece was depicted by strong black lines marking the eyebrows and nose, with the mouth set in a severe dark line. The 'female' head, by contrast, had long blonde hair, curling blue eyelashes and smiling cherry red lips.

The Body in Parts

Ethnographic material presented so far has shown how size, shape and gender describe the broad outlines of the signifying body for children. As a medium of social expression (Blacking, 1977; Polhemus, 1978) the body speaks of and to their culture, through their assimilation of wider cultural stereotypes. These set specific and particular limits to these body features, mapping out for children their own and others relative positions within the social group. Non-conformist bodies – the small, the skinny, the very fat – are remarked on. Their owners are distinguished from the majority who possess ordinary – that is, unremarkable – bodies. In this way, the physical body provides a locus for identity and personhood through mediating ideas of social conformity and individuality and establishing positions of both relative equality and differentiating hierarchies within the social body of children.

However, even bodies which are not remarked upon for being too small or too fat, may retain significatory power through the particularity of its parts. It is, for example, against the background of hair as a significant marker of identity, described above, that paediatric cancer patients find the experience of hair loss particularly demoralising, as Bluebond-Langer et al. (1991) have shown for American children. The children were attending a summer camp specifically for children with cancer and found the unconditional acceptance by their camp peers of their changed physical appearance to be one of its most positive benefits. At home, healthy friends tended to keep away from them. One eleven-year-old described how children at home refused to play, 'cause I lost my hair and they think it's dangerous and they'll catch it'; another enjoyed the camp because 'it's okay if you can't do something or don't have hair. No one makes fun of you' (Bluebond-Langer et al., 1991: 74). These comments reflect the emphasis upon equality and conformity which shapes children's culture for, in the context of the summer camp, the children's difference makes no difference; on the contrary, it unites them in a different shared identity as 'children with cancer'. It made them members of a new crowd for that summer time. This shifting between reference groups was commonly remarked on by the parents with whom I talked. Many noted that their children tended to make friends with other children whose own bodies were in some way different. Deborah, who has epilepsy, discussed this with her mother:

MOTHER: I tend to think other children steer clear. I mean one a couple of doors down she thinks you're mad.

DEBORAH: Katy . . . she's alright . . . she knows what . . .

MOTHER: Yeah, she's pretty reasonable.

DEBORAH: They say things about Katy's Mum . . .

MOTHER: Katy's Mum's in a mental home. So she accepts it a little bit more, see. Now Jenny, she's diabetic . . . she's alright . . . because she's got her own set of problems.

However, it is also the case that *any* child, not just those whose bodies are visibly and demonstrably non-conforming, runs the risk of being remarked upon or picked out. Through subtle detailing and fine discrimination, any part of anybody's body may be used as a significant representation of and for the social self. A portrait-painting competition held among a class of six and seven-year-olds revealed this process occurring in different ways. Charged with painting a picture of another child, the class collection of pictures yielded three portraits of one popular and friendly boy. In each, his teeth figured prominently. Although not protruding, as did poor Goofy's teeth, on closer observation I too began to notice how often his large and ready smile revealed an expansive set of teeth. The gleaming teeth were expressive of his friendly and welcoming personality. By contrast, a girl who was relatively isolated in the class was depicted by a small faceless figure. Painted by another girl, herself a social isolate, the head, coloured purple, took the form of a simple, featureless circle. And, in this same class, a pair of twins were distinguished, in terms of their names and their personhoods, through other children's observation of the shape their mouths took on in social interactions:

Rosemary tells me that it is easy to distinguish Billy and Brian, as Billy has the droopy face and he often has a mark on his face where he has been leaning on his hands. The next day Carol confirms this and tells me that it is easy to know which twin is which: Brian has a happy face, Billy has a sad face.

Being characterised as the smiley, rather than the sad-faced twin, of the two it was Brian who was the more popular.

This attention to the minute and subtle details of the body's appearance is one reason why conditions such as eczema can cause a child such distress. In the signification of social identity, rashes and sore skin become voluble signs. Sandy, now a beautiful young woman with a clear, tanned skin, recalls her ten-year-old body which, unremarkable for its shape and size, none the less had a noticeably different covering. This surface difference became, quite literally, more than skin deep. It gradually extended to shape her day-to-day interactions with other children and, in time, to raise questions for her about her own identity and personhood:

> They used to call me Fungus and as I got off the school bus there was a group of girls . . . who would throw apple cores at me . . . it was awful . . . [they'd] follow me round and knock into you, push you over.

For Sandy it was 'all those little things' which acted as the more important signifiers for her of the Other children's attitudes towards her body. Wishing to distance her Self from her body, Sandy took strategic action, choosing carefully the clothes she wore while, at the same time, endeavouring to follow the fashions which other girls were wearing. It was not always successful. At times, it was physically painful:

> I couldn't wear v-necked shirts. I used to cover it [the eczema patches] up because it didn't look very nice. You didn't really want to go out in your PE shorts because you're legs were covered . . . all the other kids when they were playing out were wearing flip flops. I had to wear socks and shoes. They [her feet] were just so sore and I couldn't wear flip flops because it [the eczema] was in between my toes and the rubber used to irritate me. You put on cream or ointment and then you go out in the street and then you get dirt on it.

On reflection, from the sanctity of adulthood and with a skin now free from irritation and flaking scabs, Sandy summed up her experience as follows:

> It was hard. I had my friends but the rest of the school knew. They knew you had something wrong with you. They don't make any bones about what they think and what they know. It was hard at school actually when you look back. The dinner ladies used to tell them off [the

girls who teased] at dinner time and I used to think I'll just ignore it and think 'You haven't got a brain in your head.' It's not easy but it gets to a point you think you're coping with it and then you don't. Something happens and you don't want to go. It isn't very nice. Children are cruel. They really are.

The Temporality of Different Identities

In his seminal essay on body techniques Marcel Mauss [1938] 1979) drew attention to the complexity of the body as a medium of social and cultural expression. His notion of technique instructively underlines the process of culturally acquiring, rather than simply expressing, particular body styles (James, 1986). That is to say, it allows for a consideration of the temporal processes which in the interplay between social action and cognition implicitly shape and fashion the physical body. The symbolising potential of the body lies, therefore, not simply in its form but in the cognitive awareness of that form and in those social relationships through which meaning is attributed to it: 'techniques of the body are not entirely learnt from others so much as discovered through others' (Blacking, 1977: 4). Focusing on the techniques of the body in this way, then, will underscore the temporality of identity which Schwartz (1976) has alluded to. Over time, changes in the body, together with shifting perceptions of the cultural significance of those changes, work to produce a person's personhood.

Illustration of this temporal process is found in one boy's experience. At four years old Benny started school. His physical disabilities, while meaning that he walked with a stick, did not prevent him from attending an ordinary state primary school. It was not long, however, before his poor pencil control became evident as, together with his class-mates, he began to learn to write his name. The educational emphasis placed on writing skills meant that, at five years old, he was made more aware of his own disability. As his class-mates' confidence and skill developed during their first year at school, they too began to notice his different abilities. Some children started to comment on his writing, describing it as 'scribbling'. Loftily they classed his mode of writing as that which they themselves had only just relinquished. Later that same year Benny came to realise that other children could dress themselves while he still needed help. By his second year at school he was beginning to be reluctant to go out at playtime. His class-mates, now confident of their place in the playground, could join in the boisterous games and football matches played by older boys. By contrast, he was often left alone on the edges of the playground, the spaces occupied primarily by girls (see Chapter 6). Thus, his relative immobility began to limit his choice of playmates and Benny started to looked forward to rainy playtimes when all the children would be confined indoors and where his restricted movement would be less observable and less effectively differentiating.

By six years old, after two years of schooling, Benny felt himself to be set more apart. Although this was rarely intentional, a wedge of difference was inexorably being driven between himself and other children, as new significances were given to his different abilities. However, it was also during this second year at school that he was given his first taste of direct discrimination by a confident and bullish eight-year-old. Referring directly to his disability the older boy informed him that he should be in another school.

In this process of mutual observation of child by child the visibility of bodily differences is clearly a crucial factor, but their stigmatising difference can be made to vary through information control and body management (Goffman, 1968). In the moral career of the child whose body registers the revelatory marks of illness or disability, this means learning to control other children's ascription of a cultural significance to that difference. In this respect, certain times of the day or year may prove more critical than others. PE lessons and school playtimes, for example, may be crucially and cruelly revealing of the significance which bodily differences can have. At Hilltop School, for example, a girl whose bodily difference was normally concealed by clothes, stripping to vest and pants for PE lessons at primary school was a significant moment. For the first time, her eczema was noted and commented on by other children. This may have been the first time she became conscious of the social significance that a different skin can have through the questions and derisory comments of other children. As Anderson notes, 'It is often not the child with severe handicaps who is more sensitive but rather the child who can pass as normal (1973: 134).

The social context of difference or impairment is what transforms a disability or difference into a social handicap (Shearer,

1981). It also lays the foundations for particular kinds of identities. In Maria's comments is revealed not only the 'becoming visible' of her asthma but her own acknowledgement of possible social consequences:

> I hate having asthma. When I do outdoor PE I have to take ventolin first and then I'm late coming into the playground and they all say I cheat. Sometimes I forget my ventolin and then I can't run.

Unsolicited, she drew me a picture of playtime at school. This spoke eloquently of her ambiguous feelings about her identity and sense of Self. Confident with her friends, Maria drew herself in the middle of the picture, the largest and most detailed figure. At the same time, however, the sun's rays streaming down illuminated her centrality as a static figure among others who run, jump and skip across the page. Why, she is asking, do I have to have asthma?

Although conditions – such as asthma, epilepsy and diabetes – may suddenly and dramatically become visible through an attack or seizure, such moments are rare (Scambler, 1984). Manifestations can often be well-controlled by drugs. More difficult to manage, however, is the visibility of all those 'little things' which Sandy referred to (see p. 126). In the social context of the playground these may be seized upon by other children and ascribed with a stigmatising significance. Children with asthma, who take a lunch-time medication, are seen to abruptly, and regularly, disappear to the medical room or school office. Whether alone or led by a teacher's hand their temporary absence may be remarked, and questioning and enquiry may follow. Asthmatic children may have permanently runny noses or red and sore eyes in the summer, tell-tale signs of their body's difference. In the mutual gaze shared between children such differences can, but need not, take on significance.

In following through this complex patterning of identity and personhood in childhood, played out through the body as a signifying medium, account must be taken, then, of time in two senses. First, the significance of the passage of time during childhood through which any individual child learns to see, but slowly and haltingly, the Self as others do. Second, but just as important, is the time of childhood itself, which contextualises children's culture, providing through their growing sociality, affirmation of particular identities for the Self and for one another.

Framed in this way, it becomes possible to see the range of possible identifications which the body can signal for children. It means, for example, that although any kind of difference *can* become significant – a sad face, a red nose, a different diet – there is no *necessary* relation between that physical difference and a position of social marginality or outsiderhood. That is to say, even if a bodily difference is noted, significance may not be ascribed to it; conversely, a child who for other reasons may be without friends risks *any* deviation in his or her body becoming credited with a stigmatising difference. The ebb and flow of this temporal process of identifying and personifying can be depicted diagrammatically as follows:

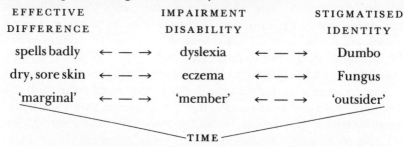

FIGURE 4.1   Diagram illustrating the range of possible changes in body signification in and through time and their relationship to concepts of identity and perceptions of personhood.

For some, the passage of time merely serves to underscore and confirm their outsider status while, for others, it allows the boundaries within which personhood is constituted to become more clearly defined. According to her parents, Lilly, unable to manage the significance of her own difference (being both small in stature and dyslexic) felt 'threatened by the fact that she thinks the others are cleverer'. She withdrew from children's company at school and took refuge in horse-riding:

> It's become her whole life. In a lot of ways it's a way of turning her own problems. She keeps talking about horses and doesn't have to worry quite so much about other things. And she gets on better with horses than people. And even up at the stables although there's lots of children up there she still very much tends to go off by herself.

Appearances are Deceiving

Involved as I was in trying to elicit some of the more subtle influences which children bring to bear on each other, I devised a number of research strategies to facilitate this. One of these was group story writing. I provided the bare bones of a story which the children then fleshed out through group discussion. The scenario was as follows: a girl or boy who had no friends decided to try and make friends. What the children were asked to do was to explain why s/he was friendless, how s/he went about making friends and what happened in the end. The stories showed a remarkable consistency, with but slight modifications introduced by the oldest children.

A key feature of the stories was the citation of the lack of social skills as being the main reason why a child might be friendless (see Chapter 5). Denoted by bullying behaviour, fighting, kicking, punching, stealing, swearing, being bossy, being selfish, and lying, this behaviour was, without exception, accompanied by a description of an outrageously ugly body, composed of a variety of stereotypical negative aspects:

> He was fat with brown hair and he looked like a girl because he had long hair in a pony tail.

> He's a punk with red, yellow, purple and blue and green stripey hair. He's fat with very long sharp fingernails.

> She has a pimpled face and a big sharp, pointed nose and holes in her trousers. Her hair came down on her face. It was green, blue and highlighted purple. She was greedy and so fat she couldn't get through the door.

It would seem therefore that, from the child's perspective, ugly behaviour is invariably and literally portrayed through an ugly body, and that children do not welcome ugly people as friends.

In the next chapter of the story the friendless child attempts to make friends. Again without variance, it was the modification of behaviour which was seen to bring this about. What is more interesting than this fairly obvious switch, however, is that it was described by the children as being mirrored in changes in the physical body. The boy depicted in the second extract above, for example, 'stopped bullying people, bit all his nails and had his hair cut off'. He also lost some weight. Other characters brushed their hair, washed their bodies and clothes or had all their 'goofy' teeth extracted. In this way, a changed physical body was made to appropriately reflect a changed social identity.

Only once did a six-year-old boy suggest that, logically, the character could not stop being ugly. Appealing to me, he argued, 'She has to be ugly, doesn't she?', a view with which the others reluctantly had to agree. But this disrupted the stereotypes to which they all adhered: that is, that good behaviour is reflected in the body's acceptable appearance. The children were at an impasse. Eventually, and somewhat charily, they concluded that, although she was still ugly, the girl's friends 'don't care any more because she is good'. Another telling story is the tale of a girl who was described as being friendless because she was in a wheelchair and 'couldn't run'. Here it was an inability to participate, rather than choosing to be anti-social, which construed for the character a marginal and friendless identity. In composing the second half of this story, the eight and nine-year-old authors were similarly at a loss. How could this situation be ameliorated? How could the girl's body be made to be the kind of body a girl with friends would have? They chose a magical resolution, a fairy-tale ending: the heroine fell out of her wheelchair and suddenly found that she could walk again.

That stereotypes of the physical body are not just the stuff of fantasy but operative in children's everyday encounters can be seen by the replication of the motifs of size, fatness and hair length in these stories. Together with dirt, spots and nits, these symbols of disorder and outsiderhood are commonly used as identity markers among children, featuring often in their jeers and taunts (Opies, [1959] 1977). More disturbing, however, is the further suggestion in these stories that there is a direct and unequivocal relationship between the body's physical form and children's social identity: ugly body equals ugly person. For children whose bodies are different this postulates a bleak social future. However, in these stories the reverse is also true – a nice person, has a nice body – which suggests that young children *are* cognisant of the cultural wisdom that appearances *can* be deceptive. Thus, although those children whose bodies are in some way unusual may be at greater risk of being stigmatised as different, of being marginalised, the risk is considerably reduced if they possess or cultivate the bodily skills, appropriate for a 'nice' person. It would seem, therefore, that the way the body is used has more significance and power to confer identity than simply how the body appears. The next chapter develops this theme.

Notes

1. Although children were aware of differences in skin colour, acknowledging this as a differentiating characteristic between children, it was rare that stigmatising significance was attached to skin colour among the younger children. The school was vigilant about racist remarks and, as noted, its ethnic mix was low. Both these factors possibly contribute to the lack of emphasis given by children to skin colour in their social relationships.

2. Birthday assembly was a weekly assembly held in the school hall to celebrate all those children and staff who had birthdays during that week. A special birthday song would be sung for these individuals but not for the rest of the children. This seems to be common practice in many primary schools.

3. Phyllis Krasilovsky (1953) *The Very Little Girl*, Grafische Industrie Haarlem, N.V., Holland. First published in Great Britain in 1959.

4. During fieldwork these were the stars of the popular Australian soap opera 'Neighbours' shown on television in the early evening and popular viewing for the girls.

FIVE

Social Children

Stories of Sociality

Giddens writes that 'a person's ease in any given situation presumes a long-term experience in confronting the threats and opportunities it presents' (1991: 57). This chapter explores the concepts and contexts through which children learn to become at ease with themselves and with Others by analysing the cultural forms through which they acquire the art of sociality, that is the skill of being social. In doing so this chapter continues to explore the possibilities of the body as a personifying medium through examining the body in performance. It begins with children's own definitions of what sociality – behaving as a social being – might consist of.

Writing their stories about a child who had no friends, nine-year-old Elspeth, Jean and Bob sat with me around a table. I acted as scribe and, collectively, the children decided exactly what I should write down. This is their story:

> *Once upon a time there was a girl who had no friends.* She didn't have any friends because she was nasty. She kept throwing stones out of a tree and kicking. She kept on getting told off because she didn't do what she's told. She always says: I don't want to play with you so they didn't play with her. *One day she decided to try and make friends at school* but they didn't want her to play with them. So she tried to be good to them. She helped them with their dinner and she used to say when they came along that she would play. She shook hands with them. In the end she went to her Mum and said, 'I'm sorry and now I have lots of friends because I've been good at school.' She said to her Mum, 'I will clean my bedroom everyday and I will read my books everyday and learn to write and read and do all my spellings right. And I will go to the shops for you.'

The story line which I provided (distinguished by the italics above) was similarly fleshed out by ten other groups of children of different ages and on different occasions. As suggested previously, what is striking about this collection of stories is their quite remarkable textual similarity. First, in all but one of the children's accounts, the story reaches a happy ending when the friendless child is eventually befriended. In all the stories too, (except the one above), the hero or heroine's physical appearance is described in glorious detail (see Chapter 4). At the start of the tale the character is depicted as being exceedingly ugly with a grotesquely fat or smelly body, an image further conceptually disfigured by features such as pointed teeth, spots and pimples or long, greasy hair. But such visually abhorrent bodies are, without exception, all transformed by the end of the tales through specific ameliorative actions taken by the central character: bodies are washed, hair is cut and combed, green teeth are brushed clean. A third significant theme running through these stories focuses upon the social distancing which aggressive or unpleasant behaviour can cause. In all the accounts it is 'anti-social' behaviour which is cited as the pre-eminent reason why a child might lack friends, for only after the character has significantly modified his or her behaviour is a resolution to social exclusion, a happy ending, achieved.

As cultural inventions these stories obviously pattern the literary form of Western fairy tales: bad becomes good and the beast grows beautiful. All's well that ends well, with truth, goodness and honesty restoring the rightful order of things. But unlike traditional fictional heroes and heroines such as the Frog Prince and Cinderella, personal happiness is not achieved simply by virtue or nobility shining through a disguise. In the children's stories, inherent goodness and beauty are not magically revealed to lie beneath the tattered clothes of a poor kitchen-maid or the damp and warty body of a frog. Neither do Fairy Godmothers or Princesses, glass slippers or kisses, aid and abet the friendless child of the children's stories. Social realists in this respect, the children instead depicted happy endings as being dependent upon choices made in interpersonal relationships and upon strategic social action. It is through radically reappraising their own social behaviour and relationships, rather than through magic or illusion, that the heroes and heroines of the children's stories gain mastery over their own fate and construct a social identity for themselves. An extract from another of

the children's stories echoes the changes in behaviour described
in the first story above:

> One day she decided to try and make friends at school.
> She wasn't so naughty and tried to be good. She helped
> the teacher and she didn't kick and didn't hurt people
> and she did wash her hair and she washed her clothes.

But, as I shall show, this restructuring of interpersonal relationships is an ideal not easily achieved in everyday life (see also
Chapter 7). A friendless child's bid for friendship may be
refused or remain unacknowledged by his or her contemporaries. Moreover, while the stories show that children clearly
rank 'social' above 'antisocial' behaviour in their interpersonal
relationships, exactly what kinds of behaviour fall into each
domain is not clear-cut for, as children know well, in the process
of everyday social interaction these are far from being fixed
and constant conceptual categorisations.

In taking sociality in children's interpersonal relations as its
focus, the task of this chapter is to outline some of the ways in
which children come to an understanding of these classifications. It does so through identifying a number of different
behavioural strategies which give most, but not all, children an
experiential rather than simply categorical sense of belonging
to the cultural world of children through knowing how to
behave as children. By this I mean that, while all children are
classed as children and have that identity conferred upon them
by the adult world, some children are recognised by their
peers as being more successful and more effective than others
at being a 'child'. This classification depends upon their ability
or willingness to conform to the implicit rules which, collectively,
structure the experience rather than simply the context of
childhood for children. These denote how a body should behave
and it is through judging each other's performances that children personify one another.

Cohen writes that 'the compelling need to declare identity is
social as well as psychological' and that it is the experience of
belonging – whether to a culture or to a smaller unit such as a
household – which allows people to mark out their 'sense of
similarity to and difference from other people' (1986: 1). By
focusing upon the ways in which such boundaries are symbolically produced it is possible, he suggests, to see how any community, large or small, 'informs its own sense of self by marking
what it is not, as well as what it is' (1986: 11). On one level,

therefore, this chapter continues to explore the boundaries to the cultural community of childhood to which all children belong by virtue of their categorical membership as children. However, it also begins to sketch in those finer symbolic boundaries and symbols of difference which, generated by children themselves, mark out identities and denote particular kinds of personhood within the community of children (Cohen, 1986). Thus, for example, while certain behaviours, such as name-calling or teasing, may from an adult perspective seem grossly to characterise social differences between adults and children, a sign that children are children, these same forms of behaviour may be invested with different sets of meanings by children themselves. They may used, for example, to personify some children as effective members of the community of children, while preventing others from belonging.

In considering the way in which behaviour acts as a symbolic identity marker I look, therefore, both to its collective and its more individual aspects, enquiring of any particular manifestation how the limits to conceptually good or bad behaviour are defined. These may be read in different ways, on different social occasions, by different groups of children. And it is this inherent ambiguity of social processes which children must gradually learn to negotiate and competently manage, for it is through these that their sociality will be constituted by Others.

The ways in which the body is used by children as a symbolic marker of social identity to create stigmatising distinctions is, as Chapter 4 showed, both subtle and fluid. The conferring and accepting identity is not straightforward, for although corporal features are fairly fixed symbolic markers – a child, unlike an adult, rarely has the power to alter his or her height or shape – none the less, potentially stigmatising bodily features *are* negotiated and manipulated by children in their social encounters. In Goffman's terms (1968), therefore, one aspect of children's social competence is knowing not only how to manage the body and its behaviour but lies also in learning the importance of being seen by others to be doing so. In this sense, social identity is both literally taken on and acted out.

Social behaviour, in its very transience, ironically, poses much more of a problem. Infinitely flexible, rather than relatively fixed, the potential for semantic creativity is the greater; its power to mark and make social identities is correspondingly mutliplex. Thus, it is not surprising that interpersonal relations between children can become fraught with tension and emotion. The process of assessing and classifying each other's behaviour in terms of belonging or in relation to friendship (see Chapter 7) slips and slides as the tussles and arguments of playground activity take their course. This chapter asks, then, how is it that, in this changing and fragile interpersonal world, children none the less are able to discover and to generate some collective ground-rules for regulating their own behaviour and that of their peers? How, individually, do they make sense of them? If, as Cohen writes, the self is 'informed by social engagement, but is not dependent on it' what kinds of encounters lead to what kinds of conclusions about Selfhood and social identity (1992: 232)?

Setting the Limits to Sociality

The children's stories indicate a wide range of anti-social behaviours. Depicted by the children as stigmatising, they are actions which exceed the conceptual bounds and bonds of friendship. However, as a set they are mostly unremarkable. They reveal a fairly stereotypical set of commonly held cultural ideals about the differences between good and bad behaviour. A first group of anti-social behaviours concern those which hurt other people, such as kicking, punching, fighting, pushing, thumping, strangling and bullying. A second group comprises behaviours, which although not physically damaging, are still widely defined as culturally unacceptable: telling lies, swearing, being selfish and being rude. A third category, perhaps more specific to the structural position of children, references opposition to authority: not doing as one's told, being naughty, not working hard, ripping books, being disobedient and unhelpful. The easy classification of such actions by children as antisocial suggests an unambiguous acceptance of cultural rules of conduct. This would imply that children have simply learnt the rules and limits of behaviour which teachers and parents maintain through the application of sanctions and rewards.

However, one last group of behaviours strikes a discordant note: stealing and popping footballs, throwing stones out of a tree, throwing stones at a window, taking eggs out of a nest and throwing them at people's windows, throwing pebbles at people's windows and throwing food. While 'throwing stones' could be said to have its condemnatory source in Christian morality, the specificity of other details in the children's stories – eggs, trees, windows, footballs – indicates that their classification of these behaviours as antisocial stems directly from their everyday encounters, rather than indirectly from socialisation practices or cultural prescription. It suggests that, through experience, a rule has been generated, a limit set and a guideline for behaviour established. Sociality is thus actively learnt rather than simply passively acquired and, in being in this sense context and experience-specific, the mean ings which children learn to attribute to particular kinds of behaviour may be both various and subject to flux and change. That is to say, the import of anti-social actions may alter in and through time and social space. Referring back to Cohen (1986) this means, therefore, recognising that a diversity of meanings may be masked by a common symbolic form and that in the commonly articulated, as well as the more idiosyn-cratic, examples of antisocial behaviour described and acted out by the children should be sought the precise implications which a lack of sociality has in terms of Self, social identity and personhood.

There is no doubt, for instance, that the contextualising of stigmatising bodies and behaviour in and through performance gives rise to variations in the process of personifying. Chapter 4 showed, for example, that while fat bodies are, in general, disapproved of by children, not all fat children will be ostracised. Nor are all thin ones inevitably acceptable. Similarly aggressive behaviour may not necessarily lead to exclusion. There is a thin and shifting boundary between social and antisocial acts which children must learn to negotiate as, gradually and tentatively, they begin to participate more fully in the cultural world of childhood (see also Chapters 6 and 7). And in looking in fine detail at the ways in which children choose to act in their social encounters, this chapter provides further illustration of how the motifs of conformity and individuality, equality and competition are played out through these encounters. These opposed cultural themes are constantly invoked in children's relation-ships, reflecting their centrality to children's experience of living in a Western industrial society such as Britain. For example, an exhortation to conformity, to abide by the rules, may frequently conflict with a child's nurtured and developing sense of his or her own individuality. Similarly, the rhetoric of equality which children encounter through the ideology of schooling is simultaneously denied by the emphasis upon physical and intellectual competition mediated through the age-bound hierarchy of that same institution.

From field material already provided, it is clear that some children are more successful than others in resolving such tensions. They may easily find a place for themselves in other children's affections and possess the necessary social skills to maintain some kind of equilibrium between these opposing social forces. For other children, however, this balance may only be achieved through considerable resourcefulness, tenacity and energy. They may need to note carefully the many subtle variations in meaning and shifts of emphasis which occur in their day-to-day relations, for it is through remarking these that identities and personhoods become well or ill-defined. For example, a knowing child is aware just when the conformity and equality, characteristic of early childhood social relations, begins to give way to the more ruthless individuality and patterned hierarchy which marks and mars the social relationships of later childhood. A knowing child learns, too, why some – but not all – children slide over the boundary which conceptually demarcates the acceptable individualist from the outcast eccentric; s/he will also know where the line between popular conformity and total anonymity is deemed to fall and what implicit rule transforms the successful strategist into a cheat, a classification which leads to summary exclusion. Through focusing on particular events in the lives of the children at Hilltop School, some of these features of sociality are documented and discussed.

Conformity: a Sense of Self and Belonging

A striking feature of three and four-year-old children's interpersonal relations is the delight which they exhibit on discovering similarities between themselves and another. This detection of mutuality can arise in any cultural domain, from names and ages through to shoes and toys:

> Mary and Julie are delighted to find that they both have a Fireman Sam sticker after the visit of the school dentist.

> Ellie comes especially to tell me that she has the same lunch box as Kate.

> SYLVIE: I had cheese biscuits and chocolate milk shake.
> VANESSA: (with obvious delight) I did too. I had all the same what you had.

In these examples social identity is expressed through 'same-ness' as if a thread of continuity links one child to another. But it is primarily a process of Self rather than Other classification, similar to that which characterises the pattern of such young children's friendship relations (see Chapter 7). A child situates himself or herself alongside another: that is to say, a child finds rather than is found a place within the social group.

In this way the idea of sameness at four years old can be interpreted as a positive aspect of Selfhood. It confirms for children that they belong. But, at four years old, this feeling of sameness is not equivalent to the notion of conformity which characterises the social relations of older children. The idea of 'sameness' does not, for instance, carry with it comparable underlying sanctions to change, to be like Others, which the concept of conformity encompasses through its implicit designation of specific forms and styles of behaviour (see James, 1986 and below). But, again unlike the idea of conformity, sameness does not have a correspondingly negative form – unsameness – in its use among four-year-olds. This absence underscores, therefore, the suggestion that the concept of sameness is only used to locate the Self in the context of Others in the social world. It is not used to make judgements about the non-conformity – the non-sameness – of those Others. Annabel, Mary and Julie demonstrate this as they sit together playing with dough:

JULIE: I'm making a bird's nest.
MARY: I'm making a bird's nest.
ANNABEL: I'm making a bird's nest.
JULIE: Everyone copies me.
ALLISON: Why do you think that is?
JULIE: Because they like it.

Julie's observation, 'because they like it' is ambiguous. She may mean that the others like the idea of making a bird's nest out of dough. Alternatively, and more importantly, she may mean that they like the idea of copying what she does: that is they want to be the same as Julie. Julie was one of the more popular girls in this class of five-year-olds, pretty, clever and well-liked by the other children. In copying her actions the other girls seemed to be aligning themselves to her, to be finding themselves an approved social niche.

By contrast, among the older children who had become more actively involved in the social world of childhood, far from

being appreciatively remarked upon, such behaviour was positively discouraged. Over time, then, the same behaviour is attributed with different meanings; 'being the same' as another
moves from its conceptual classification as a sign of sociality to
something which discriminates and stigmatises. Seven-year-old
Eliza, who has no friends at school, is sitting beside Caroline
on the mat:

> Caroline is rolling down her long white socks into a cuff
> above her ankle. Eliza does the same. 'Stop copying me,'
> orders Caroline.

By copying Caroline and rolling down her socks, Eliza makes a
bid for 'sameness', and possibly to friendship, comparable with
that made by the four-year-old girls above. It is immediately
rejected by Caroline; at this age, with more social experience and
in the social context of being in the second year at school, it is no
longer a successful strategy. Caroline accuses Eliza of copying,
displaying her displeasure and annoyance by moving away from
her. This conceptual transformation of 'sameness' into 'copying' reflects the tension which is beginning to develop between
the emergent ideas of conformity and those of individuality, a
tension which progressively, then persistently, structures the ex-
panding social world of seven-year-old children. The idea of
sameness also begins to give way to an increasing emphasis upon
competition and hierarchy and, in this way, the protective layer
with which the motif of sameness cloaks the social world of three
and four-year-old children in the nursery setting is quickly dis-
pelled soon after children enter the world of the primary school.
Here they must begin instead to learn to conform, a far more
subtle and skilful kind of social behaviour.

Put simply, the idea of conformity implies the existence of
implicit and/or explicit rules which must be adhered to. Furthermore, it suggests that any transgression of these rules may be
followed by the invocation of sanctions, the ultimate sanction
being the social stigmatisation or isolation which follows on
from non-conforming actions. As distinct from the idea of
sameness, then, the concept of conformity does not simply
involve locating a place for the Self among Others. It opens
up the opportunity to permit or forbid Others to find themselves
a place within the social group through the wielding of social
sanctions. In this sense, the concept of conformity permits the
acting out and negotiation of power relations between children
(see also Chapter 7).

For children with physical disabilities of all sorts, as earlier chapters have shown, the idea of conformity can become particularly critical to their developing sense of Self and identity. A child may become socially isolated and excluded, not because of their disability *per se*, but because of the limitations which their disability or difference places on the potential of their bodies to conform to stereotypes of what bodies should be. As Goffman (1968) describes, and as Chapter 4 illustrated, skilful management of a 'spoiled identity' masks and reduces the social impact which a disability or difference might have. Many children become skilled in the art of such strategic social action, learning both to alleviate and forestall the process of stigmatisation:

> One mother whose daughter has a hearing impediment tells me that she does not wish to sign. Attending an ordinary, rather than a special school, she wants to be like the other children. Indeed, her daughter is apt to disparage deaf people who sign, saying proudly, 'I don't do that.'

In this example, the girl distances herself from Others who are ostensibly like her, by conforming instead to the norms of ordinary childhood, rather than those pertaining among the hearing-impaired community. By not signing, she conformed with the actions of the majority of children with whom she mixed. By contrast, in one small rural school, whose pupils included a number of hearing-impaired children, the whole school learned to sign and, on one day a week, signing was the preferred mode of communication. In this way the non-conformity of signing became a conformity which excluded those who did not. For the children who did not have hearing problems, signing became a useful code for passing secret messages. Thus, as Goffman notes:

> The normal and the stigmatized are not persons but rather perspectives. These are generated in social situations during mixed contacts by virtue of the unrealized norms that are likely to play upon the encounter. (1968: 164)

Issues about social conformity and difference are not, however, limited to those children who have physical disabilities. They are a feature of *all* children's interactions with one another, continually cropping up in the minutiae of their everyday social relations. On each occasion when a demand for conformity arises children must know how to deal with it lest their identities become devalued. Children with disabilities, or who are seen as significantly different in some other way, may simply experience this questioning of their identity more intensely and more frequently (Goffman, 1968: 164). The management of non-conformity *of any kind* involves considerable creativity and mental agility and those who fail to do so may find themselves quickly cast in the role of Other.

To illustrate this I shall focus on two specific social arenas, within which differences, that is non-conformity, may be taken by other children as a significant indicator of identity and may, consequently, contribute to any individual child's diminished sense of Self and loss of personhood. The pressure to conform permeates to the more mundane and prosaic aspects of children's social life. Indeed, it may be more intensely experienced and more rigorously enforced within these everyday domains and extends beyond simply what the body looks like or what a child does with or to its body. The first social arena I shall consider is that of food and eating. As I have shown elsewhere, children often use food to structure their identities as children. In refusing normal and everyday food at meal times, while eating cheaper kinds of sweets in between meals, children assert symbolically their right to gain control over their own bodies and identities as children in the face of adult authority (James, 1979b). It is not surprising, then, that in the finer process of symbolically marking out identity and personhood, which takes place child to child, that children closely monitor each other's intake of food.

However, the multivalent nature of symbols means that the meanings with which children invest food are neither fixed nor constant. Indeed, their use of food illustrates what Cohen (1986: 9) describes as the versatility of symbolic forms for, in the shifting regard with which children observe the food they and their peers eat, is represented a complex process of staking out and claiming social identity. This is illustrated in the following example. The packed lunch, in its confusing of two important domains in a child's social experience, is a potentially highly charged and emotive commodity. It represents food from the social context of the home which is eaten within the cultural context of school and in the company of other children. Its contents – the amount and type of food – is usually decided upon by the mother and, in this sense, the packed lunch which a child brings to school also contains messages about 'life at home', open to be read by other children around the lunch table. For one six-year-old boy who was beginning to carve out a position for himself within a fairly dominant group of boys, this fuzzing of the boundaries became particularly problematic when he found that elements of his packed lunch were different from those of the other children with whom he normally ate. His yoghurt (French, set, plain and white in colour) was not like those of his friends (Mr Men, runny and brightly coloured). After some time, he began to throw his yoghurts away unopened and untasted, despite his continued enthusiasm for them at home. Unnoticed by the dinner supervisors, it was the clean spoon in his lunch-box which led to his eventual detection by his mother. By way of explanation he commented: 'They [the other children] say it's disgusting.' Social conformity is the key to understanding his behaviour: by taking strategic action the boy managed both to disguise his difference and, although rejecting what his mother provided, to avoid a direct confrontation. Through these actions he demonstrated not only his allegiance to his particular group of peers but wider cognisance of the role which food plays in British society in separating child and adult worlds and forging child and adult identities.

His social standing and identity, at least intact if not augmented after this incident, was later to be mediated again through his use of food. Rather than take a packet of crisps from home to eat at playtime, he began to take his own pocket-money to buy the crisps sold at school. In this instance, it was the social act of buying rather than the physical act of eating which was the more important to him, for most of his friends took money to school to buy themselves snacks. This stand for some independence from his mother, like the disposal of the yoghurt, helped to sustain his identity in the playground and seemed to be worth the financial sacrifice it entailed.

For children with specific food intolerances, having to eat special food may pose a more serious problem. They cannot so easily alter patterns of consumption as a strategic move in the games of identity played out in the playground. A girl with a gluten allergy, for example, had to take 'rice cakes', rather than sandwiches, for her packed lunch. Having to eat such a different kind of food began gradually to create particular problems for her: not only did she lose out on the food exchanges which take place at lunchtime – nobody wanted to swop or trade her 'peculiar' food – but, on one occasion, she was teased by the other children for eating 'polystyrene'. While

it may be fun to deride 'normal' food through analogies –
frogspawn for rice pudding – it is quite another actually to
have to consume the seemingly inedible. To forestall further
incidents her mother ensured that she always had gluten-free
bread in the house. In this way her daughter was, like the
other children, enabled to take sandwiches to school. Other
mothers with whom I spoke recalled similar incidents when
their children had been ridiculed by their peers for eating
different foods. They described the efforts they made to bake
special cakes or biscuits – without dairy produce for example.
In appearance if not in taste and ingredients, their children's
food would resemble that which their friends consumed (see
Chapter 2).

The potential stigmatising role which eating 'different' foods
can have upon a child's developing sense of Self is, as the first
example showed, not a problem confined to those children
who have specific food intolerances. Those whose familial eating
patterns are simply unusual within the social milieu in which
their children move may find that food also begins to play a
significant role in structuring their children's social relations.
Children whose families practise vegetarianism or whose
parents are concerned about additives in food, those whose
religious practices proscribe particular foodstuffs, may all offer
their children a restricted diet at home which, translated to
the context of the school, assumes a differentiating significance.
But again, this attribution of significance changes in and
through the time and space of childhood so that, while younger
children may experience few problems, older children may
find their unusual food practices being seized upon as a signifying aspect of their social identity. Two mothers confided to me
how they felt that 'being vegetarian' sometimes caused their
children more social difficulties at a small rural school than
did their asthma. In the context of an ever-growing processed
food market of alphabet chips, Monster Munchies, Ghostbuster
crisps, Haunted House pasta, Flintstone sausages, Tom and
Jerry spaghetti and Mighty White bread, all geared to the
child market, the pursuit of whole food/no meat practices may
be quite difficult for children to account for. Visits home,
school outings, and packed lunches visibly evidence their difference. It offers the potential to become significant, as brown
bread vies with white, apple juice with fizzy green pop and
nuts and raisins with sugared sweets. But, by early adolescence,

these symbolic meanings may have changed once more; among teenage girls, for example, vegetarianism often begins to take on a certain cultural cache. It is the refusal of the hamburger, rather than the consumption of it, which at this age may therefore provide the significant symbolic vehicle of identity.

In the face of aggressive child-centred marketing strategies sustaining different familial eating practices is hard. Many highly processed food products are implicitly directed at children, with brand loyalty achieved through linking foodstuffs with cartoon characters or token-and-badge collecting, free gifts or other novelties. In their different ways, all such marketing strategies tap into the culture of childhood. Explicit reference to cartoon and football heroes engage with children's (particularly boys') group allegiance to cult figures, with the novelties, cards and trinkets providing passports to shared playground games and activities. During fieldwork, the current fad was for Teenage Mutant Hero Turtles which, on the supermarket shelves, yielded food products as diverse as 'Turtle bread', 'Turtle yoghurt', 'Turtle apple crumble pizzas' as well as 'Turtle chocolate and marshmallow pizzas', 'Turtle popcorn and sweets', 'Turtle iced bakewell tarts' and 'Turtle frozen potato shapes'. Thus it could well be that, as is the case with fashionable toys, the denial of access to such foodstuffs, whether through choice or circumstance, has the potential simultaneously to deny some children access to the wider culture of childhood, so great may be the pressure on them to conform (Goulart, 1969).

Family life is the second arena in which the pressure for conformity is evidenced, illustrating the powerful pervasiveness of this motif in children's culture. In the examples introduced below, sociality – the demonstration of social skill – is again achieved through the performance of particular remedial actions by children in an attempt to deflect recognition of potentially stigmatising differences. Within the school context, even in a neighbourhood school such as Hilltop School, family life appears to intrude little into the conversations young children have with one another. While they may refer to Mummy and Daddy or to siblings, children may know few details of another child's family circumstances. Only gradually, as the children get to know one another, is background knowledge such as parental employment, types of houses and gardens, or information about the wider kinship network filled in. Even among older children much of this intelligence may be hazy. Partly this is a function of the fact that adults often actively discourage children from access to knowledge about family finances or crises. It may also be that while children find such information of tremendous importance for their own emotional well-being and sense of Self, it has minimal social currency in their encounters with Others. Detailed knowledge about another's private and personal life may have little relevance for young children whose friendships are not bound by the feelings of trust, loyalty and intimacy which characterise those of older children (see Chapter 7). Indeed, among the children at Hilltop School, of much more pressing social relevance seemed to be the familial disputes among the characters of TV soap operas such as *Neighbours* and *Home and Away*. As public knowledge these details provided currency for social exchanges, in which all could potentially participate. It was one arena through which the ideal of conformity and equality could be pursued.

Among four and five-years-old children, then, knowledge of kinship structures seemed to rest on their own experience of an immediate kinship network. But even the details of this were unclear, for as Mitchell (1985) notes, children are often shielded from information about divorce, separation and remarriage. The conceptual models of family life which a young child holds thus derive largely from their own familial experience (from whose details they may be partially protected), and from fictional situations portrayed through children's stories, television programmes and advertising imagery. And in these fictional accounts of family life it is the nuclear family – mother, father and two children – which still predominates as an image. This provides for children, whose own families differ from it, a stark contrast to their own experience.

On first entering school – the time when children really begin to socialise with others on a daily basis – the four and five-year-old children readily revealed an awareness of their own difference. Social conformity was not yet a pressing social issue. Patsy announced one day: 'I haven't got a Daddy no more,' while Tony, also from a one-parent family, enquired: 'How do you know he's got a Dad?' Clara told me, on another occasion, that she had been to visit her 'George Daddy' at the weekend, the one who always gives her sweets. Such statements, while revealing a consciousness of differences, were spoken unconcernedly.

However, as already suggested, the social pressure to conform quickly begins to impinge as five-year-old Carl recognised. From a single-parent family he sensed that his family's departure from the stereotypical model of two adults and two children was socially problematic and potentially a sign of his difference. Seated with some other children, Carl was drawing, at the teacher's request, his house and family. His picture, like those of many of the other children, was a square house with four square windows in each corner. He then drew three figures standing beside it. After a time the children examined each other's work and Carl and Roland had the following exchange:

CARL: (pointing to the figures) Mummy, Johnny and me. Daddy doesn't. [live in it]

ROLAND: (in a matter of fact tone) I suppose he died.

CARL: (uncertain) No, he always stays at work.

Roland, from a stereotypical nuclear family, presumably cannot think of any reason, other than death, why Daddy should not feature in Carl's drawing. Carl, who knows this is not the case, may perhaps also wonder why his father is not there and offers work as a reason for his absence. Or, as I suspect, he may have realised his 'error' and quickly invented an appropriate reason. This interpretation was indeed confirmed by his actions a few minutes later. Abandoning his first picture, Carl drew another. This time it had four figures in it. He explained the change to Roland:

CARL: This was when we were in London and I was a baby and Daddy was there.

In redrawing his picture Carl was surely demonstrating an unconscious awareness of the growing importance of social conformity. Now his picture resembled those of the other children seated at the table. Daddy was there.

Public statements about family life and forms of family structure seemed to be less often made by the older children, although they may have confided such information privately to one another. This absence may simply suggest that divorce or single parenthood was experienced as unproblematic or regarded as insignificant by the children and therefore as not worth discussing. However, as seems more likely, it may instead be a further reflection of the growing importance of conformity. Indeed, other research confirms that children whose parents separate or divorce rarely publicly admit their changed or different family circumstances. In Mitchell's account, for example, the children reported not only the emotional consequences for them of their parent's divorce, but also their feelings of embarrassment and shame:

> Divorce was something that happened to other families and they had often hidden the truth of their situation from their friends. Some had felt the same isolation from their peer group that prisoner's children feel. (1985: 73)

One reason for the shame and stigma which children may feel derives, in part, from the prevalence of the stereotype of the nuclear family and its reaffirmation through the patterning motif of conformity in children's culture. As Mitchell goes on to note:

> Those who had thought everyone else has two parents at primary school had tended to keep their own situation to themselves and not to tell other children or teachers. (Mitchell, 1985: 78)

Similar findings are cited by McCredie and Horrox (1985) who comment that only when children reached secondary school did many begin to realise that other children also had parents who were divorced.

The social and practical consequences of divorce or single-parenthood may be felt by children in many areas of their school life. For instance, the changes in economic circumstances which can accompany divorce may take on a particular significance for children. One mother described to me how school trips and school book-clubs were now a constant worry for her. While she did not want her child to feel left out and 'different' from his friends, she now no longer had enough money to cover such extra commitments. Another recently divorced mother told me that her ten-year-old daughter who was still attending a private school had, uncharacteristically, refused to have a birthday party. She described the school as being one where 'the children are all brought to school in Jaguars' and, as it later transpired, it was the disparity in wealth which had motivated her daughter's refusal. She did not wish her school friends to see the small house she now lived in with her mother. Thus, through discreetly managing her changed social circumstances, this young girl preserved her social standing with her friends. Outwardly, she continued to conform.

In the school where I worked about 18 per cent of the children were from lone parent or merged families of various

kinds and yet, even among older children, I rarely heard mention of it. Instead, children whose parents were divorced would,
like their friends, speak about or make reference to both their
mothers and fathers. They just made no mention that they
lived apart. Only after several visits to a child's house did one
boy realise that his friend's father did not live there. And even
in the midst of a family crisis, Judy said nothing publicly,
preferring to make a more private statement – to her Self as
well as to Others – which symbolically reinforced her continued
conformity. Despite her changed family circumstances, on the
computer screen in the corner of the classroom she typed the
words: I have a Daddy. As the little girls in Steedman's (1982)
book revealed, children's knowledge about adult relationships
and affairs is both considerable and perceptive; what is important is the timing and manner of their public revelation of it.
Through this children can confer, acquire or lose their personhood; which outcome results, depends upon their degree of
sociality, their possession and demonstration of social skills
through specific cultural performances.

Individuality: a Sense of Self and Personhood

In seeming contradiction to the emphasis placed upon conformity, a motif of individuality also patterns children's social relationships. As they grow older and more culturally experienced
it is this which becomes the more potent force. But individuality
– that complex of character traits which strongly mark a person
as being unique – is none the less still culturally patterned and
shaped. In this sense, as I shall move on to explore, individuality
is the predominant characteristic of a child skilled in the art of
sociality, that is, ironically, in the art of conforming. Individuality allows him or her to be acknowledged as 'one of the crowd',
rather than remaining anonymously, merely 'one among many
in the crowd'. However, an excess of individuality, or its inappropriate cultural expression, may confer outsiderhood, leading to the stigma of 'exclusion from the crowd'. The skill lies
in knowing how, when and where to reveal it.

Successful individualists can be defined as those popular
children who acquire their reputation internally, from within
the body of children, through their facility with or accommodation to the cultural practices of childhood. In this sense, their
very individuality is in fact established through an accommodation – although not a slavish conformity – to the implicit rules

structuring children's social relationships. Unsuccessful individualists, by definition, are far less comfortably positioned within the social world of childhood. Often, but not necessarily, bearing an externally derived 'bad' reputation, acquired through their non-conformity to the rules imposed by adults, such children find this individualising definition of the Self difficult to negotiate, particularly in the primary school setting.[1] Between these two extreme locations for the Self and for personhood, however, fall the majority of children. They gradually learn to regulate the tension between their own growing sense of individuality and an increasing pressure for social conformity. They also learn, through their mistakes, that failure to manage this tension competently risks an excess of individuality being mistaken for eccentricity, or its absence being seen as the stigmatising sign of total social anonymity. Drawing on selected events and incidents from fieldwork, I shall illustrate the complexity of the processes through which reputations are acquired, mediated or lost within the social world of children.

The importance of rules, explicit and implicit, in the framing of conformity and individuality in children's social interactions and behaviours, has been already alluded to. An example of the constraining power of explicit rules would be those, laid out by teachers, which regulate the spatial and temporal organisation of the school, restricting and controlling children's behaviour and encounters. Clearly established through verbal instruction, these contrast markedly with implicit rules which, rarely verbally articulated, may only become apparent in their breach or violation (Douglas, 1975).

On entering the world of school, the nursery-class children very quickly learned the explicit rules. Just a little later, they learned how to negotiate them. Verbally expressed in the form in which they were socially experienced, the children would articulate these rules as follows: 'You're not allowed to . . .' or 'The teacher said . . .'. Teaching themselves and each other through this constant articulation of explicit rules, the children revealed their experience of adult power as being an authoritative control system focused upon the physical body. Rules limit or direct the body's actions and movements. Pippa, who preferred to observe rather than do (and was seen by the staff as a reluctant pupil on account of her non-participation) nevertheless seemed to be particularly aware, no doubt through her constant watching, of the way in which rules structured the nursery environment. She learned too of their classificatory impact upon individuals: naughty children break rules, good children abide by or successfully negotiate them. In casual conversation with me she would frequently remark on another child's behaviour and, during the time that I knew her, was able very clearly to outline the majority of behavioural rules set down by the nursery staff. Nearly always rhetorically expressed she might say, 'You're not allowed to run in the nursery are you?', or 'You're not allowed to sit on there, are you?', or 'Sally's gone in there, you're not allowed in there are you?' On one occasion, sitting on the table swinging her legs she commented: 'You're not allowed on tables are you?', a form of self-regulation which she often adopted.

While Pippa was clearly unusual in her obsessive chanting of rules, other children also developed a good command of them, for it is in strategically invoking these rules that children endeavour to control one another's behaviour. Begun in the nursery setting the recourse to rules, explicit and implicit, increasingly acted as a restraint on certain children's individuality, constraining them to conform more fully to the culture of childhood. Often, therefore, only after the invocation of these rules had failed to curb behaviour would children call upon adults to assist them actively in the settling of a dispute. More commonly, a child would attempt to regulate another's behaviour by commenting that, 'It's not allowed.' If this strategy failed, a second and more precise second admonishment might be given, beginning with the words 'The teacher said . . .'. If this too failed to modify another's behaviour, a final threat would be issued: 'I'm telling of you.'

In their strategic use of these alternative sanctions even very young children revealed a considerable sophistication in the reinterpretation and invocation of the rules of the adult world. It also reflected the cultural value placed by children on conformity as a control mechanism to be used among themselves, for the children were highly selective about whom and on what occasions they invoked rules. Misdemeanours, for instance, were not always disapproved of. Rule-breakers could be admired. The daring complicity involved in sharing some forbidden sweets brought to school, of sniggering over a rude drawing or of listening to a Kylie Minogue tape secreted into the classroom and played on the tape-recorder brought social approval, not disapprobation, to the instigator. Reporting minor rule infringements to a teacher also ran the risk of a personal loss of social credibility if the defector was dismissed for 'telling tales'. Judging the appropriateness of when and about whom to invoke the sanctioning power of rules to constrain Others to conform involves, therefore, considerable skill in correctly reading the pattern of social relationships.

However, in some instances, there was less ambiguity over the invocation of rules. Certain children were known as 'naughty' and these individuals rarely received encouragement for their misdemeanours. Rather, their breach of *any* rule merely served to confirm their reputation and to reinforce their outsider status. These children possessed an unwanted individuality which would be compounded by constant public exposure as, made to stand up in assembly while all the others were seated or to stand facing the wall at playtime, they became visibly individualised as different. Children whose names were constantly on the teacher's lips or were written down in the 'naughty book' rarely received support from their peers. Such bad reputations, once acquired, may be hard to lose, for their very individuality as outsiders ironically makes them useful as cultural scapegoats. Children of three and four years old very soon learnt the value of having such a child in their midst and would always, even *in absentia*, name him as a culprit. Such individuality is unwelcome, as seven-year-old John sadly acknowledged. Regarded as a nuisance by the other children in his class and often excluded from their games, he was frequently chastised by teachers for fidgeting, talking when all were silent or for interfering with other children's work. Accompanying a desolate picture of playtime (see p. 176) he poignantly and with great a deal of self-knowledge, outlined his predicament for me in two short sentences:

Nobody ever plays with me. I am so norty (sic).

Although knowing that his behaviour was the primary cause of his isolation, and despite sympathetic encouragement and help from his teacher, John found it extremely difficult to change and would anxiously ask, 'Am I being good today?'

In instances such as these, classifications of behaviour as antisocial are externally derived, largely from teachers' and other adults' definitions of good and bad behaviour. With these younger children often concurred until such time when, through a more active participation in the culture of childhood, they began to abide by their own internally derived and more implicit system of behavioural rules. Being of and about children's own culture, it is this system of classification which then begins to structure different social groupings between children. Pollard (1985) noted in his work among primary school children that the value systems, generated by children for children, structured three different groups: the gangs, the jokers and the goodies. Within each of these a particular kind of sociality pertained, a sociality which literally identified group members. In this sense, although child culture 'is enabling in one respect it is constraining in another' (Pollard, 1989: 50).

The internal lines, demarcating socially acceptable and unacceptable behaviour, are amply illustrated through the children's attitudes towards fighting at Hilltop School. A main feature of the boys' conception of masculinity was their emphasis upon strength, symbolised bodily by big muscles (Chapter 4) and socially through claims to being good fighters (Chapter 6). Ironically, however, those boys who frequently brawled in the playground were far from popular, for there was a considerable and emotive difference between having a reputation as 'the best fighter' or 'the strongest boy' and being stigmatised as a 'bully'. While both kinds of reputations emphasise a particular boy's individuality, only the first expresses his sociality. The latter categorises him as an antisocial outsider.

This distinction is more easily expressed through words than demonstrated, however, for in the rough and tumble playground games which the six and seven-year-old boys played, differences in kinds of fighting could be hard to discern. But from the ways in which the boys themselves talked about fighting and represented this activity to themselves and their listeners, it was obvious that clear boundaries separated 'social' from 'antisocial' behaviour. The boys' conversations with me revealed fighting to be more a discourse about maleness than a model of masculine behaviour. Through verbal claims and boastful discussions six-year-old boys competed with one another over their fighting prowess. However, should such behaviour actually be carried out in the playground it was regarded by them as, classificatorily, 'out of bounds'. The boys' social skill lay, then, more in the way in which they told about deeds of daring do rather than in actually doing them. Consequently, the scraps and fights which did commonly take place in their playground games were usually but pale shadows of imagined exploits or tussles which would be more vividly embellished on later recall.

In the following conversation three six-year-old boys are telling me about karate and, through doing so, they make claims about their skill as fighters:

NEIL: This boy comes up to me and goes . . .
PETER: (Interrupting) . . . You have to stretch.
ROBBIE: Guess what . . .
PETER: You have to look about – they might kick you in the head . . .
ROBBIE: (standing up and demonstrating) I put the leg like that . . .
NEIL: Then you go . . .
ROBBIE: I threw him over my shoulder.
NEIL: I kicked him in the mouth and my shoe got stuck in his mouth.
ALLISON: I don't believe that. I thought you did it in bare feet . . .
ROBBIE: Guess what, I kicked this boy . . .
PETER: No, we do it at home . . .
NEIL: I don't.

During the fieldwork period, martial arts such as karate and judo were popular pastimes even for young boys of six or seven years old. It was a subject keenly discussed, and practised, by them. Neil, Robbie and Peter were all popular boys, with Robbie claiming to be the 'best fighter' in the class. This conversation was similar to many others I had with them. Full of bravado and marked with images of violence it was visually punctuated through actions and mimicry. However, its significance lies less in what it reveals of the boys' physical abilities, than in demonstrating their social skills and facility with the art of talking. Rarely were any of these three made to stand in the line of miscreants identifiable in the playground during lunch-time play, nor were their names recorded in the 'naughty book'.

Their reputations as being strong and good fighters depended, then, largely upon the art of sociality. First, the boys knew how to tell a good tale and how to engage their listeners. There are in fact three stories being told simultaneously in the extract cited above and the boys use various techniques to compete for my attention. Neil's strategy is to personalise his story by placing himself at the centre as hero: 'This boy came up to me . . .' A similar strategy is the use of recall: 'Do you remember when I . . .' Robbie, in contrast, invites his listeners to participate and be drawn into the story: 'Guess what?' he asks. Peter's technique is to grab attention by illustrating his words with a visual demonstration of the bodily skills required for karate. Humour, and the ability to make others laugh, is, as we shall see later, a critical aspect of children's social relationships and in his tale Robbie exploits this technique, through telling how his shoe got stuck in a boy's mouth. When I didn't laugh but instead challenged the integrity of his statement, Robbie, undaunted, sets off on another tale: 'Guess what?' he asks again. However, his chosen topic of kicking is unwise for, at this point in time, there was considerable concern being expressed by the staff over karate kicks being performed in the playground. Sensing potential trouble, for, as yet, they did not know me well, Peter rescues the situation. 'No,' he says contradicting Robbie, 'We do it at home,' a guarded retraction made, I suspect, just in case I thought that they were involved in the playground kicking. Neil, perhaps not so trusting, denies even this minimal involvement: I don't, he says, thus distancing himself completely.

These 'best fighters', these individualists, are in many ways therefore also ultimate conformists. Their reputations are more verbally, than violently, established through a process of individualising the Self. Popular and occupying central positions within a favoured group of boys, it was Neil, Peter and Robbie's sociality, rather than physicality, which sustained these identities. The boys who were often at the centre of playground brawls and who assaulted other children were feared and disliked. Their reputations were as bullies, not fighters. Later in the same conversation Neil, Peter and Robbie began to talk more seriously of a boy whose reputation as a fighter and potential troublemaker was well known by the staff and pupils alike:

NEIL: He's naughty . . . he trips people up.
ALLISON: Does he frighten you?
PETER: Yeah . . . he goes like that and he kicks and gets
          you and rolls you over . . .

This perception and classification of his behaviour was later confirmed by two girls:

TONIA: He kept bullying, like that.
SANDRA: He throws his bag at everybody and he thumps
          people.
TONIA: And he kicks people.

Far from inviting admiration his reputation of being physically aggressive towards other people led to social ostracism and sometimes made him the scapegoat for a variety of other misdemeanours unconnected with fighting. It was his name which was readily called to mind by the other children when investigations were under way.

While perhaps rare among young children, it is possible that later bullying behaviour has its roots in such encounters (Tattum and Lane, 1989). Children who cannot negotiate their way through the implicit rules of social behaviour, as Neil, Peter and Robbie so effectively do, may find themselves isolated. Recourse to violence and the installation of fear, rather than admiration, in others may be the only way they can see of having their individuality acknowledged. On the other hand, Steve and Bill's description of bullying is informative about potential victims of such behaviour:

STEVE: When I walk home there's these two boys, they still do it to me, they're bullying me. They still keep on saying, 'We'll beat you up when you walk home.'

ALLISON: Do you go home by yourself?

STEVE: Yeah, but I walk the other way with Bill now. My mum told the teacher.

ALLISON: Are the boys in this school?

STEVE: Yeah, but we're older.

ALLISON: So they don't do it in the playground?

STEVE: Not all the time. But when it's quite empty sometimes they do it to me, but they don't do it to him (indicating Bill).

BILL: They don't do it to me.

ALLISON: Why not? Are they frightened of you?

STEVE: No, they just don't know Bill . . . They live near me.

BILL: They probably know that I will tell their sister.

Steve was a quiet, studious boy and Bill was his one close friend. Steve disliked fighting and playing football and did not overtly display those qualities of sociality, made manifest by children through verbal or physical skill. Bill, by contrast, was more socially aware of the importance of conforming to the implicit rules shaping relations during childhood, such as playing football and particular games (see Chapter 6). This is revealed in his telling comment: 'They probably know that I will tell their sister.' This threat, derived from the cultural rules of childhood, he sees as offering him some protection against bullying – he knows the boys know that he knows which rules to use. Steve, on the other hand, has no idea why he, rather than Bill, should be the victim. He can only suggest, rather lamely, that because the bully boys live near him, they know him. However, it would seem that it is Bill's more refined social skills which allow him to get by and to avoid trouble by being, anonymously, 'one of the crowd'. Steve, quieter and more reserved, is ironically the more identifiable in standing outside the crowd. Thus it was him and not Bill whom the bullies picked on.

Such differences in personal style are particularly apparent in children's verbal skills. As the Opies ([1959] 1977) have magnificently documented, the lore and language of childhood is both immense and of immeasurable importance to children. Those who are able to use it skilfully easily acquire personhood through conformity to its principles: through telling jokes and reciting rhymes, verbal teasing and name-calling. While at four years old children may only just have begun to learn the principles and formulae around which language games are built, they have often become quite proficient in this social art by eight and nine years old.

To explore how such individual reputations are established, and what they reveal about a child's personhood – his or her socially significant identity – I shall focus on just one aspect of children's language use: the articulation of 'taboo' subjects such as those concerning excreta and sexuality. In Western cultures, where an ideology of childhood envelops children in ignorance, sexuality pertains to the adult world and speaks of adult concerns. For children, unsurprisingly, the cloak of secrecy which therefore surrounds it simply fosters their interest in it. The three and four-year-olds readily revealed their own fascination in their use of 'rude' words. 'Bum' and 'willy' and other 'naughty words' were whispered secretly between them, accompanied by giggles and squeals of shocked delight. Alternatively, they were spoken out loud in conscious breach of a known 'taboo'. The following exchange was noted between three four-year-old children:

ROB: Jimmy, would you like to be a plonker skinny.
JIMMY: No.
ROB: Pig pig.

MAURICE: Big pig pig.
JIMMY: Smelly pooh pooh.
MAURICE: Smelly pooh pooh.

Not only do the boys enjoy saying the word 'pooh', a subject
which increasingly becomes the source of a great deal of hilarity
for children along with topics such as farting, but the form in
which they speak the words prefigures the competitive language
use among older children, when name-calling and ritual teasing
predominate as a linguistic form.

At the ages of six and seven years old this skill was greatly
refined. The children knew not only what the 'rude' words
and rhymes were, but also realised their potentially strategic
use. Thus, while the implicit rules of childhood permitted
them secretly to whisper rude rhymes to one another and
to delight in their obscenity, at other times an open admittance
of these same words and rhymes could be used to identify
a particular child as being antisocial. Knowing how to speak
as a child means knowing what to say to whom and when.
The powerful child knows when to switch from the implicit
rules of childhood to those more explicit and potent ones
of the adult world in order to identify and personify an
Other (see also Chapter 6). Thus Sammy, wishing to ingratiate
himself with me, told me that Digby had said the 'a' word
(arse) and Dora, fed up with Shelia, complained that she
had used the 'f' word (fuck). In this way, they wielded power
over me as well as other children for, as an adult, I was
made to disapprove. Similarly, near Christmas time, six-year-
old Phil, tested the limits of our friendship. Boastfully, and
with style, he declared that he knew what 'virgin' meant: a
woman who hasn't had a baby, he sniggered. Ensnared again
in my adult but researcher's role, I was forced to remain
silent, neither confirming nor disavowing his claim. Phil's other
audience of six-year-old boys, knowing for sure that he had
uttered a forbidden word but unsure themselves of its meaning,
could only acquiesce to his seemingly superior knowledge.
Thus, like Sammy and Dora, Phil's strategic use of language
revealed his social skill through revealing both conforming
and individualising aspects.

The verbal arts of teasing, rhyming and tale-telling represent
a particular facility with the culture of childhood as conforming
to its implicit rules requires both flair and inventiveness. Among
the boys this was particularly significant and was a style of

speaking which the four-year-old boys were already attempting to muster:

> Callum and his friends are running about: 'Dinner, dinner, dinner Batman,' shrieks Callum, reciting the tail end of an old joke. A few moments later he alters this to: 'Dinner, dinner, dinner, desert,' at which point the boys collapse in a heap, giggling.

On such occasions rhymes and jokes would flow in a stream of competitive witticisms, with each boy trying to outdo the other:

ALLISON: When do you tell each other these rhymes and jokes?

LENNY: Playtime, don't we, most time at dinner time.

BART: Ba ba black sheep . . . smack your bum, (giggles)

LENNY: Ba ba ba black sheep . . .

ALLISON: No, Ba ba black sheep have you any wool . . .

LENNY: (interrupts) Who knows Humpty Dumpty?

BART: Humpty Dumpty sat on the wall, eating up bananas.
Where do you think he put the skins?
Down the King's pyjamas.

LENNY: I know this one . . . Humpty Dumpty sat on the wally . . .

Equality through Competition: Being and Belonging

The tension between conformity and individuality described above is mirrored in a further pair of oppositional themes which run through the culture of childhood: motifs of equality and competition also pervade and structure children's social relationships. The refrain 'it's not fair', seeming to appeal to some unwritten rule about equality, commonly echoes around children's playgrounds, but heard just as often are bouts of name-calling and insults which children use competitively to re-classify and personify one another according to hierarchies of esteem. This confirms Pollard's observation that 'children's culture develops within an informal social structure of friendship, hierarchy and status' (1989: 49). But these motifs complement, rather than complicate, the patterning of children's social relationships achieved through an emphasis upon conformity and individuality.

An insistence on equality, for example, acts as a check upon those who demonstrate excessive individuality as occurs in girls' use of the concept 'bossiness'. Being bossy, that is taking over rather then being assigned leadership, threatens to usurp other children's personhood, to reduce the social significance of the Self. It was something which the girls were particularly conscious of and guarded against, as is plainly evidenced in the emotionally volatile relations which existed between three seven-year-old girls:

FELICITY: (indicating Alice) She had an argue with Debbie this morning.

ALLISON: What happened?

FELICITY: 'Cos Alice thought that Debbie was bothering Caroline and Alice but she wasn't, only a little bit she was.

ALICE: She wasn't really, I pretended to the teacher ... I lied.

ALLISON: What did you say?

ALICE: That Debbie was bossing me and Caroline in the playground.

In such a triadic relationship, should any girl assume outright leadership the potential for the relationship to become dyadic increases. In being a favoured form of friendship for girls this relationship was frequently riven with such accusations (see Chapter 7).

In a similar way, the emphasis upon competition, so marked a feature of children's social relationships, is tempered by the necessity to conform. The children would know and repeat to one another, for example, who was the smallest, oldest, cleverest or youngest in the class, the best footballer or fastest swimmer in the school. This internal ranking and relative social positioning was of great importance to the children, despite its de-emphasis by the school staff, leading teachers to cite parental pressure as the source for such marked concern with hierarchy among the children. However, as Pollard has also noted, 'children have developed notions of who is clever and who is a thickie and this influences their friendship groups and the nature of their interaction' (1989: 90). The idea of hierarchy and competition is firmly embedded within children's own culture and nowhere more apparent than in the children's attitudes towards educational attainment and ability. Even among five-year-old children, the sense of individuality and personhood which competition brings was already being acknowledged. But, unhappily, the successful competitor often achieves this sense of Self at an Other's expense:

> Saul is sitting with some other boys at the table with felt-tip pens and paper on it. He challenges the others: 'Can you write your name?' He looks at Roland's effort: 'That ain't it.' Roland begins to defend his efforts: 'It . . .' Saul: 'No it isn't . . . that's all scribble.' Later, when I look at Saul's piece of paper, that too is covered in scribble.

On other occasions I heard the children making clear distinctions between 'scribble' – known in educational philosophy as emergent writing and encouraged as a sign of a child's willingness to write – and what they already knew and recognised as 'proper writing'. Within the reception class, when the children were just beginning to gain confidence, encouragement rather than criticism was given by the staff to these first efforts at writing. But many children realised that these were less-than-successful attempts and, when asked to write their names, remarked that they could not write. The teachers expressed surprise that the children already seemed to have what they saw as negative and self-devaluing attitudes, that they already worked with some notion of a right and wrong way of doing things. Thus, Kevin, on being asked to draw a picture of his Daddy, looked at his effort and announced: 'I can't do it . . . you finish it for me.' Of course, in one sense he was realistic: his picture of Daddy looked nothing like his own father. He could not do it. What Kevin and the other young scribblers had yet to learn were the frames through which their efforts are culturally and conventionally interpreted by adults. What the teachers failed to appreciate was that these 'negative attitudes' signified the children's growing awareness of the rhetoric of competition which pervades children's culture.

Older children revealed a considerably greater facility. At Hilltop School the masking of children's differing abilities was pursued through using colour-coded reading books. This softened the brute facts of a graded reading scheme. Six-year-old Clara and Emily, however, showed their comprehensive understanding of the workings of the reading scheme in relation to levels of reading ability. In their discussion, they openly competed with one another over who was the more able reader and knew also what level of reading book other children currently had:

CLARA: I like reading stories.
EMILY: I can read them now.
CLARA: So can I.

EMILY: I'm on blue.
CLARA: I'm on orange.
EMILY: I'm on blue.
CLARA: No you're not.
EMILY: I am.
ALLISON: Which comes first?
CLARA: Orange and blue and then you get just orange and then you go on to other books, then they've got blue and then the other books are brown and . . .
ALLISON: Is anyone on brown in this class?
EMILY: Yes – Jack.
CLARA: I'm on orange and you're on orange, ain't you?
EMILY: But you're not on the same.
CLARA: But soon I will . . .

Best friends Clara and Emily clearly articulate the competitive motif of childhood: they know that to be on a 'brown' reader is to be a better reader.

Working with mixed-ability classes, exacerbated at Hilltop School by vertical rather than horizontal grouping, led some of the teachers to organise their classes into groups of roughly similar ability.[2] These children would sit together on a 'table', composed from a number of smaller tables pushed together. In one class of six and seven-year-olds each 'table' was assigned a name connected with a current work topic. While I was there the subject was weather and the children were grouped accordingly: sunny, windy, snowy and rainy tables replaced those which, for a few weeks previously, had borne the names of birds. The children themselves were well aware of what this complex naming system in fact disguised:

ALLISON: Do you like being in this class?
GAVIN: Yeah, but my group's hard.
LEE: You two are in the same group and I'm not.
GAVIN: We're in the windy group.
LEE: And I'm in the sunny group.
GAVIN: Yeah . . . we used to talk about birds and me and him were in the sparrow group.
LEE: And I was in the kestrel group.

Whichever classification system was used the children quickly learnt to link the new names with known and established hierarchies of differential abilities through carefully monitoring

the kinds of work each 'table' was given to do. This became
clear later in our conversation:

ALLISON: It's harder in the windy group, then, than in
          the sunny group, is it?
TONY: Yeah . . . Lee's is an easy one.
ALLISON: How do you know it's harder?
GAVIN: Well, because it's all the work that people do.
LEE: Because you two do words.
ALLISON: (to Lee) What do you do?
LEE: Do pictures . . . until the middle of the morning.
TONY: We're supposed to do words. He does pictures
          all the time.
LEE: Not all the time.

While all the boys agreed that the work done by the windy
group was more difficult, significantly, it is Lee, from the less
able group, who actually pinpoints the difference: he does
pictures while his two friends do words. Perhaps he senses the
potentially stigmatising effect this may have and therefore pre-
pares his defence. To Tony's observation that he only does
pictures he is quick with a retort: not all the time he replies.

The significant difference which differing abilities can make
to social identities and personhood were recognised by some
children. Roxy, for example, revealed her understanding of
this relationship in a somewhat bizarre assertion:

ALLISON: (to three girls) Which groups are you in?
ROXY: She's in the windy and me and Annie is in the
          rain . . . but we're still cousins.

A similar understanding of the significance of difference may
also account for Sophie's peculiar observation:

ALLISON: Why do you like Carrie?
SOPHIE: I like it because she's on a bigger reader and
          I'm not and I like it . . .
ALLISON: Why do you like it that she's on a bigger reader
          than you?
SOPHIE: Well, on a bigger reader you can do lots of
          cards you see and get a superstar badge . . .

In the first example, Roxy seems to imply that a difference in
ability might seriously affect social relations – hence her comment, 'we're still cousins' – while, in the second, Sophie explains
her wish to be friends with Carrie in terms of Carrie's greater
ability. Through association, she seems to suggest, some of
Carrie's stardom might rub off on her.

That the children saw differing abilities as one route through which they could compete with one another, despite the de-emphasis within the school on overt academic ranking, was amply illustrated on one further occasion. Tina, clever and with an outstanding reading ability, was mercilessly teased by two other girls. Time after time, they moved her reading record card into a baby book and thereby symbolically demoted her. They made her conform to the levels of ability more common among the larger body of children and, in her wish to be friends with them, Tina resignedly retrieved and restored her card each time without complaint. Thus, the gifted child fairs little better than the less academic child in the demands for social conformity and equality made through the emphasis upon the individual Self through hierarchies of esteem (Freeman, 1979).

In summary, this chapter has explored the process and performance of sociality in children's culture through describing the efforts of particular individuals to achieve a recognised personhood. If, as Rapport suggests, society is 'composed of an interplay of relations of sameness and difference' then in these early attempts by children to work with and through different kinds of relations can be seen the bare outlines of the ways in which identities and personhoods come to be taken on through the negotiation of a set of shared cultural meanings (1987: 142). In this sense, for any individual child, as this chapter has shown, the process of becoming socialised is no simple taking on of social roles. As Rapport describes, at best it is a process of 'muddling through' (1987: 145).

Notes

1. This changes with age. As Corrigan 1979 notes, among adolescent boys in particular, having reputations as rule-breakers may give them admired rather than stigmatised identities.
2. Vertical integration meant that in each class there was a wider age range than is usual through the mixing of two intake years in one class.

SIX

Playing At and Learning To

Play and Personhood

Nineteenth century Britain, along with many other Western cultures, witnessed the progressive and rapid exclusion of the child from the world of work. Legislation introduced to protect the child from the harsher realities of industrial life formally ended the child's participation in adult work activities and encouraged further the already developing exclusivity of the child's play world (Plumb, 1975). Play became seen as a defining characteristic of childhood, a definitive description of the child's realm of social action and, in this way, was integral to the particular structural form which Western childhood gradually took on (Hockey and James, 1993). In this sense, just as work was to emerge as a measure of the personhood of adults during the nineteenth and twentieth centuries, similarly, play began to characterise the social personhood of children. The child who could, or would, not play appeared among the growing number of problematically deviant categories of 'the child' (Armstrong, 1983), mirroring the developing perception of unemployment as a negative, potentially disordering, aspect in an adult working life (Kohli, 1988).

In a contemporary Western society such as Britain, play is therefore seen as the prerogative of children, rather than adults. Thus, while something frivolous and easy for an adult to perform may be described as akin to 'child's play', children's own participation in play is conceived in more purposeful terms. During the twentieth century, for instance, children's play has progressively begun to take on work-like characteristics. This is primarily evidenced in the development of the concept of the 'educational toy'. Reflecting the emerging perception that play could be a learning experience, the appearance of the educational toy gave rise to the formal incorporation of 'play' activities as a learning context (children's work) in the classrooms of British primary schools. The common practice of sending three-year-old children to play-school – a movement begun in Britain during the 1960s – is now seen therefore not only to prepare them for school, in social and educational terms, but also to prefigure their later participation in the purposive play which takes place in primary school classrooms. Here time, space and materials are provided for play. Construction toys are set out on tables to encourage the development of manipulative skills and spatial awareness with social skills being fostered through the provision of space for imaginative play. In designated corners of the classroom, the Wendy house, space ship or corner shop is erected to provide a context within which children can socialise and socialise one another. In the school-room, then, children's formal learning is understood to be assisted through the relative informality of particular kinds of play. Other playforms must take place outside the confines of the classroom, in the 'playground' at 'playtime'.

This conceptual mapping between cultural categories of person and categories of activity makes the exploration of children's play particularly pertinent to the understanding of children's social identities. As preceding chapters have shown, children's ideas about the boundaries of normality for the physical body and their understanding of sociality are contextualised by the structural form of Western childhood. It is through this that their personhood is conceived. Childhood sets the broad limits and boundaries to children's culture and, therefore, also to the categories and concepts through which it is perceived and experienced by children. Belonging to a socially marginalised childhood – excluded from yet dependent on the adult world – it is as adults-in-the-making that children in British society are conceptually positioned. Thus it is also as adults-in-the-making that their comprehension of and participation in the social world, their grasp upon evolving concepts of self, identity and personhood must be understood.

This acknowledgement of the inherent temporality of the culture of childhood for individual children does not mean, however, abandoning children's perspectives in favour of more traditional socialisation accounts. As I have already shown, children begin to seek out evidential grounds for the particular cultural stereotypes about the body which they encounter through the particular social forms which characterise the culture of childhood. Similarly, it is in making social relationships with other children that they learn the possibilities which such stereotypes have as effective markers of present and future identities, and satisfy themselves about the reasoning and cultural logic which permeates the cultural fashioning of particular kinds of behaviour. Through the social processes of childhood, then, children learn to negotiate and manage differing definitions of the Self. Unfolding daily at home, at school or in the playground, children have an active and shared engagement with particular cultural framings of their own futures – as a fat or thin person, as an acceptable member of the group or as a stigmatised outsider. Thus, if play is a major defining characteristic of 'being a child', then an exploration of children's games offers further scope for exploring other facets of this process of cultural learning. It should permit consideration of how children acquire cultural knowledge, rather than just that they do, through providing illustrations of the literal playing out, the performance, of particular aspects of identity and personhood. This chapter considers just two: social status and gender.

Interpreting Children's Play

There has been a wealth of theoretical interest in play, with much attention being given to defining and/or refining the play/work distinction. For Huizinga (1949) play differs from work in being set apart from ordinary life, an activity with its own 'course and meanings' (1949: 28). For Caillois (1962), on the other hand, the special quality of play lies in it being a voluntary activity, while Ehrman (1968) and Turner (1974b) remark, respectively, on its transformatory and liminoid qualities. Others have enquired into the purpose of play and, in that play can be said to be both constitutive of and constituted by children's own experience of childhood, 'children's play' has become a specialised focus within this more general discussion. One approach has been to draw distinctions between children's play, characterised by fluid, rule-free games of the imagination, and more formalised, rule-bound children's games (Newson and Newson, 1979; Opies, 1969). Others have rejected such distinctions, arguing as Hardman does, that 'there is no such thing as play without rules or games without some imaginary situation' (1974: 186). Such a perspective is adopted here, for, as I shall show, in the temporal flow of children's social encounters 'free' or 'imaginative' play can easily be made to acquire a set of informal but inflexible rules which structure and constrain any individual player's performance. Similarly, the seeming rigidity of the rules of the games, Off Ground Tig or Bulldog, may be softened in performance through the power which one particular child has to determine the process and outcome of the game for other children.

This socialising function of children's play has been addressed by Schwartzman (1978) who interprets play as the medium through which children learn about the affective and cognitive systems of a particular culture. Sutton-Smith (1977), while also seeing play in these terms, questions the extent to which children's games can be regarded as a means-end socialising experience. He suggests, instead, that play is socialising only in as much as it 'potentiates' a child's response. In his view, children's play may be as much about nonsense as sense, as much about transformation as imitation, as much about disorder as about order. For him, play is best regarded as a 'cognitive activity which liberates thought', permitting the exploration of innovative as well as routinised roles (1977: 236). In this sense, the socialising function of children's play – play as an imitation of or rehearsal for later adult roles – has yet to be proven. Such a perspective frames this chapter as, through detailed discussion of the form and process of children's play, I depict the subtle and complex ways in which issues about social identity arise and are taken on, are negotiated and/or resolved by children through the ebb and flow of the games they play with one another.

This interpretive frame was not idly chosen for it allows the idea of cultural performance to be addressed once more. As will become clear, it is through participating in games that children become cognisant of the conceptual systems which, in Geertz's terms, enable them to 'signal conspiracies and join them or perceive insults and answer them' (1975: 13). Thus, while the games children play – Doctors and Nurses, Mummies and Daddies, Tig and Murder Ball – may well be evidence of 'conceptual structures moulding formless talents', emanating from and representative of a predominantly adult world, what is significant is that they are played out and experienced in the child's world (Geertz, 1975: 50). They can therefore be said to both present and re-present children's understanding of that world. In this way games provide a valuable account of the links 'between what [children] are intrinsically capable of

becoming and what they actually, one by one, in fact become'
(Geertz, 1975: 52).

The participative and performative significance of play was
brought home to me by a conversation with five-year-old Sylvie
and Patsy which, despite its seeming opacity, became crucial to
my developing understanding of the significance of children's
play. In the following extracts the girls are endeavouring to
explain to me the rules of a game which they had enjoyed
playing during playtime:

> Someone turns round like that and they go 'witches in the
> wood' and then you say, 'Can I play?' and you say, 'No
> . . . I'll give you a golden thing.' And then you say, 'I'll
> give you a golden story book,' and they'll say 'Yeah.' And
> you have to say what they are wearing and you have to go
> round the circle until they get to your place.

Patsy offered further clarification:

> You sit in a circle and somebody's the witch and they have
> to sing round the circle . . . they sing 'witches in the wood'
> and they stop and sit down and the witch goes to tell them
> something . . . and the witch goes round in the circle saying,
> 'Do you want a golden chair?' And when she says, 'Do
> you want a golden book?' she reads you a story.

'And then someone is the witch again,' added Sylvie helpfully.

Sylvie's and Patsy's accounts were only partially instructive
in mapping out some predominate features of the game,
Witches in the Wood. From them I learnt that the game has a
name; it has rules of a kind and a structure; it is played in a
circle; there is a repetitive motif of gold; one person plays the
witch; the witch stands up while the others sit down; the role
of the witch circulates from child to child; there are words
sung; some knowledge is secret. This much I discovered. But
what is obviously lacking in the girls' account is any detailing
of *how* the game is actually played. This omission is, however,
informative. It underlines the importance of the participative
and performative aspects of play, something which five-year-
old Naomi later confirmed. She confided that, while she too
knew of the game, she did not know how to play it:

> You sit in a circle and someone goes round but I can't
> remember the rest because I saw someone playing it but I
> never joined in.

Her last words are the most revealing: it is participation –
joining in – which counts, a message variously relayed to me

by different children through the form and structure of their talk about games. Through reference to past glories (. . . do you remember when we were playing and I . . .), through the admission of social exclusion (. . . they wouldn't let me play . . .), and through listening to disputed accounts (. . . he cheated . . . I didn't . . . it wasn't fair . . .) I was led to see the importance of participative performances. Playing a game not only permits a child to develop a familiarity with its rules and with the form of play; participation is itself a sign of a child's active engagement with the wider and more complex games of social identity which are played out through performance: the games of status and of gender.

Playing the Game

Despite the clearly established cultural linking of play with childhood, the world of children's play is characterised more by its conceptual, than its literal, separation from everyday adult social life. The adult world continues to structure the form which play takes through setting play aside as a special, childish kind of activity, an apartness underlined for children by adult demarcation of particular times, objects and spaces for play. From the child's perspective this means that the boundaries to the play world are neither fixed nor constant, for adults may arbitrarily intervene to put an end to play in both the class-room and the playground. The time for play may be cut short, styles of play disapproved of and particular games outlawed. In the nursery setting, for example, the building toys of Lego or Sticklebricks were seen by the staff as only suitable for creating technical or abstract constructions. They were deemed unfit for the more figurative representations used by children in their games. Firing guns made of Lego in a space-age fantasy and smoking 'cigarettes' made from the plastic tubes of a construction set were both forbidden as a field-note records:

> The new construction toy has great potential, for it is not long before the white tubes are being used as cigarettes. Mandy has chain smoking off to a T, lighting one of her 'cigarettes' with the end of another. Her mimicry is exceptional, as she narrows her eyes to avoid the 'smoke'. The tubes quickly get secreted in corners of the classroom and palmed in hands as the message spreads around the nursery.

Within the playground too – whether in parks, gardens or schools – limits to play are set by adults, through restrictions placed on how the physical environment is used. Children new to Hilltop School, for example, soon learnt that adult rules defined when they were allowed to play on the grass, rather than the tarmac. Adult rules designated which parts of the building they could enter freely and which areas of the playground belonged to older or younger children. The symbolic use made by adults of walls and lines in the playground to identify publicly child miscreants were visibly apparent. 'Naughty' children would be made to stand still, against the wall or on a painted line. Like statues amid the swirling hubbub of other children's games, they became temporary symbolic reminders of the social order of the school. Four-year-old children also quickly became aware that styles of play appropriate to the playground were not permissible within the structured 'educational play' of the classroom (Corrigan, 1979).

The difficulty of negotiating a path through constraints such as these is a predominant motif in children's play and most commonly achieved through processes of transformation which enable children to actively work upon and with their social and physical environment (Hardman, 1973, 1974; Newson and Newson, 1979; Schwartzman, 1978). Through their games children effect symbolic changes on the world around them which permit them to exercise a degree of both autonomy and control in a seemingly capricious and adult-centred social world. And, as I shall show, the more effective the transformation, the more social status the transformer accrues.

During play, the youngest children effected transformations on toys themselves: bikes became fire-engines and dolls turned into babies so that, despite the specificity of their form, the children did sometimes control the ways in which particular toys were used through redefining them in the context of particular games. But even among the children in the nursery class this potential was limited, for although five-year-old boys would occasionally push the dolls' pram around the classroom, the gendered specificity of prams, as belonging to a domestic and largely female environment of mothers and babies, more often limited its use in games of car-maintenance or fire-stations. The less prescribed the form of the toy the more potential it had, for in this process of redefining and transforming the environment, particular definitions imposed by particular children come to predominate. Who gets to define what and for whom has implications for social status and for identity.

It was, therefore, the wider biophysical environment which was seen by the children to have more promise. In having few specific and meaningful denotations for children it is a context which, from their perspective, appears semantically flexible in its connotations (Barthes, 1973). For instance, unlike adults, the children of Hilltop School seemed not to regard the grating over the drain as dirty or polluting through its association with the sewerage system. Instead, it was seen to have tremendous transformative potential. In the children's drawings of playtime the drains recur as an important symbolic feature. Drain covers and drain pipes, significant markers in an otherwise bare expanse of tarmac, identified for the child players the safety of the 'den' area in Drain Tig, the centrepoint for a special ball game and the space designated for a game of Babies and House played by one group of girls. On the walls of the school the down pipe was always utilised as an object to attach a skipping rope to in the skipping game Big Ben. Attributing to such items both a symbolic and a utilitarian aspect, the playground was continually 'read' by the children. Its corners, crevices and furniture were overlaid with shared significances and meanings which all children, but few adults, came to know. The playthings provided by adults for play – the climbing frames, tunnels, swings and slides – were similarly made to mean different things. As they were used by the children they became pirate islands and theatrical stages. Six-year-old Katy described for me how such transformed playworlds are accessed through play:

> When there are three of us we use the squares right down the other side of the playground – the shapes on the floor – and we use them as a house. The kitchen and the bedroom.

Elsewhere in the playground the painted lines which demarcate a netball pitch in lesson time were used at playtime to separate places of safety from those of danger in the catching game, Bulldog. But these very lines might, on another day, furnish the metaphoric tightrope along which Follow My Leader could be played (Hardman, 1974: 179). The following stories which accompanied drawings of one particular playtime were dictated by three children and show this transformation taking place in different ways through the process of play:

We are playing a house game. There is a green door to the school. There is the drain. It is raining and the sun is in the sky and a rainbow.

There was a giant in the playground one day. I am wearing my night gown because I did not know what was going on. There are some arches which were smoking. We are all coughing.

We're being naughty [riding motorbikes] on the roads knocking everyone over and everyone's coming out of their house.

They show that the skill of being-in-the-playground requires a child to know how to regard the playground: to know where to step or not step, where or where not to run and what to touch for safety. Those who fail to do so literally discredit themselves through discrediting performances in the playground.

Separated playworlds are also constituted by children through transforming their social environment. In games, new identities are adopted, so it was as cowboys, robot transformers, teachers or firemen that young children at Hilltop School would inhabit the playground. These identities, infinitely flexible, might continually transform through the process of play:

We played a ghost game, pretending to pull up all the flowers and putting them on the bench and that was our little van where we lived and we went out and then the game changed and we were all little and there was a grave where we kept crawling in traps and where there was dracula and things . . . demons, witches and vampires.

While many such children's playworlds are clearly renderings of adult worlds – games of home and hospital, war and work, for instance – they do not simply and unproblematically mimic adult life. As Walkerdine (1985a) has shown the process and experience of playing, although taking the form of adult relationships – doctors, mothers, wives – pertains to issues and concerns of the child's own social world. Thus, just as children conceptually and literally rebuild the physical environment in and for their games as a place separate from the everyday adult world, so they also cognitively reconstruct aspects of the adult social world and augment their understanding of it in terms of the present context of their *own* social relationships.

In this sense, children's play doubly socialises: children get to know about the future through getting on with life in the present. The roles and identities which children allow one another to adopt in games may, in this sense, speak loudly of the power relationships and status hierarchies which exist between them.

In sum, the transformative processes involved in play have, therefore, multiple outcomes for children. Those more skilled performers impose meaningful transformations on the environment which come to dominate a particular game or form of play. Others, less skilful or less knowledgeable, may be unable to direct its course or change its form. They may find themselves with unwelcome play-identities, on the losing side, or last in the line. These children may become subject to the deceptive and distancing strategies of their more powerful and knowing peers, an experience which can render them lonely and isolated at playtime.

One seven-year-old boy was in this position. Having no special friends at school, he was often actively excluded, as well as simply ignored, by the other children. His was a desolate picture of playtime: tall grey buildings dwarf, menacingly, two tiny, featureless stick men. The story which accompanied the picture eloquently underlined his loneliness, for it makes no reference to sharing in playground games with other children. It is, in effect, an account of his own non-participation:

I like my school. I like my friend. I like my little baby, I like my teacher. I like my school.

The emotional and social context of such social isolation is teased out in the next section which scrutinises in detail the ways in which the games of childhood are played out by children as more poignant games of status identity.

Powerful Players and Power Games

Having previously worked with older children it came as a surprise to me that the magnificent linguistic lore documented by the Opies ([1959] 1977; 1969) was largely absent from the playground activities of four, five and six-year-old children. I would hear snatches – the odd joke, the occasional rhyme – but that was all. Indeed, as I worked my way up the age range with different groups of children, I was becoming anxious that I had lost my fieldwork skills or that working in a school would prove to have been a mistake. Lots of other kinds of data, but where was this folklorist's delight? But at last, on joining a class of seven–nine-year-old children, I was flooded with jokes, rude stories, smutty rhymes, complicated games, acronyms, and body-language games. On reflection, I should have paid more attention to Naomi's observation made months earlier: that you can't play until you know how to play and you only get to know how to play by joining in. As children gradually appreciate, this takes both time and practice. It means getting to know and learning to use the implicit rules of behaviour and thought embedded in the social and cultural games of childhood.

Seven-year-old Jess and Patty confirmed for me my own growing awareness of this process. The following conversation, for example, is not simply a disagreement about the words of a rhyme. It registers instead the relative competence in linguistic lore between two friends and reveals Patty to be an acknowledged authority on this Dip:[1]

JESS: Mickey Mouse in the house,
          pulling down his trousers,
          quick mum smack his bum,
          ninety nine a hundred.
PATTY: No . . . number one.
          Mickey mouse in his house,
          pulling down his trousers,
          quick mum, smack his bum,
          and that's the end of number one.

Patty's version is meekly and unreservedly accepted by Jess who sees herself as a novice in these affairs. Patty, she told me later, 'knows them all'.

However, as the Opies' ([1959] 1977: 132) work has revealed, there is no enduring or authoritative version of such rhymes. They list two others:

          Mickey Mouse, in his house,
          Taking off his trousers.
          Quick Mum, smack his bum,
          And chase him round the houses.

          Mickey Mouse was in a house,
          wondering what to do.
          So he scratched his bun-tiddly-um
          Out goes you.

In the process of oral transmission, the telling and re-telling of rhymes from one child to another over generations of children leads to considerable variation and transformation of both words and images, as these examples show. And yet, alongside the inherent flexibility of form and the possibility for innovative performances, which this method of learning entails, there is peculiar to each group of children a sense of the correctness of a particular form of words, or, in the case of games, a style of play. This is roundly declared and rigidly observed. But who gets to dictate the form of words and which children have to follow meekly? When and in what way are changes negotiated or rejected and what do these reveal about the playing out of particular patterns of power and personhood among children?

The oral and visual mode of transmission of both rhymes and games makes children's active participation a prerequisite. This involves endless repetition and practice, careful listening and close observation of other children's performances. All of this requires both time and skill, which accounts for the relative absence of childhood lore and language among young children of four and five years old. Quite simply, most have not had the time to become proficient. But children vary both in their ability and desire to participate in this learning process, for doing so may involve a very public exhibition of failure (Sluckin, 1981). In the following three descriptions of how children learn rhymes, given to me by six-year-old girls, are subtly different perceptions of the importance which cultural knowledge has as a marker of social status and which reflect, perhaps, each girl's own confidence and ability. Eight-year-old Cassie, quiet and content to remain just 'one of the crowd', told me, for example, that 'you just hear other people doing it'. Lorna, on the other hand, had judged more shrewdly that an elevated social status accrues to those who appear to have a monopoly of cultural knowledge; thus, in rather disparaging tones she told me that 'Mary Smith kept making them [the rhymes] up and kept spreading them.' It was as if some disease had run rife through the company of children and Mary Smith was to blame. Nina, perhaps the least uncertain of her own position within a group of friends, was the most explicit: 'Jackie's sister taught Jackie, Jackie taught Polly, Polly taught me and I taught Susie and Susie taught Kim.' Despite these differences in each girl's representation of how power and authority are distributed in and through play, all of them were none the less aware that those children who are not allowed by others to play, or from whom knowledge about how to play is withheld, are effectively already becoming losers in the social world.

This signification of difference becomes most obvious in the strategic positioning of Self and Other achieved through the patterning of game ownership. Some games have open access but others are far more exclusive and excluding. These differences are not, however, intrinsic to particular types of games but arise through their playing out. That is to say, through different performative styles games can be made into closed and censored social environments which are powerfully excluding of Others. For example, in the playground at Hilltop School, willing players would sometimes be gathered democratically: two children might put their arms round each other's shoulders and march through the playground calling out: 'Who wants to play . . . ', followed by the name of the game. Anyone might join such a line and, on some occasions, this open invitation to play would transform into a game itself: as the line got longer, so the chanting became louder, and the faster it would wheel around the playground. Sometimes, however, one child would be recognised by others as having decided to play a particular game. Acknowledged as its initiator, for the duration of that playtime at least, s/he would 'own' the game and be seen to have the power, and authority, to decide who was or was not going to play.

However, from this position of authority, differentiating strategies of power were invoked. A child might use the ownership of a game purely for self-engrandisement, through arbitrarily setting limits to the number of players or excluding a particular participant, as a simple but effective demonstration of his or her power. Alternatively, being the owner of a game might give a child the chance to curry favour with more popular peers through temporarily having the authority to permit them to join the game. Conversely, s/he might choose, instead, to humiliate others, forbidding their participation and, as I shall suggest below, certain girls' games are particularly suited to this particular playing out of power. In the common playground lament – she won't let me play – the effectiveness of this personification strategy becomes quite clear.

To gain a reputation as an instigator, rather than a mere joiner, of games is therefore to have achieved a position of considerable social status in the group of children. From the perspective of those being chosen as participants, being 'allowed' to play registers a sign of their inclusion, a signal of at least temporary belonging. Being 'allowed' to play means, for that moment in time, having a recognised social identity, being allowed a personhood. Conversely, not being 'allowed' to play is the sign of a fleeting, or more permanent, designation of outsider status and, possibly, the loss of personhood. Only time will tell.

Playing children's games is, therefore, far from being child's play. Self-confidence is needed to participate in these very public performances which require overt demonstrations of both physical ability and social skill. The simple act of touching, for example, which is brought into play in games of Tig or Stuck in the Mud, may easily become a complex marker of social identity for the child who fails to play the game adequately. In these games the aim is to transfer symbolic stigmas from one child to another through touch. (In Stuck in the Mud, this 'touch' renders a child immobile until released through the 'touch' of another who is running free, while in Tig, or the more explicit Lurgy, the stigma passes serially instead. Moving from child to child the chaser continually swops placed with the chased.) For the swift and artful child such games pose few problems. Others can quickly be made to be, metaphorically, 'stuck in the mud'. The stigma of being 'it' (a non-person) can soon be passed on. But, for the fat child, the child with asthma or for the youngest child in a group, participation in these chasing games is more tricky: to be chosen as 'it', the chaser, may mean endlessly and hopelessly pursuing those others who are fleet of foot amidst their laughter and mockery. But being one of the chased, rather than the chaser, may be no better: it may entail always being the first to be targeted and the first to be caught. Differences that exist between children may, in this way, gradually acquire significances in terms of social identity and personhood. Inabilities are repeatedly made visible and made to take on stigmatised meanings through performance.

Thus, one important characteristic of a skilled performer is knowing how to manipulate the Dips which, as games of seeming random chance, lend to deciding who is 'it' – the symbolic outsider – an illusion of fairness. Jess and Patty described this skill to me and in their conversation revealed, once more, their different abilities as cultural performers:

JESS: I sometimes be on . . . but she always makes me
          on.

ALLISON: How does she do that?

PATTY: I just go . . .
I was walking down the Inky Pinky road,
And I saw some Inky Pinky men,
They asked me this, they asked me that,
They asked me the colour of the Union Jack.
Red, white or blue . . .

JESS: Blue.

PATTY: (pointing alternately to herself and Jess)
B . . . L . . . U . . . E . . . so she's on.

Such numerical facility with Dips is not uncommon after three years at school and Jess recognises that Patty uses her skill to her own advantage. But still she cannot imitate it and she admires her friend's ability and artfulness: it is seen as fair, within the rules of the game, for an illusion of parity remains. Later, however, she complained bitterly to me of another girl's unfairness. Jess told me that Maggie 'always refuses to be it' when the Dip has fairly allocated her that role. Jess regarded this, not as an admirable skill developed over time and through practice such as that which Patty had, but as an explicit rejection of the very rules of play. For this Maggie received little praise.

In this sense, the phrase 'it's not fair', which commonly echoes round school playgrounds, should not to be interpreted as an appeal for equality. Neither is it a function of the jostling for position in hierarchies of esteem which is central to much of what children do. Instead, it registers an objection to the flagrant disregard, rather than skilful manipulation, of the social relationships implicit in the games children play. Barry (who was not a fast runner) frankly told me that he uses 'Dips' at the start of games of Tig to always pick the slowest runner, because 'if they are the slowest you never get caught'.

From these examples, it is clear that acquiring playground skills, and therefore social status, involves more than just getting to know the rules of a game. Children shrewdly and candidly weigh up the balance of power and prestige, assessing their own position and skills relative to others. It is in the playground that reputations are made and lost, and stigmatised identities temporarily conferred or more permanently acquired. The following short account of a game of house, played by three five-year-old girls in the class-room, illustrates in considerable detail the ways in which power, authority and status are negotiated through play:

Three five-year-old girls, Emily, Rosie and Mary, are playing in the Wendy house, which is built in one corner of
their classroom. It is their time for 'free play', while other
groups of children are doing colouring and writing. Emily,
whose mother has had a new baby, has a pram with a doll
in it. As some boys approach the house, Emily says: 'Ssh,
the baby's crying so you have to be quiet.' The boys take
no notice and try to enter the house. Rosie says: 'Only
three people are allowed in here.' Later, Bob approaches
the house and is also forbidden entry: 'I'll go off to work
again,' he says as he leaves. Later still, Pauline tries to
enter the house. Again Rosie says, 'Only three people can
come in.' Pauline replies, 'No, it's four.' As she steps into
the house she announces: 'I'm going to make milk for the
babies.' Soon all four girls are playing in the house.

Within this separate house-world the girls are answering the
telephone and caring for a troublesome baby. No longer school-
girls, their social identities have been temporarily transformed
into those of worried mothers and sisters. However, it is a
world which Rosie, Emily and Mary wish to keep for themselves
and they endeavour, therefore, to limit other children's access
to it. Control is, however, established only indirectly for other
children are not simply forbidden to play. Adopting such an
overt position of power would invite adult intervention and
the girls would be encouraged to share the exclusivity of their
game. Whether consciously or not, Rosie chooses to adopt a
far more subtle strategy: she momentarily steps out of the
playworld, which has its own rules and order, to invoke the
higher and more authoritative order of the adult-defined school
world. Rosie claims that only three people are allowed in the
Wendy house, a rule which had been brought into force by
the teachers to prevent overcrowding. Rosie, however, has
changed it for, in fact, four had been stipulated as the maximum
number. Thus, through momentarily collapsing the boundaries
between worlds, Rosie manages to maintain the integrity and
exclusivity of her playworld: the boys are not allowed to enter.

But Pauline quickly spots the discrepancy and uses it to force
an entry from the school-world into the playworld. Her successful incorporation into the game does not, however, rest solely
on her correctly citing the teacher's ruling. Because she steps
directly into the current conceptual order of the playworld, by
making the baby's milk, Pauline demonstrates her participative

skills, something which Bob had earlier failed to do. In the domestic-interior scene of mothers caring for babies, the 'Daddy-going-to-work' identity had no part, for 'Daddies' are 'at work' outside the home. Using these strategies the girls maintain the transformation of the Wendy house into their house and retain control over their separated playworld (see Walkerdine, 1985a).

Emily, Rosie and Mary's game, although clearly very much about the adult world, is therefore played out in terms of the children's own social relations. Rosie and Mary were already close friends, having established their friendship over a long period of time, and they usually worked and played together. Emily, on the other hand, was often alone. Through participation in this game, then, Emily found her social identity temporarily transformed from that of loner to that of playmate. At least for the duration of the game she was to be part of, rather than marginal to, a friendship relationship. How she came to be included was uncertain: perhaps her knowledge of dealing with new babies attracted the other girls' attention; perhaps, she had already begun a game on her own which the other two more dominant girls took over. But, although the reasons which prompted the trio to play together are not clear, the social ramifications of their game is more certain: they had no wish to share it. And, as owners of the game, the girls were able to define who was and who was not allowed to play.

Social status is central to their successful performances. It is significant, for example, that it is Rosie who takes it upon herself to defend their mutual interests by standing up to the threat of intruders. Rosie, one of the more articulate and academic girls, was a confident and popular member of the class. Of the two girls who try to forbid the boys' intrusion into the game, it is Rosie, rather than Emily, who is successful. But the two girls adopt markedly different strategies. Emily stays in the playworld and invokes a rule of play; she tells the boys that they will wake the baby. It is a rule which the boys could have well ignored. Rosie, more shrewdly, invokes an adult, rather than a child's, rule and the boys, perhaps recognising the sanctioning power of the latter, acquiesce and withdraw from the scene. Perhaps they also acknowledge Rosie's centrality within the class and leave in deference to this. Significant too may be a growing awareness of the implicit gender separation which gradually comes to characterise young children's play at school and which makes certain types of games suitable for girls rather than boys (see below). Rosie, however, is less successful in her territorial defence against Pauline's demand to join the game. Pauline, although less popular than Rosie, is as articulate and, like her, enjoys a central social position within the class of children. Pointing out Rosie's error Pauline forestalls any resistance and completes her successful entry through immediately stepping into the conceptual world of the game: 'I'm going to make the milk,' she announces.

Children's games are, therefore, simultaneously the vehicle for more consequential games of social status, often played for high stakes. Children whose performances become discredited, or who are denied for whatever reason the opportunity to participate, risk more than the loss of a game: they may seriously diminish their social standing, acquire signs of an unwelcome identity and place their personhood in doubt.

Boys and Girls Come Out to Play

Participation in the cultural activities of childhood, as the previous examples have shown, is a key element in children establishing particular social identities. Those who cannot or do not perform effectively may jeopardise their personhood, becoming anonymously marginal, unnoticed and unremarked. Or, worse still, they may be stigmatised as outsiders. 'Playing the game' means knowing what to play, where to play, how to play and who to play with in the complex marking out of social status between children. In this section, I consider how gender identity is also instructively played out by children through their games. It is, however, by no means an exhaustive account of how knowledge about gender is acquired nor of the processes through which children learn about gender stereotypes through the school experience. This has been variously explored elsewhere (Delamont, 1980; Walkerdine, 1984; 1985a, 1985b; Whyte, 1983). Instead, the focus is more specific: what significance does gender have in children's play, what do children learn about gender through their games and to what use do they put this knowledge?

In the context of the school gender looms large as a significant symbol of difference among children, operating as the other major social classifier, besides age, through which adults conceive of and order the category, 'children'. In Hilltop School, for example, gender worked to separate the boys from the girls at morning registration and allocated them different washing and toilet facilities.[2] In contexts outside the school, despite some changes in consumer-marketing, gender remains a prominent signifier for children's sense of Self, shaping choices in clothes, toys, sports and books. Unsurprisingly, therefore, children use the classificatory power of gender to structure their own social relationships. As Chapter 4 explored, for example, it crops up in the accusations of Otherness with which children daily taunt one another: 'You've got girl's hair,' 'Those are boys shoes,' 'That's a girl's story,' and so on.

That gender retains its salience in the primary-school playground, despite advances made in largely de-genderising the classroom, supports Hastrup's contention that the 'semantics of biology' remain a significant area of social enquiry (1978: 49). Becoming a boy or a girl is not simply a matter of responding to biology, nor yet one of donning a ready-made identity as male or female.[3] Rather, as field material will explore, it is more a process of discovering, confronting and experimenting with the gender stereotypes embedded within particular cultural practices. In this the 'culture of childhood' is pivotal, a fact often ignored in discussions of gender-role acquisition. There is still a tendency to assume that it is just adults whom children are observing or copying in the socialisation process, forgetting that older children in the playground or siblings at home also loom large in children's social relations. They may also, therefore, play a significant part in the shaping of gender identity. It is, then, against the changing background wrought by age and social experience among children between four and nine years old that the following account of children's games of gendered identity must be set. It is these differences which are significant for the ways in which gender is variously perceived, taken on and publicly declared by children. It is these differences, then, which are significant in acquiring a gendered identity.

At Hilltop School in the relatively free-form play of the very youngest children, who were just beginning to enter the culture of childhood, gender identity remained fluid and shifting. Distant from the Self it seemed to be primarily located in the future. In this sense, although reflecting wider cultural stereotypes of gender, the concept of gender difference had only just begun to impinge on their present social lives and social experiences. Four-year-old boys and girls still often played together and shared their toys and games as, in the nursery setting, the boys shared the bathing of dolls and girls made (forbidden) guns out of construction toys.

But in the rulebound games played by older children, gender took on much more significance. In life outside the playworld, too, it began to provide a constant reference point for the Self and for Others, becoming a more fixed and stable aspect of social identity. But the conceptual boundaries separating male from female, boys from girls, were not simple replications of an adult model for, through their games, the children themselves set particular limits to gender roles. It was clear from my conversations with six, seven and eight-year olds, and from my own observations, that at this age boys and girls rarely played together, a separation shored up through playing radically different sorts of games.

This finding – that gender becomes increasingly prescriptive between the ages of four and eight, shaping both games and friendship – is well-known and continues to be confirmed in research work (Eder and Hallinan, 1978; Lever, 1976; Whyte, 1983). But the persistence of gender as a strong and cleaving difference in child culture has recently come to be seen as problematic within social psychology, given contemporary moves towards gender equality in adult society (Henshall and McGuire, 1986). Why, despite changing family structures and parental roles, do children continue rigidly to adhere to stereotypical gender roles? Henshall and McGuire proffer one reason: that there is a deal of difference between 'the meaning implicit in what parents do' and 'simply what they do' (1986: 156). Thus, they suggest, stereotypes of gender may remain as underlying or implicit cognitive frames of reference in the adult world despite apparent surface changes in gender roles. But another explanation can also be proposed: that the culture of childhood itself may, through its mode of transmission from child to child, act as an influential and conservative force in shaping children's consciousness of Self and Others. Quite simply, then, those children who perceive alternative gender models in their parents' behaviour or that of other significant adults, may keep this knowledge secret. In public, before their friends, they may acquiesce to the roles and models which seem the more commonplace and culturally appropriate. In the culture of childhood conformity is at a premium (see Chapter 5).

To flesh out this argument I return to the home corner located in the nursery class. Usually, but not always, initiated by girls, scenes from daily domestic life were here enacted out. Conscripted to play the male roles – you're Daddy, right – boys were often refused a more active part in the domestic environment constructed by the girls around babies and future maternal roles. A four-year-old girl established this world as she played, drawing a boy into her script where necessary:

'They're out of my house,' she says to no one in particular as she brings plates and cups to a table. 'I haven't no peas in my house.' (To a boy standing watching): 'Will you look after my food? . . . You're Daddy, right? Come on, hurry. You can have milk-shake and I've got some peas. I know where they are . . . lost them . . . in the pink jug. Where's the milk jug because I need it? No. We don't need it there. I gave it to Dad and he was losing it. I'm going home.' (To the boy again) 'You come to my house, Dad, there's your hat.' (She gives him a straw hat) 'Go away.' (She pushes away another boy who attempts to join in)

On another day, hanging around outside the Wendy House in the reception class and refused access by the girls for the third time, five-year-old Saul reluctantly announced: 'I'll go off to work again.'

In such games the gender stereotypes which are played out concern the future: 'Mummies' feed their babies, cook the dinner, go shopping, control their husbands, speak on the telephone and smack their children. 'Daddies' go off to work. For much of the time they are forced to stay outside the house, only gaining entry by permission of the 'Mummies' or, when refused, by violence and force (see Newson and Newson, 1979: 104). When under the boys' control the Wendy house was more frequently a place of male work in the public world – a fire station, a garage or a Ghostbuster's den. The goings-on inside were less specific, the characters less clearly defined, for five-year-old boys may have little idea about their futures as male workers besides knowing that that is what the future should be. I shall return to this point later.

In general, then, the gendered play of little children concerns their future identities as men and women, rather than their present identities as boys and girls. But these future gender identities may, none the less, be used strategically in the present as the above example showed. Similarly, one five-year-old girl's access to nominally male space was gained by an alliance made in terms of future gender roles. Sally was pushed away from the computer by some boys and Roland, a peacemaker, defended her right to be there:

> No, no she's my friend. She loves me. She only likes me
> . . . anyway I fell in love with her. Anyway, I'm going to
> get married to her, serve you right.

Roland takes Sally's hand in his and later tells another boy: 'I fell in love with Sally.' The next day, the romance forgotten, he asked her what her name was.

In another corner, on another day, five-year-old Verity and Pamela were playing in the sandpit with Jon. A few minutes later Shirley joined the group:

> VERITY: (to Shirley) You marry Jon and I'll be your
> baby.
>
> SHIRLEY: No, you can be two babies.
>
> PAMELA: I'm fed up with babies. You can be big sister.

And in another corner of the classroom, Robin challenged Alice: 'You love Helen.' 'No, I don't,' she retorted.

In all these examples, then, the future is anticipated through stereotypes of male and female roles but knowledge of what these might consist of is unequal: boys can be husbands, possibly fathers, while the possibilities for girls are many; as mothers, wives, sisters or babies. Boys would seem to have but one future, (which is obscure), while girls have multiple futures (about which some things are quite well known): true love is expressed physically; marriage is based on love; boys love girls; girls can't love one another; marriage entails having babies; and, as Shirley later announced to Pamela, 'You can't marry people who live in your house.' Among young children these observations transform into a set of generalisable rules, a clutch of stereotypes, with which they begin to explore the complexity of their present social relationships through future gender roles. This emphasis on the *future*, rather than the present, importance of gender means that four-year-old boys may push prams and girls mend cars without jeopardising their present social identities.

Snapshots of slightly older children who have entered school tell another story: that gender differences have begun to have significance in their present lives. Although some of the girls still play the game of Babies, having and being babies, boys are no longer included. It is a girl's game and while the girls get down to their domestic chores of child-rearing and cleaning, groups of loud and boisterous boys play games of chase. Colours, books, stories, clothes and toys are all beginning to be seen as gendered in terms of their suitability for boys or for girls. That this developing consciousness of gender identity is a socialised identity was clearly illustrated in the following incident which took place at Hilltop School.

On a work-table in the reception class, dolls and dolls' clothes were laid out for the children to play with and, as the children moved from table to table, it was soon the turn of a small group of boys. Avidly they dressed and played with the dolls, making no disparaging remarks to one another, and seemed greatly to enjoy this legitimated opportunity to play with the dolls and enact out fantasies. It was an activity over which they had no choice: being school-work provided for the children by the teacher, it did not necessitate the public affirmation of their male identities. However, when a short while later they were able to choose for themselves, the boys refused point-blank to don pink painting shirts. These they saw as being a 'girls' colour. This rejection is a clear sign of the significance which gender starts to have for the presentation of the Self in terms of the here and now – today, tomorrow and the next day – as well as in relation to a more distant future (Goffman, 1971).[4]

Such gendered meanings are embedded in the cultural practices of childhood. Passed between different generations, as children become familiar with them, so gender inevitably takes on a greater social significance with respect to present identity and personhood. And it does so – for the Self and for Others – through the signification of difference. Thus the games played by six, seven and eight-year-olds increasingly emphasised the difference between the genders, distinctions reinforced through gender stereotyping. No longer simply a fact of adult life, gender had become part of child life, so that, in their games, seven-year-old girls referred to boys as present 'boyfriends' rather than, as when younger, future 'husbands' or 'fathers'. This was despite their frequent condemnation of the boys they knew for being 'rough and horrible' and their equally clamorous insistence that they *never* played with boys. Boys, likewise, claimed to have a 'girlfriend'. For them, it seemed to articulate their present maleness, being something to boast about and to be admired for. At the same time, however, they never considered including girls in their *boys* games. John told me why: 'Girls are boring because they go like this: chatter, chatter. chatter.'

The importance of gender as a signifier of difference, as a reflexive device for distinguishing between the Self and Other, is clear in the assertions the children made about gender which, through vehemently promulgated stereotypes, established both limits and possibilities. The six and seven-year-old boys and girls, for instance, used many traditional taunts to tease each other in the process of signifying the gulf which lay between them, switching genders where appropriate: the boys yelled in delight, 'Girls are rubbish, chuck them in the bin,' to which the girls replied, 'Boys are elastic, girls are fantastic.' However, despite vociferous proclamations and denials of contact between boys and girls, at the same time, the game of Kiss Chase provided a welcomed opportunity for breaching the conceptual wall erected between them:

GILLIAN: Me and Sylvie was chasing Peter and Garth said we had to kiss him. He has to kiss me and Sylvie before we go in class.

ALLISON: And did he?

GILLIAN: Yeah.

RUTH: He did kiss you?

GILLIAN: No . . . Peter tried to kiss us and Garth did but he didn't kiss us because we got away.

RUTH: I wish I could play with you.

GILLIAN: Tomorrow you can. Being as we chased them today they've got to chase us tomorrow.

In her wistful request, 'I wish I could play with you,' Ruth indicates the symbolic value which such participation has. It would confirm her gender identity: for boys kiss girls. But what is also significant in this conversation is that Gillian and Sylvie depict themselves as initiators of the chase. Later confirmed by the boys, this suggests that the traditional cultural stereotype – passive female/active male – is not yet beginning to structure children's behaviour or, alternatively, that gender stereotypes are in the process of change.

Among eight and nine-year-old children, concepts of gender had shifted again, a change reflected once more in the games they played. These children seemed more certain about gender identities, their games were more rigidly gendered. In the playground at Hilltop School the girls played traditional singing, skipping and clapping games while the boys more often chased or duelled each other or held football matches in the playground. Kiss Chase had been abandoned and even to the most casual observer the most obvious feature of school playground activity at this age would have been the extent to which boys and girls did *not* play together. In discussion with me, the girls vehemently denied ever playing with boys at school, with two eight-year-old girls remarking on the boys' different use and domination of the playground. Unprompted, they observed that the boys 'use all of it' and 'we go on the corners and the sides', which was a style of colonisation already beginning to be established in the nursery setting. The boys, confirming this gender segregation at school, described girls' games as 'boring' and not worth playing. Outside school, however, this strict separation did not necessarily occur. Some girls, and boys too, confessed to me that, at home, they played in mixed sex groupings. At school these would be temporarily abandoned. It was as if an invisible dividing wall snaked through the playground to separate the boys from the girls.

Thus, in contrast to four and five-year-old children, for whom gender is meaningful largely in terms of the future, by the age of eight and nine it has become a significant difference around which present activities are organised. Games provide a particular cultural context for exploring the gendered nature of the Other and for shaping and limiting the possibilities of Self-expression. The next section lays out in detail the structuring of this perception through the particularity of the games children play.

Boys will be Boys and Girls will be Women

Lever's (1976) research on children's games reveals six major differences between girls' and boys' games. These range from the kinds of games played by each gender – boys preferring public and competitive games in large age-based groups, girls playing more private, turn-taking games played in smaller age-mixed groups – to the observation that although girls sometimes join in boys' games, boys rarely join in girls' games. My own research supports these findings which are, I suggest, contextualised by the growing significance of gender as a mark of difference more generally in children's social relationships (see Chapters 4 and 7). As children familiarise themselves with the cultural practices of childhood, passed down from child to child, so they begin to establish a place for themselves within their peer group. And in this process of placing the Self, gender takes on an increasing salience as I have shown. No longer is it simply a future identity marker – the Self as a mother or father – but, instead, it confirms present social identity. A further skill of 'being-in-the-playground' involves, therefore, the active demonstration of this identity. But as noted previously, the variability in skill among individual children inevitably means that some boys are better at being boys than others, just as some girls are better at being female.

Around the age of six the boys at Hilltop School began to play together in large groups. Their games were usually structured around factional collectivities: Goodies and Baddies, Cowboys and Indians, Cops and Robbers, Japs and Commandoes, Thundercats and Mutants, Transformers and Decepticons (see, Opies, 1969). During the period of fieldwork, Hero Turtles and the Evil Shredder's gang became adopted as yet another pair of conflicting forces to add to the battery of oppositional identities which the boys could assume in their games. Although each generation of boys might have its own particular combatant armies, therefore, the form of battle remains traditional: good always triumphs over evil, with the outcome of the power game being culturally predetermined:

KEVIN: Sometimes I like being a baddy and sometimes
            I like being a goody.
ALLISON: Which is the best to be?
KEVIN: A goody.
ALLISON: Why's that?
KEVIN: 'Cos they always win.

From this conversation it is clear that, just as in their understanding of the body and behaviour, stereotypes are integral to children's understanding of gendered social action, providing those images of difference around which identity is hung (Rapport, 1990a). Thus, although some experimentation is possible during the playing of such games in relation to specific events and characters – a kind Indian, a nasty policemen or even the domestic home life of cowboys – variation in these boys' games is limited by the overdetermination of form: good must ultimately be seen and made to triumph. The championing of the male 'baddy' is, essentially, what defines the identity of a male 'goody'. In this sense, the games six-year-old boys played celebrated the contested nature of power through emphasising both competition and hierarchy.

The games played by six-year-old girls – schools, Mummies, babies – also comprised fairly fixed and stereotypical roles. Girls became 'Mummy', 'baby', 'teacher' or 'pupil'. Like the boys' games, these too were games about power relations but, for the girls, there was greater potential for experimentation. Drawn from daily life – from being a daughter, from being a pupil, from being chastised – the characterisations were more rounded, the plots more intricate. The goodies and baddies of the boys' games were, by contrast, more the stuff of fantasy, based on representations of the lives others live – television characters, American policemen, mid-west cowboys, cartoon drawings or plastic mutant figures.

Quite simply, then, the girls had more knowledge about gender to play with. In small groups girls investigated in some detail the nature and working of systems of power in the home or at school and, as Steedman (1982) has shown, their knowledge may be quite considerable. Such play is not just passive imitation but, as Sutton-Smith (1977) has termed it, an 'adaptive potentiation' involving the creative exploration, rather than simple replication, of the stereotypes of gender which the girls variously encountered. Thus, although the form of their play was traditionally structured, its content and performance varied extensively. It was, for instance, the context of the 'game' which enabled Lucy and Annie to play at being 'naughty girls' in the same classroom where daily they, as girls, had to be good. As Walkerdine has argued, outside the game, girls are more restricted in the identities they can assume: 'boys will be boys' and so it is that girls are often seen by teachers 'as the custodians of the moral order and not, like the more "active" boys, responsible for its demise' (1985a: 41).

Genders at Risk

The above examples have begun to sketch in the ways in which games provide a cultural framing for gender during early childhood. Through their goody/baddy games younger boys have little opportunity to experiment with their identities as men, for the stereotypes of masculinity they embrace provide few alternatives from which to contemplate their futures. Girls' games, in contrast, furnish more effective 'groundworks for anticipating the future' through the opportunity to experiment with many different stereotypes of 'femaleness' (Rapport, 1990b). In this sense, boys' games lock boys into the present through the proffering of surreal or uncertain futures while the future in girls' games is essentially knowable. This difference may help explain why the present of childhood becomes effectively dominated by boys and why it is in boys', rather than girls', social relations that hierarchy and competition are the most explicit (see Chapter 7). It may also explain why, in their uncertainty about their futures as men, that it is conceptually worse for little boys to be 'sissies' than for girls to be 'tomboys' (see below).

By eight and nine years old the gendered difference in games is firmly established and, at Hilltop School, the boys of these ages played games which involved a more active demonstration of stereotypes of manliness – of power hierarchies and of competitiveness – than those played at a younger age. It was no longer enough to take on the victorious role associated with the 'goody' identity; success in battle had to be proven, toughness had to displayed. In contrast to the six-year-old boys for whom this was primarily encapsulated in the idea of having 'big muscles', eight and nine-year-old game participants obliged each other to perform as men. Eight-year-old Toby revealed this in his admiration of a younger boy whom he thought was developing this social skill:

> He's the only one out of Year 3 [who plays football] . . .
> It's a rough game when we play. Most don't like playing
> because its tough.

Being 'tough' has always been central to boys' games of physical endurance when losing, or worse still crying, earns the label 'cry baby' (Opies, 1969; Hardman, 1974). But that this stereotype rarely fits well at the age of eight or nine years old and yet is one to which boys must pay lip-service, was readily acknowledged. At Hilltop School, those boys who actually participated in playground brawls, rather than play-fights, were regarded by their classmates (male and female) as more foolish than famous (see Chapter 5). Toughness was therefore a verbalised image of masculinity, performed and acted out through talk rather than physical violence, which may explain why the boys who did not participate in 'tough' football games received little social condemnation. Although not receiving any approbation as 'the best footballer' or 'the strongest in the class', as long as they played other boys' games – Build Ups, Follow My Leader, Tig – they were not stigmatised as a 'sissy'.

Assessing this male self-image nine-year-old Penny's observations reinforce this interpretation:

> They say, 'I'm a cool dude and all that stuff.' They show off. We know they are weak but they act tough. We see their weaknesses.

Penny described for me how, in a play-fight, a boy's face will redden while he simultaneously declares that he is not being hurt as, heroically, he plays out his masculinity.

What then do traditional girls' games teach eight and nine-year-old girls about being female? In contrast to those of the boys their games are played on the edges of the playground and in this less visible and more private marginal zone, girls teach each other the words of clapping, skipping and circle games. Boys, while sometimes knowing these songs and rhymes, use few verbal formulae, except the Dips which start a game or certain ritual words which lay claim to the first and last positions of play (Opies, 1969). That girls control the transmission of a verbal culture of childhood is seen by Grugeon (1988) as 'empowering', as providing them with an exclusive and excluding knowledge. This can be seen in the game of Wallflowers, for example, during which girls disclose to one another the names of potential boyfriends. After the first part of the rhyme is sung, a girl must name a boy whom she likes. This done, the girls' friends chant: 'Stamp your feet if you hate him, clap your hands if you love him; pull a funny face if you want to marry him.' Many of the other traditional games which the girls enjoyed playing similarly prefigured and reflected on their futures as women in terms of a discourse of romantic love and, through divination techniques, they plotted out in detail their lives to come (see Figure 6.1).

As Chapter 7 will describe, for the eight and nine-year-old girls at Hilltop School, 'going out with' a boy or 'having a boyfriend' did not mean, however, literally going out with them. Indeed, a boy might not even know of his involvement in an affair of the heart. But by claiming a boy as her boyfriend in these games, a nine-year-old girl symbolically identified him as a future husband, affirming as she did so her own identity as female. The effect of this in the present, was in some instances to cause rifts in the community of girls, with jealousies and arguments developing over who had the right to 'name' a boy

ALL THE BOYS IN OUR CLASS,
AREN'T VERY NICE,
EXCEPT FOR . . . . . .*   (Fills in boy's name)
WHO HASN'T GOT A WIFE.

HE TOOK ME TO THE PICTURES
AND SLAPPED ME ON THE LEG*   (Possible alternative)
AND SAID, 'OH MY DARLING,   'sat me on his knee')
WILL YOU MARRY ME?'

WHERE DID YOU GET MARRIED?
– CHURCH, TOILET, PIGSTY
– CHURCH, TOILET, PIGSTY etc.

WHAT DRESS DID YOU HAVE?
– SILK, COTTON, WOOL, RAGS
– SILK, COTTON, WOOL, RAGS etc.

WHAT RING DID YOU HAVE?
– DIAMOND, RUBY, PLASTIC
– DIAMOND, RUBY, PLASTIC etc.

WHERE DID YOU LIVE?
– BUNGALOW, CHURCH, HOUSE
– BUNGALOW, CHURCH, HOUSE etc.

HOW MANY CHILDREN DID YOU HAVE?
– ONE, TWO, THREE, FOUR
– ONE, TWO, THREE, FOUR etc.

WHAT COLOUR WERE THEY?
– WHITE, PINK, HALF CASTE
– WHITE, PINK, HALF CASTE etc.

AND DID YOU EVER GET DIVORCED?
– YES, NO, MAYBE SO etc.

FIGURE 6.1   *Divination Skipping Rhyme.* Two girls hold either end of a rope and sing this rhyme as they twirl it for another girl to skip over. As the questions are asked, the rope is swung faster and faster, the answers repeated in sequence until the girl fails to clear the rope. The answer spoken at that precise moment divines her future. In this way a girl receives a detailed account of her own future.

as their boyfriend. In this sense, these were power games, comparable with those more actively engaged in by the boys. But in these girls' games, the motifs of competition and hierarchy worked as far more subtle and implicit signifiers of social as well as gender identity.

Despite the rigorous separation between the genders, defended daily by both boys and girls in the playground, there were two important exceptions. During my time at Hilltop School, the games of Football and Bulldog were gradually infiltrated by a small number of nine-year-old girls. Both games, by tradition boys' games, monopolised the playground and were central to the public exhibition of a rough and tough masculinity. The girls' request to be allowed to play was, consequently, viewed suspiciously by the boys.

In Bulldog, the boys were least troubled by their intrusion and, in time, seemed to enjoy the opportunity which it provided to outrun the girls, to demonstrate how much tougher and faster they were. From time to time, Bulldog was also banned by the staff for being potentially dangerous, a move which united boys and girls in their resentment. Together they sought ways in which Bulldog could surreptitiously be reinstated, under the guise of another game. However, football was an entirely different matter. Having opted for a non-gendered social environment the teachers were willing supporters of the girls' claim to be allowed to play. Grudgingly, the boys gave their permission, keenly resenting this more dramatic invasion of a traditional male arena. But the football teams which resulted were never mixed. Instead, they formed along gender lines, allowing the differences between the genders to be grimly played out:

ALLISON: What happens if you win against the boys?

LETITIA: They go mad.

ALLISON: Do you win?

LETITIA: No, they never let you have the ball. When they touch [the ball] they won't let us have a penalty or anything or a handball. Right, they tell us what to do, what goal we've got to score in. They tell us all these things, you know, the ins and outs.

ALLISON: And what do the boys say when they get beaten by the girls' team?

BIDDY: They go, that ain't fair or that's cheating, 'cos when we get ten and they get eight.

ALLISON: Why do they say you're cheating?

BIDDY: 'Cos we can do it. And when they're cheating they say they're not.

In this way, while Bulldog temporarily dissolved gender differences between boys and girls, the girls' participation in football merely served to reinforce gender roles and to add to disharmony between them.

Why, then, did the girls insist on being allowed to play? Possibly, through challenging the boys' domination of physical space, the girls were symbolically challenging the stereotype of the dominant male; possibly, changing gender roles in the adult world had filtered down to shape the girls' demands. What is more certain, however, is that the girls delighted in their successful intrusion into the boys' sphere and enjoyed their newly acquired and sanctioned freedom to race around the playground.

The boys, by contrast, never asked to join the girls in their games:

ALLISON: And so, do they ever want to play your games?

LETITIA: (to Abby) I don't know really. They don't do they? Some boys like playing, they must be sissy or something.

ALLISON: Do you let them, or do they sometimes decide to play on their own?

LETITIA: They are a bit of a copy-cat, boys. Say, like we're playing a game and they like it, they won't play with us but they'll start playing another one with the boys . . . Like Time Bomb. [a ball game]

Although the girls could not explain why it was that the boys did not join in girls' games, the difference can be accounted for in terms of the disparate conceptualisations of gender identities which are mediated through children's present social relations.

Playing games entails developing particular and effective play-skills to avoid being stigmatised as a loser, an outsider or as being seen as simply odd and different. Through skilful performances children can gain reputations as powerful persons, people who are able to manipulate both games and players to their own advantage. With respect to gender identity, the same skills are necessary. For boys this means manipulating the important signifiers of masculinity – 'toughness' and 'physical prowess' – in the process of play; for girls it means demonstrating through play the nurturing skills of wives, mothers and managers. But, as suggested, knowledge of gender roles is unequal. Boys' games give boys few clues about their future roles as men and few opportunities to experiment with any they might have gleaned. Their knowledge about 'being men' is both sparse and precarious, necessitating a continual demonstration and active affirmation of the little information they collectively have. To play girls' games would be a risky move indeed. Not knowing precisely what the future holds, the boys were, consequently, trapped into preserving their present male identities in which they had more confidence. By contrast, the games girls played were often explicitly directed towards their futures as women, providing for them a more certain knowledge of what it means to be female and giving them the chance to add to these traditional games ideas about gender which they had obtained from other sources. Playing in mixed age groups from a young age, the girls learnt from their older caretakers in the playground and, more certain about their own futures, could safely experiment with boys' games as they grew older. Unlike the boys their gender was not at risk.

However, there were limits to how far girls could take such experimentation before they too jeopardised their gendered identities, as occurred for one girl, whose reputation rested on her ability to act like a boy – to fight, cheat and run fast. Because of her fiercely competitive stance and her vehement, sometimes violent, refusal to accept the rules of the game, she was given 'lives' in Bulldog or Tig and allowed to escape the power of touch. But in her monopoly of both male and female games and styles of performance her social identity, derived from belonging to the group of children, was far from secure. This she registered in frequent outbursts of temper and tears, in accusations levelled against other girls and in broken friend-ships. Endeavouring to break out of the stereotypes of gender she encountered – to literally beat the boys at their own game – she effectively sacrificed the safety of her social position among the girls. Often, therefore, it was through more bullying tactics that she tried to maintain the appearance, if not the status, of being a popular girl.

This chapter has raised a number of questions. First, do the different temporal orientations of the games played by boys and girls confirm the growing documentary evidence presented in previous chapters that 'childhood' is dominated by boys? Second, do girls, as keepers and transmitters of the traditional lore and language of childhood, playing more often than boys in mixed age groups, actually contribute to their own social marginalisation and muteness (Ardener, 1975) through the perpetuation of gender stereotypes which many girls later resent and which anti-sexist education is endeavouring to erad-icate? Grugeon (1988), for example, has suggested that boys may feel excluded by the girls, as they watch their play or catch their own names being whispered by the girls in secret chants. This Grugeon sees as empowering for girls. In one sense this is certainly true, for, as shown, boys dare not risk participating in girls' games and therefore never develop a comparable expertise in the lore and language of childhood (Opies, [1959], 1977). But, in another sense, the girls' monopoly of this traditional lore may also work to disempower them. Despite their exclusion from this childhood knowledge, the boys' physical and aural domination of playground activity enables them publicly to belittle what girls do. Moreover, the very visibility and audibility of boys' games – running, jumping, fighting, kicking, pushing, shoving – serves to symbolise children's play more generally. It is what adults observe and come to expect of playgrounds, of the context where boys will be boys. Indeed, it is precisely this kind of activity which makes boys 'real' boys. What makes girls girls is, as Walkerdine (1985b) has argued, their silent obedience and sensible behaviour. Unnoticed on the boundaries of the playground, therefore, girls skip and clap out their time until adulthood or learn to care for the little ones in the playground. The discourses of romantic love and stereotypical gender roles which permeate the games girls teach one another, therefore, act as a conservative force on girls' more public aspirations. As each childhood generation passes its knowledge to the next, the stereotypes of what it means to be female remain potentially unchallenged.

Notes

1. A 'dip' is a counting out rhyme which children often use at the start of a game to decide who will be 'it'. Alternatively, it is used to decide who will be included, if too many children want to play. In seeming to allow fate and chance to decide, children see 'dips' as fair. However, children also know how to manipulate the counting out to ensure desirable outcomes, as described later in this chapter.
2. Hilltop School was very keen to eradicate gender differences between girls and boys, in terms of their activities and school experiences (see later in the chapter). Despite this the children themselves used gender as a differentiating factor at school.
3. Biology may not itself prescribe gender as Brigg's (1982, 1986) work on Inuit childhood has shown.
4. In a lesson about India, six and seven-year-old boys similarly avidly dressed up in the sari costumes provided. As a legitimated activity it was not seen by them as threatening, but rather as fun, a good laugh.

SEVEN

Friends and Acquaintances

Defining Friendship

The complex and often volatile, patterning of children's interpersonal relationships described through this volume has revealed a kaleidoscope of subjective reflections about the Self
and Other by which means social identities are created and
enhanced, devalued or destroyed during childhood. For any
particular child, participation in this tangled web of social relationships helps shape the identity and sense of Self which is
assumed as s/he moves towards adulthood to become a person
in society. But, although in this sense the socialised child may
in adult life bear eventual witness to its orbit and effectiveness,
the actual process of socialisation can only ever be but haltingly
documented. Preceding chapters have separated out some of
the varied aspects of this passage to personhood for children
in British society as, through a series of unfolding cameos, the
dynamics and import of children's social relationships with
one another have been gradually teased out.

   An implicit but repetitive theme running through this depiction of children's social lives, and their own commentaries
upon them, has been the impact which different modes of
behaviour, styles of interaction and personal presentation can
have upon friendship choices and patterns. One implication
to be drawn from this, then, is that children's experience of
both having and being friends plays a critical part in their
acquisition of social identity and Selfhood. A second conclusion
is that the experience of friendship is pivotal in engendering
a sense of belonging. Those children who find difficulty in
making friends risk becoming socially marginalised in the everyday companionship of the class-room and playground; conversely, as I have already shown, children who overstep the
limits of sociability or who are considered to be significantly
different in some way, may easily find themselves without
friends. While for eight-year-old Christian, wandering alone

around the playground seemed outwardly to pose few problems for him, other children found such a public revelation of their social isolation less easy to manage. Clinging to the teacher's hand at playtime, hovering on the edge of other groups of playing children or climbing on the apparatus, they could be appear to be alongside, if not belong to, the friendship groups of other children (Putallaz and Gottman, 1981). That children themselves readily acknowledge the importance of the social relation friendship is indicated in their considerable and early fluency with the terminology of friendship relations. At Hilltop School, although articulated only occasionally at four years old, the words 'friend', 'best friend', 'like' and 'hate' very quickly began to pepper children's conversations as their social experience broadened on entering school. Such words become useful to differentiate between individuals in a range of social encounters: she is my friend, Johnny likes me, I don't like him and so on. In this way, by nine or ten years old, being and having friends had become a central feature of children's social relationships: anxieties about changing school were exacerbated by the future absence of friends or assuaged by knowledge of their continued presence and the threat of the withdrawal of friendship was used as a powerful social sanction to influence or curb a friend's behaviour.

However, children's seeming verbal and practical competence with the interpersonal relations involved in friendship is, at the same time, apparently belied by the frailty of those relations. Frequent squabbles, arguments and 'fallings out' pattern many young children's friendships leading Bigelow and La Gaipa to observe that 'stability is not very characteristic of children's friendship's until about 16 years of age' (1980: 38). This makes these disagreements seem tiresome to adults for, if the relations were truly those of friendship, should they not weather differences of opinion and changing moods? Drawing on the cultural ideal of 'real' friendship (Allan, 1989) adults may trivialise or irritably discount the rupture of a relationship, brushing aside the tears, in the knowledge that the next day will most likely see a restoration of that friendship relation. At the same time, and somewhat paradoxically, the very instability of children's friendships creates anxiety in the adult world about children's happiness and well-being. It is, for example, this concern which has contextualised the considerable psychological research undertaken to discover factors which help or hinder popularity and marginality in children's social relations (Putallaz and Gottman, 1981) and which underpins much contemporary interest in research into bullying (Tattum and Lane, 1989).

The paradox which surrounds such adult judgements about the pattern and quality of children's friendships stems, I suggest, from the assumption that children's friendships are characterised by the same forms of intimacy, trust and mutuality which are held ideally to shape adult friendships in Western cultures (Allan, 1989). But is such a concept of 'friendship' a natural, unvarying, instinctual aspect of all human relations, fundamental to human sociality? Or is it as Paine (1974) has argued, culturally specific, being of and about particular social worlds?

Against the background of these broader issues about the nature of friendship this chapter focuses on two specific questions. First, what forms do children's friendships take and what meanings do children attribute to a range of affective relationships with one another? Second, through looking at gendered friendship, this chapter asks what import these bonds of affection have in children's everyday social relations? That is to say, is the concept of friendship as a shared, intimate and voluntary relation an appropriate framework within which to explore and understand the affective relationships of children of all ages? Or does the cultural specificity of this friendship relation mean that children only gradually and falteringly learn to participate in its subtle complexities as they slowly come to an understanding of its precise semantic range? Thus, if children have to learn to take on and participate in culturally specific friendship relations, might not this explain the seemingly brittle nature of their early attempts at making friends?

The following two conversations between children of different ages are suggestive of the wide rather than narrow range of meanings which children attribute to the concept of friendship. They indicate, too, the importance of contextualising those meanings, for although in both extracts the word 'friend' is used grammatically by the children, there is considerable semantic slippage between the two accounts. Moreover, the different discourses within which the term 'friend' appears are framed by quite disparate emotions and attitudes, which alter the contextual meaning of the apparently simple term, friend. In the first conversation, three four-year-old boys are talking together in the class-room:

ROGER: Are you my friend?

TONY: Yes.

ROGER: You can come to my party. (pause)

ROGER: Are you my friend?

SAUL: No.

ROGER: I'll punch you up the face.

This conversational exchange is brief and to the point. A series of short, direct questions and replies appear satisfactorily to define, for these four-year-old boys, what friendship is about. Essentially, it is an exchange relationship. Forthright in the extreme, friendship is presented as involving a direct trading of favours. Any emotional investment is at a minimum. Only Roger's reaction to Saul's refusal to classify him as a friend – his threatened punch – suggests that the boys might be beginning to recognise friendship as being a more shared and participative relationship, rather than one involving mere functional exchange.

By nine years old, however, 'friendship' seems to have become a far more complex social relation. In stark contrast to the small boys' unambiguous conversation, Emily confided to me that her close involvement with another girl was marred by a constant and emotionally charged ambivalence. In the following extract, therefore, friendship is not depicted as a relationship which can be quickly and unambiguously established by bestowing favours or offering threats. Nor yet is it simply an exchange relationship. The boundaries to friendship are uncertain, unleashing a range of emotions which are difficult to gauge and with an uncontrollable internal dynamic:

When she [her friend] don't like somebody and you like them she says, 'Well, do you like her?' and I goes, 'Yes' and she goes, 'Well, I don't like you then.' And I says, 'Well, you can't be much of a friend because friends are supposed to like people all the time.'

I shall have cause to return to these brief snatches of conversation. It suffices at the moment, however, to note the very different meanings of friendship which they present. The subtlety of the emotional ties of friendship described by the girl are entirely absent from the boys' conversation. While in this instance the contrast can undoubtedly be attributed to differences in both age and gender between the children, this chapter will explore other factors which also shape the pattern and course of children's friendships. In doing so, it will show that *affective* friendship relations are primarily cultural relations, which are socially and contextually acquired over time as children develop their *effective* participation in the culture of childhood.

Words and Meanings

Clearly, the cultural construction of friendship as a channel for affective relationships between people makes its study problematic (Allan, 1989). What one definition is it possible to use when, even within cultures, the concept may become slippery and ill-defined, shifting between social encounters and social spaces? Paine (1974) identifies two main approaches which, from within anthropology, have attempted to deal with this problem. The first of these explores the 'moral' qualities of affective relationships, contenting itself with identifying types of friendship. In this tradition distinctions are drawn between friendship which is inalienable and 'true' and relationships of a more expedient kind. The second avenue of research concentrates on the social functions which friendship has in particular societies. Work within this sphere enquires whether and in what ways the social relation – 'friendship' – differs in its social role and practical outcomes. For instance, although the universal need for affectivity in human relationships might have been established (Leyton, 1974), the extent to which this 'need' can be said to be satisfied through 'friendship' rather than other types of social relationships varies considerably. Indeed, Paine (1974) sees the Western ideal of friendship as a unique vehicle for the affections and a very particular kind of interpersonal relationship, amounting to a 'sociological "luxury"' ill-afforded in many other cultures (1974: 127). In non-Western contexts the sentiments associated with friendship may be overlaid on to or combined with other kinds of social, political or economic relations through kinship or clientship. What is required, therefore, is a re-conceptualisation of the study of friendship which, through combining both strands of enquiry, might seek out the 'ploys and strategies' people actually use in their encounters with one another (1974: 13). The understanding of children's friendships presented here embraces such a perspective.

One way in which affectivity is culturally 'managed', for example, is through the symbolic power of language which metaphorically moves people between classificatory domains.

Thus, although feelings of friendship are universal 'between whom such sentiments may exist cannot be designated . . . [for] . . . the term friend is, in many languages, non-existent or indistinguishable from kinsman' (Schwimmer, 1974: 49) In the close-knit society of the Tangu in Oceania the kinship system forms the basis for all social, economic and political alliances. This means that, although friendships *are* made between non-related people, the terms used to describe such relationships are necessarily drawn from the kinship system. What distinguishes these relations as those of friendship is that such classificatory kin remain free from the obligations and constraints imposed on 'real' kin. While affections are therefore in practice exchanged outside the kinship system, their expression is articulated within its terms (Schwimmer, 1974). The New Zealand Maori traditionally used a similar device to incorporate affective relations within the orbit of the kinship system. Prior to any form of social intimacy, kinship links would be established which meant, in effect, that the Maori had no friends who were not also kin. The existence of an extensive genealogical record among the Maori, extending ambilaterally over twenty generations, meant that in practice the number of possible friendships was limitless (Schwimmer, 1974).

Besides exemplifying the role which social classification plays in friendship designation, the New Zealand Maori provide another significant point of comparison. Although traditionally they had no separate category of 'friend' – all friends were also kin – affective friendly relations between non-kin were acknowledged by the term *hoa*. Roughly translated as mate or friend it was a reciprocal term used to express an 'unrestrained, warm, affectionate, co-operative, equal, personal and private relationship' (Schwimmer, 1974: 52). Does the logic of this inconsistency mean that, in effect, although the Maori did not *have* friends, they could nevertheless *be* friends? Such a distinction is instructive. It highlights the necessity of documenting the process and experience of friendship as well as its more mundane classificatory function, a feature crucial to understanding children's friendships. Comparative material suggests, therefore, that any analysis of friendship must take account of its 'idioms of discourse' (Schwimmer, 1974: 53). The Western experience of friendship as a relation which binds people to one another through simple bonds of affection is clearly just one form. Indeed, this may account for the potential fragility of Western friendship: as a voluntary, (rather than obligatory), a personal (rather than public) relationship, friendship in Western cultures is both unpredictable and terminal (Paine, 1974). Unlike cultures where bonds of affection are linked with or expressed in terms of kinship systems, Western friendship has no explicit external framing, no pattern of ritual obligations to shape and sustains its course. Enjoined in the spirit of mutuality, trust and intimacy, it is potentially an exceedingly strong and exceedingly brittle interpersonal relationship.

However, even in Western cultures on a day-to-day basis friendship relationships may be experienced as more prosaic encounters (Allan, 1989). They may be engendered by shared interests, through physical propinquity or daily association. These differences are shaded in through the levels of intimacy and range of affection expressed in the English terms, 'pal', 'mate', 'chum', 'crony', 'companion', 'acquaintance', 'buddy' and 'friend'. But how are these terms realised in practice? How do we judge, for example, which 'friends' to invite to dinner and which to ask for drinks? (Douglas, 1975).

In seeking to find out what differences make a difference in children's friendships (Bateson, 1973), their culturally specific nature must be attended to. This chapter will follow three broad lines of enquiry which, although not leading unambiguously to a definition of friendship, will enable the patterning of relationships between children to be traced out and some of the meanings which they attribute to these relationships to be identified. First, because the words spoken about friendship can as easily obfuscate as illuminate social meanings, the different contexts of their utterance will be explored. Second, the ways in which children use the terms of friendship to classify and limit the boundaries of affection and significance will be documented and situated in the flow of their interpersonal relations, for it is through these encounters that the meanings of friendship emerge. Third, the quality and temper of these interactions will be traced out over time, to chart the changing obligations and orbit of children's friendships.

The two conversations cited earlier have already shown the considerable explanatory power unleashed by adopting such an approach. It is, for example, possible to see that the social experience gained by nine-year-old Emily has enabled her to flesh out the skeletal form of the concept of friendship held by the four-year-old boys for whom the term 'friend' is relatively unambiguous. It is used as a rudimentary conceptual tool to negotiate social encounters through a process of simple binary classification: friend or foe. But by nine and ten years old the experiential quality of social encounters, which draws on and contrasts with those in the past and the future, has transformed that act of classification into a complex and exceedingly emotional process of negotiation.

However, this is not to suggest that time alone is the key to change. Nor does it imply that children's friendships progress naturally and uneventfully from a simple to a more complex form. Such a perspective would, again, involve making value judgements about the quality of children's friendships – that they are not as 'good' or 'stable' as adult friendships – or lead to the establishment of a developmental model showing a unilinear progression from child to adult types of friendship relationships (Bigelow and La Gaipa, 1980). This would simply bring the argument back full circle through drawing implicitly on some notion of 'true' or 'real' friendship. It would shed little light on the social significance which friendship has in children's contemporary social relationships nor on how that significance changes over time. For these reasons, therefore, I shall not attempt to predefine what children's friendships are. I shall be content to let this emerge through descriptions of how those encounters, which children themselves define as about being and having friends, actually take place. That is to say, I shall explore friendship in and through its performance. Adopting such a strategy not only works from children's own understandings of the nature of friendship (and is therefore reflective of those understandings at any point in time), but also effectively mirrors the way in which children gradually learn the different shades of meanings which friendship can have in the context of contemporary British society.

Having and Being Friends

For some children friendship is a matter of sheer expediency, a consequence of their shared isolation or social exclusion from the main body of children. It is a muted expression of solidarity, arising out of a common experience of being identified by other children as in some way 'significantly different' (see Chapter 2). As other research has indicated, while such children may team up to play together – so that in the public demonstration of sociality which playtime represents they do not wander around alone – this visible togetherness signifies little about the quality of their relationship (Gottlieb and Leyser, 1981; Putallaz and Gottman, 1981). Is it one involving trust and intimacy, or simply one of association? At the other extreme, friendship may be characterised by considerable emotional investment and expression of commitment. To understand these different kinds of friendship entails careful detailing of the contexts which distinguish the experience of being friends from that of having friends.

It is clear, for instance, that parents often exert influence over young children's friendships, encouraging their son or daughter to invite one child, rather than another, home for tea. Similarly, a pre-established friendship between mothers may, over time, encourage the development of friendship between their children. Thus, while six-year-old Annie and Phoebe denied that they liked boys, Annie admitted to me that she was fond of Ewan because '[her] Mum likes his Mum.' More deliberate structuring of interactions between particular children may occur at school. The staff of Hilltop School, for example, judged one six-year-old girl to be becoming too dependent upon another and, in the yearly reshuffle, she was purposefully separated from her soul-mate. For the next year the girls were to be in different classes, a move made to encourage their self-reliance. In the same way, the disruption and distress caused by personality clashes and conflict between particular children was reduced by physically separating them.[1] In this sense, then, sheer propinquity and patterns of daily interaction in the class-room may, like the behavioural and social factors identified in earlier chapters, help shape the overall composition of children's friendship groups. Indeed, this may partly account for the close correspondence which is often found between class-room seating plans and the patterning of children's friendships (see Chapter 5).

However, the quality of those experiences of friendship are less easy to assess. In her analysis of young children's conversations, Garvey comments, for example, that 'playing together, avoiding serious fights and sharing things and activities . . . is a definition of friendship that a pre-schooler will give, if asked' (1984: 171). During my own fieldwork experience, such explicit and abstract reflection on the nature of friendship was far more common among older children. Younger children rarely volunteered definitions of this or any other social relationship.

Instead, I was left to tease out their understanding of the nature of friendship from the ways in which they employed its terminology, from passing comments and through observation of encounters between children. Non-verbal cues might reveal their affection for one another: a reciprocated smile, a look of distress, a thump or cunning pinch, holding hands, playing side by side, approaching or walking away from a group of children. Some of the principles of friendship – kindness and reciprocity, for example – could be seen as nascent in these encounters, as Garvey notes. But, for the children themselves, I suspect that these remained largely implicit and unacknowledged as frames of reference, for it seemed that many of the four-year-old children were more concerned about their status as someone who has friends rather than the experience of being friends. Indeed, as I shall show, the one logically precedes the other.

In the nursery class, which I joined when the children had been playing and learning alongside one another for nearly nine months, the term 'friend' could be frequently heard. To the casual listener it might have seemed, therefore, that friendships were already clearly established among the group. However, closer attention to the structure of the children's conversations would have revealed that the term 'friend' was most often used in interrogative statements. In this sense, questions, rather than certainties, about the nature of friendship were being raised: 'Are you my friend?' or ' You're my friend, aren't you?' More rarely, positive and negative declarations might be made: 'I'm your friend'; 'I'm not your friend.' More rarely still, a child might make a pronouncement about a third party: 'Josephine is my friend.' But what meanings were children attributing to this word? What did they understand when hearing and using it and what were the social consequences of its usage?

A first interpretation might be that four-year-old children employ the term 'friend' simply as a classificatory tool. However, this categorical placement of one child as a 'friend' of another may be temporary rather than permanent. It may only last for a few moments, the time it takes to walk the length of a room together; it may last for the duration of a game, or for a morning, a day, a week. In this sense, the term 'friend' cannot be said to denote necessarily any continuity of affection or the desirability of mutual affiliation when used by four-year-old children. What its usage appears to do instead is to register the current social positioning of Others relative to the Self.

'Are you my friend?' and 'You're my friend, aren't you?', were two typical opening gambits to a sequence of interactions between children (Corsaro, 1979). These questions were often asked by four and five-year-old children shortly after mutual play had been initiated. But, although the question is ostensibly about the placing of the Other – you – in practice, its concerns are focused upon 'I'. Have 'I' got any friends? Is this person my friend? In this sense, 'having a friend' can be said to presage a child's own status and identity of 'being a friend'. This latter experience involves a far more complex process of interaction and engagement with others, as I shall discuss later. Hence, when Peter asked Robin, 'Are you my friend?', he was, in effect, asking Robin to confirm that he – Peter – had a friend, that he – Peter – was socially acceptable to be or to become a friend. Such examples confirm Paine's (1974) tentative suggestion that friendship in Western cultures may consist more of 'the act of finding a hand which will clasp one's own' rather than, as is more commonly assumed, 'the act of proferring the outstretched hand' (1974: 119). As such it is a process of classifying the Self rather than the Other, more a seeking out of personal identity than of reciprocal relations.

But how to identify when the hand is there? Garvey suggests that among young children the 'term friend usually refers to what they conceive of as friendly behaviour' (1984: 171). The converse is also true: children may reject as friends those whose behaviour is interpreted and classified as unfriendly. Again, careful detailing of the contexts in which children use the term 'friend' shows the ways in which children begin conceptually to fill in its various shades of meaning. Interpreting encounters as 'friendly' rather than 'hostile' is the first step as a field-note observes:

> Toby and Joel are seated side by side doing jigsaws at a table. They do not regularly associate with one another. After a while Toby looks up and says to Joel: 'Let's go down the bottom.' He means to the 'messy' end of the room where the painting and water activities are. Joel looks pleased, smiles and says: 'Yeah . . . we're friends, aren't we?'

Toby interprets Joel's invitation to move elsewhere as a sign of his own acceptability. He asks Joel to confirm that he – Toby –

has a friend and is therefore to be categorised as someone's friend. But the phrasing of his question – 'aren't we?' – also hints at his awareness that reciprocation is a feature of 'being friends'. He knows that this condition must also be satisfied before the self-referential statement – 'Toby is my friend' – can be made. Although of but brief duration – the time it took to walk the length of the room – through this encounter the boys were beginning to piece together a workable concept of friendship. As Fine observes, 'children learn through the response of others that their behaviours have consequences' (1981: 32).

Among younger children particularly, friendship may therefore be quite dynamic and fluid, with allegiances changing swiftly during the course of short interactions. Through implicit comparison with a model of stable and enduring adult friendship, this patterning of social relations inevitably leads to pathological interpretations of children's interpersonal relations. There is an unarticulated yet clear feeling that 'it would be somehow "better" if children did not change friends so often' (Bigelow and La Gaipa, 1980: 39). However, such worries seem to impinge little on four-year-old children's conception of friendship; only later does durability begin to assume significance as a feature. In the following conversation, for example, Saul's expressed anxiety is less about the possible termination of a friendship – the breakdown of some reciprocal kind of relationship, being friends – than a concern about his own changed social status and, hence, his personhood, *vis-à-vis* another child: has he a friend or not?

> (Piers and Saul are playing with some cars and the garage. After a while they begin to argue and Piers hits Saul.)
>
> PIERS: (anxiously to Saul) Are you my friend now? (They continue to play. A while later Barbara approaches the boys and starts to play with the garage. Saul removes her car.)
>
> BARBARA: Get off, that's my car.
>
> SAUL: (to Piers) We're not her friend, are you?
>
> (Piers does not reply. Piers and Barbara whisper together.)
>
> SAUL: (more urgently) Why aren't you my friend, Piers?
>
> PIERS: Shut up.
>
> SAUL: (casually and invitingly) I'm going out to play.
>
> PIERS: We ain't.

(Saul remains sitting sulkily in his chair.)

BARBARA: (to Saul) We're not your friend.

SAUL: Why aren't you my friend, Piers?

(Piers and Saul punch one another.)

BARBARA: Let's go outside.

(They leave Saul sitting in the chair.)

Loyalties and affections change abruptly in this scene. Piers, after his initial antisocial act (hitting Saul), receives no confirmation that Saul remains his friend. Later, acting from this premise, he teams up with Barbara and, friends together now, they leave Saul on his own. Saul, who presumably dislikes being hit, refuses to affirm his friendship with Piers instantly and only later realises his error of judgement when Barbara arrives. He tries to prevent her intrusion into his friendship with Piers by taking away her car. Her stout retaliation is unnerving. It prompts Saul to try to re-establish his former intimacy with Piers more urgently. This can be seen in his somewhat peculiar statement-cum-question: 'We're not her friend, are you?' In using the plural pronoun 'we' Saul risks his identity by clearly aligning himself with Piers and in rejecting Barbara as a friend. But in adding the question, 'are you?' Saul shows, at the same time, an awareness that his overtures of friendship with Piers might be rejected. The ensuing interactions hinge on this statement; in the event, Saul is left to interpret the whispering between Piers and Barbara that follows as a sign that his friendship with Piers is over. Having risked rebuttal there is nothing left to lose: Saul asks Piers directly why their friendship is over and, in the silences which follow, makes a last-ditch attempt to win back his 'friend'. When Piers fails to follow him out to play, Saul is at a loss. His final classification is as a 'non-friend', for this moment in time is firmly established by Barbara and Piers' exit from the classroom. Later that day Piers and Saul are again to be seen playing happily together in the sandpit.

The examples given so far reveal children seeking knowledge of their own classification and socially positioned identity within the body of children. They confirm that 'being a friend' means first, 'having friends'. Thus it is that on contemplating their move to a distant middle school, older children spoke first to me of their concern that they would not have any friends, before regretting the loss of particular friendships.

But in the nursery at Hilltop School some children did appear more certain about their position *vis-à-vis* others. They had begun to participate in the durable relationships – the being friends – more characteristic of older children (Bigelow and La Gaipa, 1980). Particular clusterings and pairings of children became evident as the children moved freely between activities in the nursery class-room, and these children made different statements about friendship. More certain of their own position, they ventured comments and opinions about other children's social standing. Thus, one day Ruth who always played with Elspeth asked Timmy: 'Is Joseph still your friend?' Through the inclusion of the adverb 'still' she acknowledged that, for her, durability was already an important feature of friendship relationships. The existence of this more subtle understanding of the nature of friendship, alongside the use of the term 'friend' as a rudimentary classificatory tool in the same class of four-year-olds, is why developmental models of friendship tied to chronological age are ultimately unsatisfactory. It is social experience, rather than simply time passing, which is the more critical. It is this which permits the acquisition of the necessary social skills to be able to make and keep friends.

The qualitative, rather than classificatory, aspects of the term friend were beginning to be grasped by some four-year-old children. Thus, although 'liking someone' (the affective relations of friendship) was rarely distinguished from 'being friends with someone' and was less commonly used, opinions were none the less sometimes expressed about another's sociality in relation to the boundaries of friendship (see Chapter 5).

(Conrad comes to tell me something).

CONRAD: Arthur's not my friend any more. He snatched the scooter.

This example indicates that the sanctioning power of friendship characteristic of older children's relations, although as yet rarely used, was nevertheless employed by some children. Thus, Jimmy told me that: 'Oliver's not my friend 'cos he follows me around,' and Tommy described how: 'Piers fighted me when he wasn't my friend.' In the nursery class I rarely heard four-year-old children ask the question, 'Do you like me?' or say of another 'I don't like him.' And on only one occasion did a child use the word 'hate' about another. Instead, what might be regarded as dislike – an affective relation of friendship – was more probably simply expressed as indifference, and expediently effected: four-year-old children would simply ignore one another's presence. The following exchange between three four-year-olds struck me, therefore, as being relatively unusual in its discussion of affectivity:

CONRAD: Danny, you like me, don't you?
NEIL: Do you like Adam?
CONRAD: (to Danny) I like Neil and you.
NEIL: (to Conrad) I saw you in my van.
CONRAD: (smiles and looks pleased: Yeah, you saw me.

Here Conrad, who frequently tried to assess his relative social standing, once again anxiously endeavours to check up on his identity and personhood. Danny is refusing to answer, so Conrad, rather bravely, shows his own hand by unilaterally declaring that he likes both him and Neil. But – and Conrad is surprised – it is Neil and not Danny who responds warmly to this declaration, showing a willingness to be friends by mentioning that he saw Conrad in the street. Conrad is well-pleased at this memory; it proves to him that he has a recognised social identity, a recognisable personhood: 'Yeah, you saw me' he says proudly.

This extract introduces another theme in children's friendships: its performative aspect. Friendship is not simply a cognitive relationship of affectivity. It must be affirmed, confirmed and reaffirmed through social action. This explains how the emphasis upon 'sameness' and conformity in children's social relationships – wearing the same clothes, eating the same food, liking the same football teams – works to mitigate the significance which any differences might have. It represents one visible demonstration of friendship, for it is through such public performances that children evaluate and acknowledge their friendships with one another: being friends must not only be experienced but be seen to be experienced. Through their everyday social interactions with one another children discover the boundaries to friendship and the degree of commitment which particular relationships entail. It is a process of fine-tuning affective relationships which are publicly acted out between children.

However, the style of these performances varies in relation to age. As children grow older, the meanings which they attach to friendship, and the expectations they have of its dramatic enactment, begin to change. Some of the ways in which this occurs I have already alluded to but, as I have also insisted, this does not therefore mean that chronological age has an invariant impact. While there are a number of different stages

through which friendship logically progresses, types of friendship are not contingent on age. Thus, although it has been
argued that only at eight years old can children cognitively
empathise with others, (which means that prior to this age,
mutuality in friendship may not be possible), a simple hierarch-
ical development model of friendship cannot be sustained
(Bigelow and La Gaipa, 1980). There may be a considerable
blurring of the categories of 'friend' and any individual child
might be at different stages of friendship with different people.
It is therefore through its discrete performance that children
learn about and experience friendship, which means that the
social contexts in which children find themselves, not simply
their age, play the greater part in shaping children's understanding of the concept. Thus, on reflection, nine-year-old
Bobby and Samuel were able to classify their past association
in previous years as friendship. From the perspective of their
present experience of companionship, durability was now
understood by them to be an important feature:

ALLISON: So you two are best friends. Have you always
been?
SAMUEL: We started being friends in the second –
BOBBY: No, it was in the third year.
ALLISON: So you've been friends for two years?
SAMUEL: And he had another friend but he's moved away
now.

Thus, while chronological age may minimally shape a general
path along which concepts of friendship develop, there may
be considerable variation in the meanings which friendship
has. As Bigelow and La Gaipa noted, 'Little is known as yet
about what children expect from their friends, how these expectations change over time and the impact of such social
cognition on friendship choice' (1981: 15).

Naming Names: the Performance of Friendship

The classificatory processes, so characteristic of young children's friendships, is fundamental to all social relations.
Through its application, 'them' are distinguished from 'us'
and a place for 'me' is established in a 'we' relationship. Children, as Fine notes, do not develop a 'conception of Self (or I)
until after a conception of others has been acquired' (1981:
31–2). And, as children begin to appreciate the significance of
such boundaries, this social positioning of the Self relative to

Others through friendship designation becomes increasingly sophisticated. The symbolic power invested in naming or being named as a friend starts to give shape and substance to children's social encounters. In earlier chapters I showed how insulting nicknames can work to exclude or marginalise particular children, something which in later childhood works as an extraordinarily powerful classificatory device (see James, 1979; Morgan, O'Neill and Harre, 1979). But among young children, simply naming ordinary names has this potential. Through the act of naming, labels can be applied and individuals picked out. When children warn, 'I'll tell of you', the potency of the threat lies in the implied intention to inform on one another by naming names to a higher and adult authority. With such a warning miscreants soon learn to change their tactics.

The symbolic power invested in names has, however, been relatively unexplored by those researching children's friendships and social relations, an omission all the more surprising given that this work has at its core the naming of names. Since the 1930s, under the general rubric of 'sociometry', many different techniques have been developed for assessing children's social relationships. Through plotting children's friendships these purport to map out peer-group interactions and alliances. From the resultant network diagrams, assessments are made about the relative popularity of individual children and conclusions drawn about children's relations with one another. Data collection is usually carried out by asking each child in a class to nominate either their best friend or, alternatively, to name four or five friends. These are then aggregated and the results plotted diagrammatically to reveal relations of affectivity and clusters of popularity.

Such techniques have not been without their critics, from both a theoretical and practical viewpoint (Hallinan, 1981). Mannarino (1980), for example, questions whether it is friendship or popularity that sociometric tests reveal. The two, he suggests, are not equivalent, for friendship, unlike popularity, should include some degree of mutual affection. Few sociometric techniques test for the reciprocation of nominations and, as Mannarino writes, 'children may create the illusion that their positive feelings are reciprocated but this perception may have no basis in reality' (1980: 46). On a methodological point, it has also been suggested that many sociometric techniques have inbuilt assumptions about children's range of friendship; asking a child to list four or five friends limits their friendship nominations and, effectively, makes the rest of the class members fall into a category of non-friends (Foot, Chapman and Smith, 1980). In everyday life this may not be the case; children may simply be indifferent to these others or, indeed, may have wished to include them as friends (Denscombe et al., 1986; Thirkell and Worall, 1989). In this respect Hallinan notes that the actual form of many sociometric techniques exclude the possibility of certain outcomes:

> Most social scientists have considerable difficulty obtaining data on negative affect because authorities – especially school personnel – are reluctant to have questions asked that might elicit unfriendly or hostile feelings. (1981: 101)

A further methodological problem is that children may have friends who are not in their class, or their school, or indeed have friends who are not children. My own fleeting use of sociometric tests, discussed below, revealed for example that when restrictions are not placed on the number of names a child can give, some children listed an extremely wide range of people. These included children attending different schools with whom they played at home, siblings, cousins and teachers. On one occasion my own name was included in a child's list. For these children, then, what does friendship mean?

Such criticisms are instructive in revealing the model of adult friendship which implicitly frames many sociometric techniques and which assumes that children's expectations of friendship are built upon similar foundations. As already noted this is not the case. This is especially so among younger children who are just beginning to understand what such a relationship might possibly entail. Thus, for instance, children who may be quite socially acceptable to others, may not feature centrally in the resultant sociograms. But this omission should not necessarily be taken as a sign of social isolation nor yet of a distressing social experience. Conversely, the inclusion of a child's name on a sociogram may be equally misleading for, as Mannarino writes, 'in no way . . . does a child's level of peer group accept-ance suggest anything about his [sic] personal intimacy with other children, his [sic] age or his [sic] capacity to form and maintain close friendships' (1980: 47).

Merely using the naming of names as a technique for assessing children's friendships would seem, then, to yield at best only a bare indication of the patterning of social relations and, at worst, a distortion of those patterns. More recent commentators recommend their use only alongside ethnographic research methods, a suggestion which this research endorses (Denscombe et al., 1986). By using a variant of sociometric techniques I added very little to my knowledge of the children's friendship patterns, previously gathered through participant observation. And my own knowledge was certainly far less than that of their class-room teachers: the already acknowledged popular children were readily nominated and those known by the staff to be socially isolated, as expected, did not appear on the plotted map of social relations. Particular clusterings and dyadic pairs were simply graphically confirmed. However, what the experience did alert me to was the power which the naming of names can have. This became glaringly apparent as I tried out a number of different techniques.

While working with six and seven-year-old children I made each of them a small booklet containing four sentences about friendship. Heeding the critiques of sociometry, these sentences contained no direct reference to friendship but, instead, aimed to establish a general range of personal contacts and associations for each child. There was no limit set to the number of names to be named and the children filled in two sentences at first, completing the task about six weeks later. As Foot et al. (1980) note that 'children's choices of their best friends are at least partially – if not substantially – affected by momentary factors like besides whom they are standing or sitting when they complete the test', I sat with each child as they filled in their books (1980: 3). I gave help, when asked, with the mechanics of writing and through doing so hoped to eliminate some methodological problems: anxiety over spelling names correctly might mean unusual names being omitted; poor writing skills or simply a lack of interest in the task might lead to lists being artificially curtailed. It was while watching and talking with the children, as they wrote names down, that the power that naming names can have was vividly enacted for me.

First, it became apparent that the absence of 'best friends' or durable friendship relations does not necessarily mean that a child is socially isolated. Some of the six and seven-year-old children relied on earlier patterns of interaction established at four or five years old and drifted between groups of friends. For them friendship still had rather temporary associations. The names named by such children often represented those with whom they had played races at playtime or who had held their hand that morning. On another day an entirely different set of names might have been written down and, in their books, the two lists of names, gathered six weeks apart, were often quite different. The children who lacked any firm friendships, by contrast, simply recorded the names of those they found socially acceptable without expressing any particular preference. In this sense the naming of names just continued to classify, to sort out the good from the bad and to identify the children who were skilled in the art of sociality. Field-notes record such a situation:

> Carol seems unsure about what names to put down. Sucking the end of her pencil she looks about the class while she is filling in her book. She finishes and looks at what she has done, appearing satisfied: 'I've got lots of friends,' she says. This seems to come as a pleasant surprise to her. Matthew is also rather vague when it come to his turn. He too constantly looks around the classroom as he thinks of what names to write down.

Both these children were known to the teachers to be often on their own and to lack close friendships. Both, however, obligingly wrote down a list of names for me. For Carol, the result was pleasing. She smiled, although rather quizzically, at the list in front of her. Perhaps the naming of names gave her the sense of belonging which in her daily encounters with other children she did not often experience?

Matthew's list was long and varied, too, and included the most popular boys in his class, his teacher and children from other classes. While being conscious of his own isolation, none the less, the act of naming names to register friendship afforded him a momentary pleasure and was a strategy he tried out on another occasion. While recording a conversation with a group of boys one day, Matthew joined us in our discussion about playtime. Although I and the other boys were unaware of it at the time, Matthew repeatedly makes a bid for friendship through naming the same name at three points in the conversation. The first occurs in context as the boys were telling me whom they liked to play with:

MATTHEW: I like Charles.

Later, breaking into the conversation, Matthew asks me a question:

MATTHEW: Can you tape, I like Charles?

ALLISON: Its taping everything.
Later still Matthew's voice can be heard again in the background
as as he stakes his claim again:
MATTHEW: I like Charles.
The poignancy of this episode only later became apparent
when the tape was transcribed. At the time of recording,
Matthew was desperately seeking a friend in Charles who was
extremely wary of his approaches, a situation which was being
monitored by the teaching staff.

Many six and seven-year-old children had, however, begun
to form quite close relationships with others and these children
did not hesitate to name names. When the sociogram was later
drawn up, these nominations were reciprocal, reflecting the
strong bonds of affection between the children. However, in a
few cases, some nominations stood alone. In these can be seen
the desirability of a future, rather than present, friendship.
Tonia, for example, very quickly wrote down a number of girls'
names, many of which she again listed six weeks later. Not one
of these were, however, reciprocated and, on a day-to-day basis,
Tonia remained on the margins of this particular group of
girls. She was included in their games but not in their affections
(see Figure 7.1). Debbie and Pamela, on the other hand, were
tied firmly into a triadic relationship with Ellie. As a threesome
they often played and sat together but their friendship was
marred by frequent quarrels. It was both a stormy and emotionally tense relationship. Through their naming of names, each
girl revealed her desire to make other friendships outside this

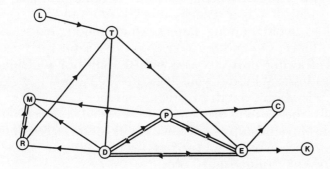

FIGURE 7.1   Tonia (T) receives nominations and makes nominations trying
to join the triadic relationship D–P–E.

difficult triadic relationship in which they were all currently enmeshed (see Figure 7.2). A similar pattern of looking for new friendship can be seen Sid's relationship with Bobby (Figure 7.3).

For the oldest children, those of nine and ten years old, the naming of names took on the greatest significance. For them the act of naming names no longer merely reflected the patterning of everyday social relations but, instead, could be put to the more practical ends of directly manipulating friendships and social interactions. Among the girls, in particular, to name and thereby class as a friend was a strategy they often used to manoeuvre their own position relative to Others within the network of girls. Being friends had become a very complex affair for the girls after just five years at school.

My use of sociometric techniques with one class of nine-year-old children graphically illustrated how such processes are played out in everyday encounters. When asked to name friends and best friends, some members of a dominant group of girls let it be known whose names they had chosen to write down. Those who had been included hurriedly added names to their own lists, while those who had been omitted crossly scribbled out the namers' names. New pieces of paper were requested, rubbers urgently looked for, and hands carefully placed to cover the listed names. Some asked each other directly: 'Did you put me down?', 'Who did you write down?' Answers, knowingly withheld, made the emotional tension run high until one girl devised a solution. She wrote down an acronym based on the letters of all her friends: A.C.L.H.E.N.S. In this manner the whole group of girls metaphorically became one girl, a best friend to all. It was a strategy quickly adopted by others who wished to avoid naming names which might, inadvertently, cause offence. On another occasion, these same girls used the task of drawing portraits as a similar indicator of friendship relationships: 'Why did you draw her?'; 'I drew a picture of Sally,' 'Why didn't you draw a picture of me?'

Finally, the naming of names also revealed children's understanding of friendship as a distinctive kind of social relationship:

ALLISON: You've got two best friends. Who are they?
AUSTIN: Jimmy and Toby.
ALLISON: Jimmy, who's he? Is Toby in this class?
AUSTIN: No...
ALLISON: Is Toby in another class?

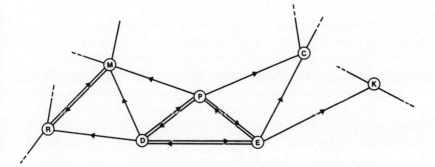

FIGURE 7.2   P–D–E=The triadic network. Each girl seeks other friendships.

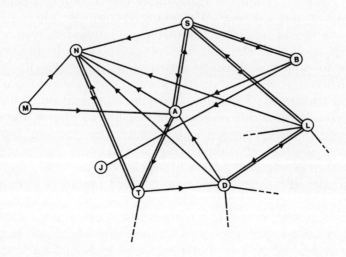

FIGURE 7.3   S–B is a strong dyadic relationship, but linked into other relationships in this large group of boys.

AUSTIN: Yeah, a big one.

FRANK: Toby can't be his mate because he's his cousin.

In this exchange Frank and Austin reveal their knowledge of the different kinds of affectivity which are possible in a Western culture. Cousins may be good companions but they are classified primarily as kin rather than friends, which is what making claims to kinship the ultimate accolade of friendship: older boys may become blood brothers and girls may pretend to be sisters. Twins are in a unique situation for as age-mates in a class they are also bound by kin relations. At Hilltop School I encountered three sets of twins, all of whom listed their twin as being one of their best friends.

Gendered Friends: the Experience of Friendship

The power to include or exclude, to name or not name, to signify friendship or to ignore another is central in children's social relations. Children can control one another's behaviour through issuing a threat – 'I'm telling of you,' – or, alternatively, temporarily terminate a friendship – 'I telled of you.' This process of literal identification plays upon both differential access to power – through which children effect change or restitution in their social relations – and upon the performative demonstration of friendship, which enables children to allocate identities, to personify one another. In this way particular relationships become charged with considerable emotion. But the manner in which the identifying and personifying power of friendship is wielded differs between boys and girls and it is the gendered nature of friendship which this next section explores.

While gender exerts few constraints upon young children's social relations, permitting a relatively unproblematic engagement in mutual play between boys and girls of four and five years old, children's passage into and through the culture of childhood bears witness to a growing awareness of gender difference from the age of six or seven. The pattern of strict gender separation which, in the school context, develops in children's play is replicated in their friendship relations. In this sense, gender has a double significance for children. Its differentiating potential both reinforces and is reinforced by particular forms of play and patterns of friendship which, in turn, generates cultural models of and for particular gendered identities. Thus, it is unsurprising that the tightly bound and structured form of girls' games reflects and refracts the strong dyadic patterning of their friendship bonds. Similarly, the looser but competitive team structure of boys' games attests commonly to their admittance of less intimate forms of friendship (see Chapter 6). And, just as girls' participation in games may be both exclusive and excluding, so their friendships are binding affairs of the heart involving considerable emotional commitments, while the team spirit infecting the games typically played by the seven, eight and nine-year-old boys de-emphasises the personal in the public world.

Thus, although by no means solely a girl's experience, the close bonds of affection, seen as central to the Western concept of friendship, are more commonly articulated by girls than boys. This difference can be interpreted as simply a function of children's growing socialised awareness of the implicit binary classification linking the expression of emotion with stereotypes of gender, which continues to proclaim that in Western cultures boys don't cry and that it is girls who do the caring. However, while undoubtedly this occurs, girls gain other kinds of experience from their participation in such friendship forms: they come to know and to use the intricacies of power. This is a significant cultural experience which, in other spheres of their lives, is often denied to them.

The dyadic, indeed didactic, nature of girls' friendships has been well-documented (Lever, 1976) and, at Hilltop School, was particularly marked in the case of two seven-year-old girls. They spoke publicly and often of their close friendship, frequently articulating the meanings which it held for them through images drawn from the world of marriage and romance. On being asked how long they had been friends, Shona phrased her reply as follows: 'We've been together for four years.' From time to time, however, they would argue. Then, aware of my interest in friendship, they would solemnly detail for me, like a lover's tiff, the changing pattern of fortunes in their metaphoric courtship:

> I have been talking to Helena about friendship and soon afterwards she comes to tell me that she and Shona have had a 'break up'. Helena has drawn a picture of her cousin and Shona is jealous; she is cross that Helena didn't draw her portrait.

On one such occasion, the girls embroiled me in their complex game of love and hate, with each in turn coming to tell me of the twists and turns in their changing affections. But, even as they did so, they maintained a careful watch that this teasing of each other was not presaging a more permanent change in their affairs.

An important lesson in getting to know the meaning of friends seems to be gained, therefore, through the experience of rejection and jealousy. Among girls the boundaries and bonds of friendship intensify as the identities 'my friend' or 'best friend' come under threat. The eight and nine-year-old girls would watch anxiously for subtle signs of disloyalty from their friends, while, at the same time, remaining cannily watchful for any new overtures of friendship that might come their way. Choosing partners in PE, holding hands while going out to play, sharing a book or being allowed to brush and plait another girl's hair, could all be read as signs of shifting patterns of affection, as Paula described in telling me about her friendship with Tanya:

ALLISON: Do you ever fall out with your friends?
PAULA: She [Tanya] falls out with me.
ALLISON: Why?
PAULA: Just because I won't hold her hand.
ALLISON: Why won't you hold her hand?
PAULA: Because I'm holding Janet's.
ALLISON: Couldn't she hold your other hand?
PAULA: We're not allowed in threes.

Eight and nine-year-old boys, however, were less keen to talk openly of their friendships and, in this respect, Samuel and Bobby's discourse on friendship (p. 216) was unusual. Like those of the girls, their dyadic relationship was exclusive; they rarely allowed others to enter in it and they had had time to reflect on their experience of being friends. Other boys rarely spoke of friendship in this way, preferring to offer in discussion an account which emphasised its instrumental rather than its affective aspects. For them friends were people to play or fight with or members of the daily football team which congregated in the playground. This is not to say that the boys did not have particular and close friendships. I am certain that many did. A number of boys identified for me a 'best friend' in our more private conversations. Rather, it suggests that they had learnt not to speak of them or to be demonstrative in their relationships with one another in the public context of the class-room and playground. They realised that 'children who too readily admit to affection become the objects of teasing and scorn' (Fine, 1981: 35). This may have been at the root of Matthew's dilemma (see p. 220), a cause of his social isolation. Thus, the classificatory status of having friends which four and five-year-old boys anxiously sought through their open quizzing of one another: 'Do you like me?', 'Are you my friend?' becomes translated by eight and nine-year-old boys into a performance. Being friends must be publicly enacted through a shared participation in loud and boisterous games. And it was precisely such games that Samuel and Bobby, quiet and studious in their friendship, avoided. For girls, however, the status of 'having friends' is less visibly encoded in their playground behaviour. Thus it may be that, for them, the more private and personal experience of 'being friends' is where the classificatory power of friendship comes to reside.

One five-year-old girl demonstrated a shrewd and uncommon early awareness of the power which friendship has to personify through its bestowal of a significant social identity. Beatrice and Penny often played together, having been playmates in the nursery school. Val, new to the school, outspoken and confident, quickly recognised the closeness of their relationship. She also realised that, of the two girls, Beatrice was the more popular in the class. During the first weeks of school, Val offered herself as a rival to Penny in Beatrice's affections. The following field-note describes one such occasion, when Penny, called away from the work table by the teacher, was forced to leave Beatrice and Val alone:

> Val and Beatrice are drawing side by side. Beatrice knocks a picture on the floor. 'Oh that's Penny's,' says Val, adding disparagingly, 'It's not very nice anyway.' Beatrice hesitates to pick up the paper.

In her momentary reluctance to retrieve Penny's drawing, does Beatrice perhaps heed Val's account of her friend's ability? Is she a little intimidated by her forthright manner or, by her unkind comment, prompted to revise momentarily her previous perceptions of Penny? In such instances, whose meanings will predominate may depend upon which child has the social expertise to tip the balance of social relations.

This exclusivity of girls' dyadic relationships has been well-documented (Lever, 1976; Steedman, 1982). Less has been said about how they come into being or about the power relations which structure their performance. These are the keys to understanding the experiential aspect of girls' friendships which are both structured by, and provide the contexts for, the caring-control which, in their future role as adult women caring for dependent others, they are being elsewhere socialised to adopt (Hockey and James, 1993). That is to say, the power to care for others can, at the same time, be construed as a form of control and it is through their dyadic friendships that the double-edged quality of care is both experienced and made manifest to girls. In the drama of a playground accident it is the girls who take control through the act of caring:

> Whenever a girl or first-year boy falls over in the play-ground the older girls immediately surround them, offer-ing advice and sounding the alarm. There was such a drama today. I am told that Cindy fell over and, with greater poignancy, that 'she lay still for a bit'. Cindy herself demures from comment. As in all such instances the injured child remains passive, while the older care-givers speak up on their behalf.

The girls' socialised identities as carers find expression in and through the friendships which they espouse. In time, moreover, it helps structure the very exclusivity of those friendships through the powerful controls which caring can bring with it. Thus, the 'friends' which many six-year-old girls told me they had among the little – that is the younger – children, can be understood in these terms. From the point of view of a six-year-old girl, confident as I have shown in the prestige which age and size bring with them, these little(er) children can be cared for and mothered in the same moment as a girl's own 'bigness' is made public. For their part the little children wel-come such attention in their concern first to have friends, so that later they can be friends. Made into the object of older girls' fussing may signal for them the public acknowledgement of their social identity, of their personhood.

The potentially powerful control upon social relationships, which a caring friendship unleashes, may only slowly be realised. It may also remain context specific; even among the older girls of seven and eight at Hilltop School, affectionate ties of friend-ship were not always continued beyond the school gate. Despite its mirroring of romantic love, Helena's relationship with Shona, for example, was kept within its boundaries. When Helena was away from school for three days, Shona did not know why she was ill nor did she admit to having made any enquiries. While partly this may have been because Shona did not have the means of making such an enquiry at her disposal – for example, the freedom to decide to telephone or to send a card – Shona's growing awareness of the restrictions which such a dyadic friendship places upon the Self may also account for this seeming lack of interest. Remarking that it was important to have a friend, so that you have someone to play with, she also pointed out the dangers of being too exclusive in friendship choices: 'If you only make one and she's away you've got no one to play with so you've got to make lots.'

But by nine years old, however, many of the girls' relationships were bound by just these ties of care and control. Their friendships were patterned by the signs of caring noted by Prout (1989) in his discussion of childhood sickness, and the girls saw themselves lucky in having close friends who would care for them:

ALLISON: What's important about friendship?

BETH: Well, when you hurt yourself, they'll look after you and sit with you and when you get told off they come to you and say, 'Are you alright?'

At the same time, however, they were wary of the limitations which those same friendships placed on establishing wider social relations. Of particular concern was the ability which some girls seemed to evince to 'take away' friends and to deprive others from participating in a caring relationship. It paralleled the monopoly of power which some girls established through the ownership of games and which they used to exclude Others from playing (see Chapter 6).

In summary, then, girls' friendships are constituted by fickle patterns of close and emotional alliances, which in turn are shaped by subtle shifts in power relations. By contrast, in the boys' larger groupings of 'us' – the footballers, the Bulldog players or the karate enthusiasts – which is distinct from a more disparate 'them', friendship is less publicly binding, although the experience of rejection is no less keenly felt. Kate and Ally, in their still rather uneasy and somewhat fragile friendship, reflected back for me upon how it had developed:

ALLY: When I didn't like her, she used to take my friends away.

KATE: No, I did not. I asked them if they liked me and they said, 'Yes,' and I said, 'Do you like Ally?' And I said, 'Would you like me if I still like Ally?'

The significance which the power to define and allocate friendship has on the attribution of personhood was not lost on
seven-year-old Tamsin either:

> Carol (a popular girl) don't like me . . . She does but every
> time we go swimming she says: I don't like you. She only
> jokes me . . . she always jokes me.

Tamsin, without a close friend, is ambivalent about her own
position in Carol's affections and acknowledges the power which
Carol wields has over her through permitting or withholding
the possibility of friendship and, consequently, the possibility
of personhood. Unsure and uncertain, Tamsin prefers to interpret Carol's avowed dislike of her on swimming days as a joke.
But, at the same time, her complaint testifies to the hurt which
Carol's rebuttal causes. Six-year-old Marina's difficult relationship with Paula rests upon similar oscillations of power:

> 'Cos Paula wants to be horrible to me. She be's nice for a
> while until dinner-time and then she gets all angry and
> then she makes friends again.

This power to include and exclude on the grounds of affectivity,
wielded by some girls over Others, refines and builds upon
the more simple classificatory and identificatory function of
friendship, noted previously as a feature of young children's
relations. It is a process of personifying which identifies 'we',
plural and together, as opposed to 'you' on your own:

> (Four-year-olds, Barbara and Rosemary, are sitting in the
> armchair looking at books. Anthea approaches, sits down
> on the arm of the chair. Barbara and Rosemary say nothing,
> but continue to talk together ignoring her presence. Then
> Barbara speaks.)
>
> BARBARA: (to Anthea) You're not sitting next to us. You're
> not our friend. You can't sit down here next
> to us.
>
> (Anthea continues to sit and says nothing. A while later
> she gets off and goes away.)

Here the excluding pronouns 'we' and 'us' invoked by Barbara
can be seen to prefigure the patterning of older girls' relationships when the subtleties of the sanctioning power of 'taking
friends away' or withdrawing friendship become more fully
exploited. It is a learning process which evolves gradually into
a powerful form of social control. In the following example,
four-year-old Karen seems to be already aware of the potential
which the phrase, 'I won't be your friend,' will later have.

While the conversation reflects the process of self-identification, the 'having friends' noted earlier, it is clear that Karen already realises the power which she has to give 'friendship' to others. It is the power to personify. She relishes the delay in answering the perennial question raised by boys about their own positioning: 'Are you my friend?':

> (Karen, Clark and Robin are sitting on the floor doing jigsaws together.)
>
> CLARK: Are you my friend, Karen?
>
> (Karen smiles, looks away and carries on with her jigsaw, and, still smiling, appears to ponder this question. Clark stops making the jigsaw, and watches her, waiting for her answer. Finally, she speaks.)
>
> KAREN: Yes.

In that boys' relationships are less exclusive, being friends often being coterminus with their participation in a larger grouping of 'us' as opposed to 'them', any changes in the group's personnel is less noticeable. This contrasts with the girls' smaller friendship pairings where any rupture may immediately precipitate the re-alliance of other dyadic relationships. Being less tied to one another, boys more easily drift between different groupings, their departures and arrivals being seen as less dramatic. For girls, in contrast, the loss of a friend is always an event:

> DEBBIE: And Estelle came up to me and Trish and kept saying: 'Why don't you like Mary?' and Trish already liked Mary.
>
> ALLISON: Why did she say that?
>
> DEBBIE: Because we was playing with Mary first of all and then we went off because only three players could do it.

Among the older girls the subtle playing out of power relations was, as in the example above, often mediated by the use of intermediaries. Sent as an emissary, a girl might be asked to settle an argument or repair a friendship on another's behalf, to find out information or to offer a reconciliation.

This practice prefigures the later use of intermediaries during adolescence for the instigation of cross-gender relations, but at this age such friendships are rare. More correctly, they are rarely admitted to. At Hilltop School, for example, although cross-gender associating was common in the nursery setting, on entering school, children quickly drifted into single sex groupings, a form of social relations furthered and made public through the differentiating games which they learned to play. But, as with their games, outside the school context, cross-gender relationships were not uncommon. Thus although Bobby was Nina's close friend at home, someone whom she often met, at school they rarely spoke and never played together.

During fieldwork, I only came across one instance of a cross-gender friendship, after the age of five. Existing between a boy and girl of nine years old, their friendship was regarded by the other children as an oddity. Harry, eschewing the team games of the boys, told me that he rarely played football and liked to play imaginative games of TV reporters with Kirsty, his friend. However, although he was often teased for his public admittance of this friendship, he also bore a certain and ambiguous distinction. It may be that his nine-year-old peers, although registering his difference, were nevertheless also aware of the attesting to masculinity which 'having a girl-friend' might have. This was certainly already becoming part of the six-year-old boys' perception of what it means to be a man. Although denying that they ever played with girls, they sought, simultaneously, to espouse their developing manhood by announcing to me, an adult and impressionable woman, that they had girl-friends (see Chapter 6). Was Harry's unusual relationship with Kirsty to be taken, then, as a sign that he was a sissy in having a friend who was a girl? Or, conversely, was Harry to be admired? Was he the more mature in already having a 'real' rather than fanciful girl-friend?

Nine-year-old girls were more certain of the social value and prestige which attached to having a boy-friend. However, it was a relationship which the boys in question rarely had knowledge of, a secret affair of the heart celebrated in their singing games (see Chapter 6). Two five-year-old girls revealed a precocious familiarity with this discourse:

(Sylvie, John and Vera are playing in the sand.)
SYLVIE: I love John.
VERA: So do I.
SYLVIE: (to John) Who are you going to marry? Me or Vera?
VERA: He's going to marry me because I really love him. Kiss me on the lips.
(John obliges but takes no other part in the conversation. He seems merely to be pleased to be somehow involved.)

VERA: Good boy, good boy.

Here Sylvie and Vera vie with one another for the upper hand in their relationship. Expressed through motifs of care, they seek control over John, moving him through the course of their argument from the role of passive lover to that of passive child. John himself, immature and ill-regarded, without any friends among the boys, complies with their demands, grateful perhaps to at last and at least be noticed.

For the nine-year-old girls, having a boy-friend was a mark of status, of personhood, It was used by them to map out distinctions between themselves and, on occasion, to facilitate the ending of particular friendships. In this sense 'having a boy-friend' was essentially about the girls' relationships with each another, but it was talked of within the familiar, future discourse of love and marriage which their games also encompassed. Sheena and Collete revealed themselves to be skilled and powerful negotiators, their power masked by framing their conflicts and intentions toward each other through this discourse of romance:

SHEENA: I had a boy-friend.

COLLETE: Yeah, the whole school knew about that.

SHEENA: Yeah, and I didn't want him to know about it. They knew about it and I thought, 'Oh, God,' and then after Christmas he bought me a present and then when we got back to school he went off with Carol and then after the holidays – when you went out with him.

COLLETE: Yeah, and I broke up with him because he was going out with Carol again. I'm not really interested in him any more because he lied to me.

SHEENA: And he asked me out with him again and I said, 'No.'

COLLETE: It's lies, lies, lies.

SHEENA: I'm going out with somebody but I don't know if he's still going out with me though.

In this conversation the girls renew their own relationships with one another, uniting in their opposition to the boys whose affections they desire. The idiom of romantic love, prefiguring their own futures, disguises the struggle for power in which their present friendship is enmeshed, but it is a relationship in which the boys themselves have no part to play. Thus, Sandra's fear of Nancy found a comparably safe cultural expression within this frame:

SANDRA: Nancy goes to Dicky all the time and she says that she hates him one minute and I go: 'Do you fancy Dicky?' and she goes: 'No, I never even fancied him in the first place.' And I go: 'Well, I can go out with him, then, can't I?' and she goes: 'No, because I never said I wasn't going out with him.'

Sandra and Nancy's friendship was riven by arguments and fallings out, with Nancy, although a year younger, seeming always to wield the more effective power. Talking with Sandra after her transfer to middle school she remarked that the one good thing about moving school was that Nancy was not there. And yet, as she less hopefully remembered, in a year's time the struggle would recommence when Nancy joined the school.

*   *   *   *

Persons Identified

The power to personify which friendship unleashes for children has been variously traced through the course of this book. Through showing how the body interposes and intervenes between the Self and Other selves, I have set out some of the contexts and conditions through which personhood is acquired by children. Working from children's own understandings and comprehension of the particular social worlds which they inhabit, I have explored how styles of behaviour and the body's appearance come to image the Self in relation to the Other and, through performance, how they begin to locate for the child a social and more personal experience of identity. In a very real sense, then, there can be no conclusion to this book. Just as it is for children growing into adulthood, the project of seeking out identity and personhood remains inevitably incomplete, for it is through the process of social life and engagement, rather than as its product, that personification takes place.

Note

1. This was made possible by its large pupil intake and the system of vertical integration at Hilltop School (see note 2, for Chapter 5 above). At other smaller schools this would not necessarily be possible. Children may therefore not be so easily helped to avoid such confrontations.

Bibliography

Ablon, J. (1990) 'Ambiguity and difference: families with dwarf children', *Social Science and Medicine,* 30 (8): 879–87.

Allan, G. (1989) *Friendship: Developing a Sociological Perspective,* London: Harvester, Wheatsheaf.

Anderson, E. M. (1973) *The Disabled School Child: a Study of Integration in Primary Schools,* London: Methuen.

Ardener, E. (1975) 'Belief and the problem of women', in S. Ardener (ed.) *Perceiving Women,* London: J. M. Dent.

Ardener, E. (1987) 'Remote areas: some theoretical considerations', in A. Jackson (ed.) *Anthropology at Home,* London: Tavistock.

Ariès, P. (1973) *Centuries of Childhood,* Harmondsworth: Penguin.

Armstrong, D.(1983) *Political Anatomy of the Body: Medical Knowledge in Britain in the Twentieth Century,* Cambridge: Cambridge University Press.

Attwood, M. (1989) *Cat's Eyes,* London: Bloomsbury Publishing.

Barley, N. (1986) *The Innocent Anthropologist,* Harmondsworth: Penguin.

Barthes, R. (1973) *Mythologies,* London: Paladin.

Bateson, G. (1973) *Steps to an Ecology of Mind,* London: Paladin.

Bauman, R. and Scherzer, J. (eds) (1974) *Explorations in the Ethnography of Speaking,* Cambridge: Cambridge University Press.

Benedict, R. (1955) 'Continuities and discontinuities in cultural conditioning,' in M. Mead and M. Wolfenstein (eds) *Childhood in Contemporary Cultures,* Chicago: Chicago University Press.

Benthall, J. (1992) 'A late developer. The ethnography of children,' *Anthropology Today,* 8 (2): 1.

Bernardi, B. (1985) *Age Class System: Social Institutions and Polities Based on Age,* Cambridge: Cambridge University Press.

Bertaux, D. (ed.) (1981) *Biography and Society: the Life History Approach in the Social Sciences,* London: Sage Publications.

Bigelow, B. J. and La Gaipa, J. J. (1980) 'The development of friendship value and choice', in H. C. Foot, A. J. Chapman and J. K. Smith (eds) *Friendship and Social Relations in Children,* London: John Wiley.

Blacking, J. (ed.) (1977) *The Anthropology of the Body,* London: Academic Press.

Bloch, M. (1985) 'From cognition to ideology', in R. Fardon (ed.) *Power and Knowledge,* Edinburgh: Scottish Academic Press.

Bluebond-Langer, M. (1978) *The Private Worlds of Dying Children,* Princeton: Princeton University Press.

Bluebond-Langer, M., Perkel, D. and Goertzel, T. (1991) 'Pediatric cancer patients' peer relationships: the impact of an oncology camp experience', *Journal of Psychosocial Oncology,* 9 (2): 67–80.

Boas, G. (1968) *The Cult of Childhood,* London: Warburg Institute.

Booth, T. A. (1978) 'From normal baby to handicapped child: unravelling the idea of subnormality in families of mentally handicapped children, *Sociology*, 12 (2): 203–21.

Booth, T. A. and Statham, J. (eds) (1982) *The Nature of Special Education*, London: Croom Helm/Open University Press.

Booth, T. A. and Swann, W. (eds) (1987) *Including Pupils with Disabilities*, Milton Keynes: Open University Press.

Boyden, J. (1990) 'Childhood and the policy makers: a comparative perspective on the globalization of childhood', in A. James and A. Prout (eds) *Constructing and Reconstructing Childhood*, Basingstoke: Falmer Press.

Bradley, B. (1986) *Visions of Infancy*, Cambridge: Polity Press.

Briggs, J. (1982) 'Living dangerously: the contradictory foundations of value in Canadian Inuit society', in E. Leacock and R. Lee (eds) *Politics and History in Band Societies*, Cambridge: Cambridge University Press.

Briggs, J. (1986) 'Expecting the unexpected: Canadian Inuit training for an experimental lifestyle.' (Paper given to the 4th International Conference on Hunting and Gathering Societies at the London School of Economics, London.)

Bromley, R. (1988) *Lost Narratives: Popular Fictions, Politics and Recent History*, London: Routledge.

Burton, L. (1975) *The Family Life of Sick Children*, London: Routledge & Kegan Paul.

Caillois, R. (1962) *Man, Play and Games.* London: Thames and Hudson.

Campbell, A. T. (1989) *To Square With Genesis*, Edinburgh: Edinburgh University Press.

Caplan, P. (1988) 'Engendering knowledge: the politics of ethnography', *Anthropology Today*, 4 (5): 8–12.

Carrithers, M. (1988) 'The anthropologist as author. Geertz's "Works and Lives"', *Anthropology Today*, 4 (4): 19–22.

Carrithers, M., Collins, S. and Lukes, S. (eds) (1985) *The Category of the Person*, Cambridge: Cambridge University Press.

Cheater, A. (1987) 'The anthropologist as citizen: the diffracted self', in A. Jackson (ed.) *Anthropology at Home*, London: Tavistock.

Clifford, J. (1988) *The Predicament of Culture*, Cambridge, Mass: Harvard University Press.

Clifford, J. and Marcus, G. E. (eds) (1986) *Writing Culture*, California: University of California Press.

Cohen, A. P. (ed.) (1982) *Belonging: Identity and Social Organisation in British Rural Cultures*, Manchester: Manchester University Press.

Cohen, A. P. (ed.) (1986) *Symbolising Boundaries*, Manchester: Manchester University Press.

Cohen, A. P. (1989) *The Symbolic Construction of Community*, London: Routledge.

Cohen, A. P. (1990) 'The future of the self'. (Paper presented at the Association of Social Anthropologists Conference, Anthropology and the Future, Edinburgh University.)

Cohen, A. P. (1992) 'Self-conscious anthropology', in J. Okely and H. Callaway (eds) *Anthropology and Autobiograhpy*, London: Routledge.

Corrigan, P. (1979) *Schooling the Smash Street Kids*, London: Macmillan.

Corsaro, W. A. (1979) 'We're friends right? Children's use of access rituals in a nursery school', *Language in Society*, 8: 315–36.

Coveney, P. (1957) *Poor Monkey: the Child in Literature*, London: Rockliffe.

Crick, M. (1976) *Explorations in Language and Meaning: Towards a Semantic Anthropology*, London: Malaby Press.

Davies, B. (1982) *Life in the Classroom and Playground*. London: Routledge & Kegan Paul.

Davis, A. G. (1982) *Children in Clinics,* London: Tavistock.

De Jong, W. (1980) 'The stigma of obesity: the consequences of naïve assumptions concerning the causes of physical deviance', *Journal of Health and Social Behaviour,* 21: 75–87.

Delamont, S. (1980) *Sex Roles and the School,* London: Methuen.

De Mause, L. (ed.) (1976) *The History of Childhood.* London: Souvenir Press.

Denscombe, M., Szulc, H., Patrick, C. and Wood, A. (1986) 'Ethnicity and friendship: the contrast between sociometric research and fieldwork observation in primary school classrooms', *British Educational Research Journal,* 12 (3): 221–35.

Donaldson, M. (1978) *Children's Minds,* London: Fontana.

Douglas, M. (1973) *Natural Symbols,* Harmondsworth: Penguin.

Douglas, M. (1975) *Implicit Meanings,* London: Routledge & Kegan Paul.

Eder, D. and Hallinan, M. T. (1978) 'Sex differences in children's friendships', *American Sociological Review,* 43, 237–50.

Ehrenreich, B. and English, D. (1979) *For Her Own Good: 150 Years of the Expert's Advice to Women,* London: Pluto Press.

Ehrman, J. (1968) 'Homo Ludens revisited', *Yale French Studies,* 41.

Ennew, J. (1986) *The Sexual Exploitation of Children,* Polity Press: Cambridge.

Fabian, J. (1983) *Time and the Other: How Anthropology Makes its Object,* New York: Columbia University Press.

Featherstone, M. Hepworth, M. and Turner, B. S. (eds) (1991) *The Body: Social Process and Cultural Theory,* London: Sage Publications.

Fine, G. A. (1981) 'Friends, impression management and pre-adolescent behaviour', in S. R. Asher and J. M. Gottman (eds) *The Development of Children's Friendships,* Cambridge: Cambridge University Press.

Firth, R. (1983) 'Review of D. Freeman', *Royal Anthropological Institute Newsletter,* 57: 11–12.

Foley, W. (1974) *A Child in the Forest,* London: BBC Publications.

Foot, H. C., Chapman, A. D. and Smith, J. R. (1980) *Friendship and Social Relations in Children,* London: John Wiley.

Freeman, D. (1983) *Margaret Mead and Samoa: the Making and Unmaking of an Anthropological Myth,* Cambridge, Mass: Harvard University Press.

Freeman, D. (1984) 'Samoa and M. Mead: a rejoinder to Paula Brown Glick and Rosemary Firth', *Royal Anthropological Institute Newsletter,* 60: 6–8.

Freeman, J. (1979) *Gifted Children,* Lancaster: MTP Press Ltd.

Frith, G. (1985) 'The time of your life: the meaning of the school story', in C. Steedman, C. Urwin and V. Walkerdine (eds) *Language Gender and Childhood,* London: Routledge & Kegan Paul.

Fyfe, A. (1989) *Child Labour,* Cambridge: Polity Press.

Gabbay, J. (1982) 'Asthma attacked; tactics for the reconstitution of a disease concept', in P. Wright and A. Treacher (eds) *The Problem of Medical Knowledge,* Edinburgh: Edinburgh University Press.

Gamble, R. (1979) *Chelsea Childhood,* London: British Broadcasting Corporation.

Garvey, C. (1984) *Children's Talk,* London: Fontana.

Geertz, C. (1975) *The Interpretation of Cultures,* London: Hutchinson.

Geertz, C. (1983) 'From the native's point of view: on the nature of anthropological understanding', in Geertz, C. *Local Knowledge,* New York: Basic Books.

238 CHILDHOOD IDENTITIES

Geertz, C. (1988) *Works and Lives: The Anthropologist as Author,* Cambridge: Polity Press.
Giddens, A. (1991) *Modernity and Self-Identity,* Cambridge: Polity Press.
Glick, P. (1983) 'The attack on and defence of Margaret Mead', *Royal Anthropological Institute Newsletter,* 58: 12–14.
Goffman, E. (1968) *Stigma,* Harmondsworth: Penguin.
Goffman, E. (1971) *The Presentation of Self in Everyday Life,* Harmondsworth: Penguin.
Gottlieb, J. and Leyser, Y. (1981) 'Friendship between mentally retarded and non-retarded children', in S. R. Asher and J. M. Gottman (eds) *The Development of Children's Friendships,* Cambridge: Cambridge University Press.
Goulart, R. (1969) *The Assault on Childhood,* London: Victor Gollancz.
Graham, H. (1984) 'Surveying through stories', in C. Bell and H. Newby (eds) *Social Researching: Politics, Problems, Practice,* London: Routledge & Kegan Paul.
Grugeon, E. (1988) 'Children's oral culture: a transitional experience', in M. Maclure, T. Phillips and A. Wilkinson (eds) *Oracy Matters,* Milton Keynes: Open University Press.
Gumperz, J. J. and Hymes, D. (eds) (1972) *Directions in Socio-Linguistics,* New York: Holt, Rhinehart & Winston Inc.
Hallinan, M. (1981) 'Recent advances in sociometry', in S. R. Asher and J. M. Gottman (eds) *The Development of Children's Friendships,* Cambridge: Cambridge University Press.
Hardman, C. (1973) 'Can there be an anthropology of children?', *Journal of the Anthropology Society of Oxford,* 4 (1): 85–99.
Hardman, C. (1974) 'Fact and fantasy in the playground', *New Society,* 26 September.
Hastrup, K. (1978) 'The semantics of biology: virginity', in S. Ardener (ed) *Defining Females,* London: Croom Helm.
Hayes, E. N. and Hayes, T. (1970) *Claude Lévi-Strauss: The Anthropologist as Hero,* Cambridge, Mass: MIT Press.
Hegarty, S. and Pocklington, K. (eds) (1981) *Educating Pupils with Special Needs in Ordinary Schools,* Windsor: NFER.
Hendrick, H. (1990) 'Constructions and reconstructions of British childhood: an interpretive survey from 1800 to the Present', in A. James and A. Prout *Constructing and Reconstructing Childhood,* Basingstoke: Falmer Press.
Hendry, J. (1986) *Becoming Japanese,* Manchester: Manchester University Press.
Henshall, C. and McGuire, J. (1986) 'Gender development', in M. Richards and P. Light (eds) *Children of Social Worlds,* Cambridge: Polity Press.
Hockey, J. (1990) *Experiences of Death,* Edinburgh: Edinburgh University Press.
Hockey, J. and James, A. (1993) *Growing up and Growing Old: Ageing and Dependency in the Life Course,* London: Sage.
Holt, J. (1975) *Escape From Childhood,* Harmondsworth: Penguin.
Holly, D. (1974) *Beyond Curriculum,* London: Paladin.
Honigman, J. J. (1976) *The Development of Anthropological Ideas,* Illinois: Press.
Huizinga, J. (1949) *Homo Ludens,* London: Routledge & Kegan Paul.
Hymes, D. (1971) 'Sociolinguistics and the ethnography of speaking', in E. Ardener (ed.) *Social Anthropology and Language,* Tavistock: London.
Jackson, A. (ed.) (1987) *Anthropology at Home,* Tavistock: London.

James, A. (1979a) 'The game of the name: nicknames in the child's world',
    New Society, 14 June.
James, A. (1979b) 'Confections, concoctions and conceptions', Journal of
    the Anthropology Society of Oxford, 10 (2): 83–95.
James, A. (1986) 'Learning to Belong: the Boundaries of Adolescence', in
    A. P. Cohen (ed.) Symbolising Boundaries, Manchester: Manchester University
    Press.
James, A. and Prout, A. (eds) (1990a) Constructing and Reconstructing Childhood,
    Basingstoke: Falmer Press.
James, A. and Prout, A. (1990b) 'Re-presenting childhood: time and transition
    in the study of childhood', in A. James and A. Prout, (eds) Constructing
    and Reconstructing Childhood, Basingstoke: Falmer Press.
Jenks, C. (ed.) (1982) The Sociology of Childhood, London: Batsford.
Just, R. (1978) 'Some problems for Mediterranean anthropology', Journal of
    the Anthropology Society of Oxford, 9 (2): 81–97.
Kohli, M. (1988) 'Ageing as a challenge for sociological theory', Ageing and
    Society, 8: 367–94.
La Fontaine, J. S. (1985) 'Person and individual: some anthropological
    reflections', in M. Carrithers, S. Collins and S. Lukes (eds) The Category of
    the Person, Cambridge: Cambridge University Press.
Lever, J. (1976) 'Sex differences in the games children play', Social Problems,
    23: 478–87.
Ley, P. (1979) 'Psychological, social and cultural determinants of acceptable
    fatness', in M. Turner (ed.) Nutrition and Life Styles, Barking: Applied
    Social Science Publishers.
Leyton, E. (ed.) (1974) The Compact: Selected Dimensions of Friendship,
    Newfoundland: University of Toronto Press.
Macbeth, H. (1989) 'Nature/culture: the false dichotomies', Anthropology Today,
    5 (4): 12–15.
McCredie, G. and Horrox, A. (1985) Voices in the Dark: Children and Divorce,
    London: Unwin Publishers.
McDonald, M. (1987) 'The politics of fieldwork in Britanny', in A. Jackson
    (ed.) Anthropology at Home, London: Tavistock.
MacKay, R. (1973) 'Conceptions of children and models of socialization', in
    H. P. Dreitzel, (ed.) Childhood and Socialization, London: Macmillan.
McRobbie, A. (1978) Jackie: An Ideology of Adolescent Femininity. Birmingham:
    Centre for Contemporary Cultural Studies.
Malinowksi, B. (1922) Argonauts of the Western Pacific, London: Routledge.
Mannarino, A. P. (1980) 'The development of children's friendships', in H.
    C. Foot, A. J. Chapman and J. R. Smith (eds) Friendship and Social Relations
    in Children, London: John Wiley.
Marcus, G. E. and Fisher, M. M. J. (1986) Anthropology as Cultural Critique,
    Chicago: University of Chicago Press.
Martin, G. (1981) 'Readers, viewers and texts', in G. Martin et al. Form and
    Meaning 1, (Popular Culture, Block 4), Milton Keynes: Open University
    Press.
Mascarenhas-Keyes, S. (1987) 'The native anthropologist: constraints and
    strategies in research', in A. Jackson (ed.) Anthropology at Home, London:
    Tavistock.
Mauss, M. [1938] (1979) 'A category of the human mind: the notion of the
    person, the notion of the "Self"', in B. Brewster (1979) Sociology and
    Psychology, London: Routledge & Kegan Paul.

Mayer, P. (ed.) (1970) *Socialisation: the Approach from Social Anthropology,* London: Tavistock.

Mead, M. [1928] (1963) *Coming of Age in Samoa,* Middlesex: Penguin.

Mead, M. [1930] (1968) *Growing up in New Guinea,* Middlesex: Penguin.

Measor, L. and Woods, P. (1984) *Changing Schools: Pupil Perspectives on Transfer to a Comprehensive,* Milton Keynes: Open University Press.

Mitchell, A. (1985) *Children in the Middle,* London: Tavistock.

Morris, B. (1984) 'Ruth Benedict: popular success, academic neglect', *Royal Anthropological Institute Newsletter,* 62: 4–6.

Morgan, J., O'Neill, C. and Harre, R. (1979) *Nicknames,* London: Routledge & Kegan Paul.

Musgrave, P. W. (1987) *Socialising Contexts,* London: Allen & Unwin.

Munday, E. (1979) 'When is a child a "Child"? Alternative systems and classification', *Journal of the Anthropology Society of Oxford,* 10 (3): 161–72.

Newson, J. and Newson, E. (1979) *Toys and Playthings,* Middlesex: Penguin.

Okely, J. (1975) 'The self and scientism', *Journal of the Anthropology Society of Oxford,* 6 (3): 171–88.

Okely, J. (1978) 'Privileged, schooled and finished: boarding education for girls', in S. Ardener (ed.) *Defining Females,* London: Croom Helm.

Okely, J. (1983) *The Traveller Gypsies,* Cambridge: Cambridge University Press.

Okely, J. (1992) 'Anthropology and autobiography: participatory experience and embodied knowledge', in J. Okely and H. Callaway (eds) *Anthropology and Autobiography,* London: Routledge.

Opie, I. and Opie, P. (1969) *Children's Games in Street and Playground,* Oxford: Oxford University Press.

Opie, I. and Opie, P. [1959] (1977) *The Lore and Language of Schoolchildren,* London: Paladin.

Orton, C. (1981) *Learning to Live with a Skin Disorder,* London: Souvenir Press.

Paine, R. (1974) 'Anthropological approaches to friendship', in E. Leyton (ed.) *The Compact: Selected Dimensions of Friendship,* Newfoundland: University of Toronto Press.

Paine, R. (ed.) (1985) *Anthropology and Advocacy, First Encounters,* St Johns: Institute of Social and Economic Research.

Philip, M. and Duckworth, D. (1982) *Children with Disabilities and their Families,* London: NFER.

Pinchbeck, I. and Hewitt, M. (1969) *Children in English Society,* Vol. I, London: Routledge & Kegan Paul.

Pinchbeck, I. and Hewitt, M. (1973) *Children in English Society,* Vol. II, London: Routledge & Kegan Paul.

Plumb, J. H. (1975) 'The new world of children in eighteenth century England', *Past and Present,* 67: 64–95.

Pocock, D. (1973) 'The idea of a personal anthropology'. Paper presented to the Decennial Meeting of the Association of Social Anthropologists, Oxford.

Polhemus, T. (ed.) (1978) *Social Aspects of the Human Body,* Harmondsworth: Penguin.

Pollard, A. (1985) *The Social World of the Primary School,* London: Holt, Rhinehart & Winston.

Pollock, L. (1983) *Forgotten Children: Parent-Child Relations 1500–1900,* Cambridge: Cambridge University Press.

Prout, A. (1989) 'Sickness as a dominant symbol in life course transitions: an illustrated theoretical framework', *Sociology of Health and Illness*, 4 (11): 336–59.

Prout, A. and James, A. (1990) 'A new paradigm for the sociology of childhood? Provenance, promise and problems', in A. James and A. Prout (eds) *Constructing and Reconstructing Childhood*, Basingstoke: Falmer Press.

Putallaz, M. and Gottman, J. M. (1981) 'Social skills and group acceptance', in S. R. Asher and J. M. Gottman (eds) *The Development of Children's Friendships*, Cambridge: Cambridge University Press.

Quicke, L. (1985) *Disability in Modern Children's Fiction*, Beckenham: Croom Helm.

Qvortrup, J. (1990 'A voice for children in statistical and social accounting: a please for children's rights to be heard', in A. James and A. Prout (eds) *Constructing and Reconstructing Childhood*, Basingstoke: Falmer Press.

Rafky, D. M. (1973) 'Phenomenology and socialisation: some comments on the assumptions underlying socialisation', in H. P. Dreitzel (ed) *Childhood and Socialisation*, London: Macmillan.

Rapport, N. (1987) *Talking Violence*, St Johns: Institute of Social and Economic Research.

Rapport, N. (1990a) 'And we shall build a new Jerusalem: stereotypes, clichés and the individual construction of the future.' Paper presented at the Association of Social Anthropologists conference, Anthroplogy and the Future, Edinburgh University.

Rapport, N. (1990b) *Personal communication*. Talk given at the Association of Social Anthropologists Conference, Anthropology and the Future, Edinburgh University.

Rapport, N. (1991) 'Writing fieldnotes: the conventionalities of note-taking in taking note in the field', *Anthropology Today*, 7 (1): 10–13.

Reynolds, P. (1985) 'Children in Zimbabwe: rights and power in relation to work', *Anthropology Today*, 1 (3): 16–20.

Reynolds, P.(1989) *Childhood in Crossroads: Cognition and Society in South Africa*, Claremont, South Africa: David Phillip Publisher.

Richards, M. and Light, P. (eds) (1986) *Children of Social Worlds*, Cambridge: Polity Press.

Richardson, S. A., Goodman, N., Hastorf, A. H. and Dornbusch, S. M. (1961) 'Cultural uniformities in reaction to physical disabilities', *American Sociological Review*, 26: 241–6.

Robinson, D. and Henry, S. (1977) *Self-Help and Health: Mutual Aid for Modern Problems*, London: Martin Robertson.

Rutherford, F. (1971) *All the Way to Pennywell*, Durham: Institute of Education.

Scambler, G. (1984) 'Perceiving and coping with stimatising illness', in Fitzpatrick, R. (ed.) *The Experience of Illness*, London: Tavistock.

Schwartz, T, (1976) 'Relations among generations in time-limited cultures' in T. Schwartz (ed.) *Socialization as Cultural Communications*, London: University of California Press.

Schwartzman, H. (1978) *Transformations: the Anthropology of Children's Play*, New York: Plenum.

Schwimmer, E. (1974) 'Friendship and kinship: an attempt to relate two anthropological concepts,' in E. Leyton (ed.) *The Compact: Selected Dimensions of Friendship*, Newfoundland: University of Toronto Press.

Shearer, A. (1981) *Disability – Whose Handicap?* Oxford: Basil Blackwell.

Sluckin, A. (1981) *Growing Up in the Playground*, London: Routledge & Kegan Paul.

Solberg, A (1990) 'Negotiating childhood: changing constructions of age for Norwegian school children.' in A. James and A. Prout (eds) *Constructing and Reconstructing Childhood*, Basingstoke: Falmer Press.

Steedman, C. (1982) *The Tidy House*, London: Virago.

Steedman, C. (1986) *Landscape For a Good Woman*, London: Virago.

Sutton-Smith, B. (1977) 'Play as adaptive potentiation', in P. Stevens (ed.) *Studies in the Anthropology of Play*, New York: Leisure Press.

Synnott, A. (1989) 'Truth and goodness, mirrors and masks – Part II: a sociology of beauty and the face', *British Journal of Sociology*, 40 (4): 607–36.

Tattum, D. P. and Lane, D. A. (eds) (1989) *Bullying in Schools*, Stoke on Trent: Trentham Books.

Taylor, S. E. (1981) 'A categorization approach to stereotyping', in D. L. Hamilton (ed.) *Cognitive Processes in Stereotyping and Intergroup Behaviour*, New Jersey: Lawrence Erlbaum Associates.

Thirkell, B. and Worall, N. (1989) 'Differential ethnic bias in Bengali and white children,' *Educational Research*, 31 (3): 181–8.

Thomas, D. (1982) *The Experience of Handicap*, London: Methuen.

Tizard, B. and Hughes, M. (1984) *Young Children Learning: Talking and Thinking at Home and School*, London: Fontana.

Tonkin, E. (1982) 'Rethinking socialisation', *Journal of the Anthropology Society of Oxford*, 13 (3): 243–56.

Turner, B. S. (1984) *The Body and Society*, Oxford: Basil Blackwell.

Turner, B. S. (1987) *Medical Power and Social Knowledge*, London: Sage.

Turner, V. (1974a) *Dramas, Fields and Metaphors*, London: Cornell University Press.

Turner, V. (1974b) 'Liminal and liminoid in play, flow and ritual: an essay in comparative symbology', *Rice University Studies*, 60 (3): 53–92.

Vosey, M. (1975) *A Constant Burden: the Reconstitution of Family Life*, London: Routledge & Kegan Paul.

Walkerdine, V. (1984) 'Developmental psychology and the child-centred pedagogy: the insertion of Piaget into early education', in J. Henriques *Changing the Subject: Psychology, Social Regulation and Subjectivity*, London: Methuen.

Walkerdine, V. (1985a) 'Child development and gender: the making of teachers and learners in the classroom', *Early Childhood Education: History, Policy and Practice*, Bulmershe Research Publication, 4.

Walkerdine, V. (1985b) 'On the regulation of speaking and silence: subjectivity, class and gender in contemporary schooling', in C. Steedman, C. Urwin and V. Walkerdine (eds) *Language, Gender and Childhood*, London: Routledge & Kegan Paul.

Wedell, K. and Roberts, J. (1982) 'Special education and research – a recent survey', *Special Education: Forward Trends*, 9 (3): 19–25.

Weil, S. and Weil, M. (1987) 'Anthropology Becomes Home: Home Becomes Anthropology.'in A. Jackson (ed.) *Anthropology at Home*, London: Tavistock.

Whiting, B. B. and Edwards, C. P. (1988) *Children of Different Worlds*, Cambridge, Mass: Harvard University Press.

Whyte, J. (1983) *Beyond the Wendy House: Sex Role Stereotyping in Primary Schools*, Schools Council: Longman.

Wilson, A. (1980) 'The infancy of the history of childhood: an appraisal of Phillipe Ariès', *History and Theory*, 19 (2): 132–54.

Woodhead, M. (1990) 'Psychology and the cultural construction of children's needs', in A. James and A. Prout (eds) *Constructing and Reconstructimg Childhood,* Basingstoke: Falmer Press.

Woods, P.(1987) 'Becoming a junior: pupil development following transfer from infants', in A. Pollard (ed.) *Children and their Primary Schools,* Lewes: Falmer.

Wright-Mills, C. (1959) *The Sociological Imagination,* New York: Oxford University Press.

Young, M. (1990) *An Inside Job,* Oxford: Oxford University Press.

Zakay, D. (1985) 'The influence of information and daily contact on children's attitudes towards aphasic children', *British Journal of Educational Psychology,* 55 (1): 1–10.

Index